The Marvelous Ones

The publisher and the University of California Press Foundation gratefully acknowledge the generous support of the Lisa See Endowment Fund in Southern California History and Culture.

The Marvelous Ones

DRUGS, GANG VIOLENCE, AND
RESISTANCE IN EAST LOS ANGELES

Randol Contreras

UNIVERSITY OF CALIFORNIA PRESS

University of California Press
Oakland, California

© 2024 by Randol Contreras

Library of Congress Cataloging-in-Publication Data

Names: Contreras, Randol, 1971- author.
Title: The marvelous ones : drugs, gang violence, and resistance in
    East Los Angeles / Randol Contreras.
Description: Oakland, California : University of California Press,
    [2024] | Includes bibliographical references and index.
Identifiers: LCCN 2023036714 (print) | LCCN 2023036715 (ebook) |
    ISBN 9780520295087 (cloth) | ISBN 9780520295094 (paperback) |
    ISBN 9780520967977 (ebook)
Subjects: LCSH: Mexican Mafia (Gang) | Mexican American
    gangs—California—East Los Angeles. | Prison gangs—California—
    East Los Angeles. | Drug abuse—California—East Los Angeles. |
    Violence—California—East Los Angeles.
Classification: LCC HV6439.U7 E2254 2024 (print) | LCC HV6439.U7
    (ebook) | DDC 364.106/60979494—dc23/eng/20231107
LC record available at https://lccn.loc.gov/2023036714
LC ebook record available at https://lccn.loc.gov/2023036715

33   32   31   30   29   28   27   26   25   24
10   9   8   7   6   5   4   3   2   1

I dedicate this book to the East Los Angeles Chicanos and Chicanas who got swept up in gangs and drug addiction. I also dedicate it to their parents, children, and loved ones who suffered as they helplessly watched the anguish and violence.

Publisher's Note

This book contains quotes from interview subjects that use racial slurs and other offensive and derogatory terms. We acknowledge that encountering these may be disturbing or triggering for readers. In consultation with the author, we chose to retain this language to accurately document these stories in their tellers' own words.

Contents

Photographs follow page 146

Acknowledgments

I would like to thank some of the people who have supported my career and research for the last several years.

Kimberly Hoang: It has been a long time, but thank you for your support of my research. I have learned so much from our conversations and your brilliant work, which serves as a model for what I want to achieve.

Eric Klinenberg, Mary Patillo, and Patrick Sharkey: It has also been a long time, but I truly appreciate your backing of my work, and your push to show its importance. This means so much to me.

Jooyoung Lee: Thank you for your fantastic support of me, and for our numerous conversations on writing for clarity and wider audiences. I truly miss having you as a colleague who I could just shoot the breeze with.

Eduardo Bonilla-Silva: Thank you for always providing guidance on sensitive research and academic matters. Your selflessness is amazing, and your enthusiasm for bettering the world is inspiring. Gracias, hermano!

Dennis Rodgers: Thank you for your friendship and insights, and for making sure that my work reached international audiences. I cannot express how much that means to me. You're mi broder!

Michaela Soyer: Thank you for your wonderful comments on my manuscript and research (and for your wonderful humor!). You have been so generous with your help and time. I hope that I can return the favor one day.

John Eason and Waverly Duck: Thank you both for our deep conversations on methodology and on life in general. Your breadth of knowledge is amazing, and I always look forward to speaking with you.

Michael Walker: Thank you for your wonderful insights on my manuscript. I truly appreciate your friendship and honesty, and your brilliance has influenced my understanding of the world. Thank you for picking up the phone every time.

Naomi Schneider: Thank you for your continued faith in me as a writer. You have always given me the freedom to be creative in writing about the world. This has helped me make complicated arguments and connections easier to grasp, a main goal of mine.

Gail Kligman: Thank you for being a steadfast champion of my work, and for putting yourself on the line to help a kid from the Bronx. I am honored and forever grateful that you think so highly of me and have tried to advance my career.

Philippe Bourgois: Thank you for always advocating on my behalf, and for understanding what I am trying to accomplish. And you not only champion me, but also all the promising unprivileged students and scholars you come across. This is so inspiring to see. You are an amazing human being.

Lauren McDonald (my wife): Thank you for your love, patience, understanding, and support as I continue dealing with a health issue. Just know that I appreciate how you have believed in me from day one, and how you always make time to read my work and listen to my ideas. You are special.

Introduction

As I made my way through unincorporated East Los Angeles—the area east of Boyle Heights—I marveled at its tranquility. Everywhere I turned, the streets were empty. No children playing or teenagers hanging out. The often flat, sometimes inclined blocks resembled each other. Their mostly small, peach-colored cement homes stared blankly. A few homes had trees, but most featured cement yards. Excitement came about every fifth house, when a dog or two rushed out of hiding with only a chain-link fence checking them, *bark, bark, bark*. Their commotion stopped with a last warning, a hoarse *woof!*

East LA's simplicity confused me. Past media coverage showed streets teeming with bald Mexican gangsters wearing white T-shirts, baggy khakis, and long white socks that reached the knees. Iconic East LA gang movies like *Blood In, Blood Out* and *American Me* also glorified them. Their characters had street handles like Popeye, Huero, and Little Puppet. These *vatos locos*, or crazy ones, rode a roller coaster of drugs and violence—a life of *pura locura*. I did not see them. *A dónde están?*

East LA's main boulevard, Whittier Boulevard, provided a partial answer. The busy street interrupted the community's calm: Mexican restaurants, fast food joints, clothing stores, music stores, street vendors, hot dogs here, tacos there, crowds of people, standing here, walking there—all of it provided energy. And underneath the boulevard's whirlwind of feet and faces, underneath its mariachi and corrido music, underneath its defining feature, an arch proclaiming "WHITTIER BOULEVARD"—like a gold rainbow crossing from one side of the street to the other—I got glimpses of the legendary Maravilla gangsters.

They were not Maravilla's younger generation, nor the youngsters who spent most of their time indoors to avoid police harassment. The Maravilla legends are the *veteranos*, or the older, retired gang members. One knew them through their tight grip on the past: brushlike mustaches; traditional comb-backs with no fade; creased khakis or blue jeans; Buster Brown or Stacy Adams shoes; thick plaid Pendleton shirts; and a fedora or *tango* or *tando* hat. Old-school. They come from close to twenty separate, unrelated gangs, or "neighborhoods," that call Maravilla home. Maravilla, which means "marvelous" or "wonderful," is a local term for East LA and is often attached to a gang name. For instance, several Maravilla neighborhoods took on the following names based on the street the gangs formed on:

Arizona-Maravilla	Lomita-Maravilla
El Hoyo-Maravilla	Lopez-Maravilla
Ford-Maravilla	Lote-Maravilla
Fraser-Maravilla	Marianna-Maravilla
Gage-Maravilla	Moeriya-Maravilla
High Times-Maravilla	Pomeroy-Maravilla
Juarez-Maravilla	Raskals-Maravilla
Kern-Maravilla	Rock-Maravilla

A legend would introduce themselves to others by saying, "I'm Joe from Ford-Maravilla," "I'm John from Lopez-Maravilla," "I'm Tempo from Arizona-Maravilla," "I'm Guano from Juarez-Maravilla," and so forth.

Then they sometimes told outsiders (like me) their history.

During the early 1990s, the different Maravilla neighborhoods—whose gang members often battled each other—united against the most powerful prison gang in the United States, the Mexican Mafia, or La Eme. This homegrown Mexican American gang controls all the Southern California Latino gangs.[1] In fact, it demands that all Southern California barrios follow its rules and pay a tax on its drug sales. If any gang resists, then La Eme puts a "greenlight" on its members. This means that all Southern California barrios must assault resistors on sight. In return, La Eme provides structure and protection in jail and prison. Since the Maravilla gangs united to resist La Eme, a greenlight was put on them. The Maravillas then endured a brutal twelve-year period, from 1994 to 2006, that was perhaps unrivaled in the gang world.

I met many aging Maravillas who experienced the greenlight. Surprisingly, the physical and emotional traumas they experienced in prison became a lifelong source of pride for them. Even evangelical Maravillas, who battled inner demons not only with Christian love but also with Christian rage—felt proud of their greenlight status. I wanted to dig deeper into how this Maravilla pride came from extraordinary pain and harm.

For guidance, I perused the gang literature in the United States. I found that the research, though important, generally focused on the situational themes of youth gangs: gang-related status, structure, bonds, income, symbols, and thrills.[2] But I wanted to follow C. Wright Mills, who argued that we must link history, social structure, and biography to comprehend society.[3] Most people understand themselves within personal orbits, such as family, work, and neighborhood. Mills, though, urged us to link immediate experiences to changes in the economy, technology, and social structure. In other words, we must understand people through history.

I also wanted to heed the call of sociologist David Brotherton. He criticized gang scholars for bracketing historical moments; for making the gang experience seem timeless or transhistorical; and for taking the existing social arrangement (which favors the privileged) for granted.[4] Such researchers made gangs appear as cultural misfits or system errors that just needed alignment—which stripped them of humanity and context.

I did find the rare scholars who integrated gangs into history.[5] Sudhir Venkatesh and Steven Levitt showed how crack cocaine's rise during 1980s changed Chicago Black gangs from a "family" into selfish crack dealers.[6] Similarly, Dennis Rodgers showed how crack cocaine's rise in Nicaragua during the late 1990s changed *pandillas* (gangs) from beloved barrio protectors to feared crooks and drug dealers.[7] And historian Deborah Levenson showed how Guatemala's history of corrupt politics, political coups, labor uprisings, military cruelties, state-sponsored torture, and poverty all changed the harmless peer-based *maras*, or gangs, of the 1980s into violent gangs obsessed with "necro-living," or death, by the late 1990s.[8]

Those historical studies inspired me to focus on the period between the 1960s and early 1990s, during which La Eme became the most powerful prison gang in the United States. This period later set up the clash between the Maravillas and La Eme. If La Eme had not formed, the Maravillas would likely have experienced typical gang violence. But since it did form, the Maravillas experienced La Eme's greenlight wrath. The violence they experienced increased, which changed how they regarded their lives. History mattered in how the Maravillas lived and understood themselves.

Maravilla Matters

I committed my research to the Maravilla old-timers for a few reasons. First, most gang studies focus on the crime, violence, thrills, and status pursuits of young gangsters. But old gang members matter too. The O.G.s, or *veteranos*, pass the torch onto the youngsters because of death, faltering health, drug addiction, and finding Jesus. Second, the aging Maravillas die quickly. Drug-related health issues, such as liver and heart disease, strokes, and heroin overdoses, shorten their lives. Since I began my research in 2012, seven Maravillas have died before the age of sixty-five. Others I met in passing also died during the COVID-19 pandemic.

Third, I found that the aging Maravillas wanted to *matter* as complete human beings. This theme of *mattering* guides this book, which I credit to critical scholars Luke Billingham and Keir Irwin-Rogers.[9] To explain violence among young people, they show how *mattering* means more than just earning status and power on the streets. Mattering is an intrinsic human need regardless of social position and location. It starts at infancy and continues into adulthood as one interacts with family, peers, community, and society. To matter is to feel needed and heard, to feel like a provider of joy and stability. At best, one feels valued and impactful. At worst, one feels the "trauma of failed influence"[10] and falls into a "terrifying abyss of insignificance."[11]

The story of mattering is the story of the Maravilla participants. They felt like stars because of their bloody battle with La Eme, and they wanted to matter as violent men. Just as gender scholars R.W. Connell and James Messerschmidt note about marginal men, the Maravillas had little chance to exert power in society's mainstream social, economic, and political institutions.[12] As a result, they showed hypermasculine toughness, aggressiveness, competitiveness, and domination on the street and in jail and prison. In such spaces, violence determined where one stood on a masculine hierarchy. Many of them then became experts in violence. They had to matter as courageous men.

But they also struggled to matter as men to children, friends, neighbors, and lovers. Sometimes they felt important through religious activities or community building. Other times they felt worthless because of drug addiction and declining health. This is when they struggled to negotiate their various identities, when they seemed not to know which identity to portray: a dopefiend versus a Christian; a violent person versus a friend; a masculine man versus a vulnerable one. And when they fell into the abyss of pain and misery—of insignificance—it seemed as if they wanted to erase their existence or die. I would see it all: their hope and laughter, their crying and despair. Their deaths.

Last, I want to emphasize that the Maravillas matter historically. As citizens of the world, they have much to say about current events. They offer political commentary on immigration policy, former president Trump, and religion. They also discuss the volatile race relations between Mexicans and Black people, and the distrust between the old and new generations of gang members. They say this all to matter in a world that they perceive makes them irrelevant or relics of the past. But mattering in such ways is not uniquely Maravilla. Their views tie into larger political and social movements across the country, and even across the world. The Maravillas do not stand outside of history; rather, they reinforce political and cultural narratives about certain people and places. They matter to our times.

The Format

In my research, I always ask three basic questions:

1. How do history and social structure shape who people become?

2. How do people make meaning of what they do?
3. What are the consequences, good or bad, of being who they are and doing what they do?

To answer these questions I have divided this book into three parts. In the first part, I discuss the history of Los Angeles and East Los Angeles, where racist policies and rising drug markets set the stage for the participant's lives. Then I reveal the family and neighborhood factors that shaped their biographies as gangsters and drug addicts. I also discuss their prison experiences, which reinforced their Maravilla identity and violence. Finally, I document their conflict with La Eme, which led to unprecedented violence and victimization. In the second and third parts I analyze the everyday lives of the aging Maravillas. Here I document their homelessness, drug addiction, street life, and religious experiences. I also examine how they negotiate politics, racism, fatherhood, and aging as they try to matter in the world.

Maravilla: A Day in the Life

The revival lowrider scene on Whittier Boulevard was amazing. On Saturday evenings you would see lowriders, or bombs, the classic, immaculate cars from the 1940s to the 1960s. Shiny ones, sparkling ones, small ones, large ones. The Bel-Air, the Riviera, the Monte Carlo, the Torpedo, the Coup de Ville in all colors (hot pink, lime green, cherry red, rich purple, royal blue) and in all styles (iron top, cloth top, convertible down)—a throwback to another era. And the oldies music was all around us, a time capsule that made us emerge within a wall of 1960s sounds:

♪
It's just like heaven, being here with you,
You're like an angel, too good to be true,

But after all, I love you, I do
Angel baby, my angel baby . . .
♪

It was the music that solemn-faced drivers played, wearing shades, cruising with an arm around their lady; the music that made the crowd feel giddy and brought them back to their teenage years. It reminded them of being young men who gathered in *ranflas*, or cars, and drove down the boulevard looking for *rucas*, or girl-friends, for the night; or of being young women, dressed up, hair high, makeup on, looking for vatos, for someone to slow dance with for the night.

♪
When you are near me,
My heart skips a beat,
I can hardly stand on
My own two feet,
Because I love you,
I love you, I do,
Angel baby, my angel baby
Woo-hoo, I love you
Woo-hoo, I do
No one could love you
Like I do . . .
♪

Getting ready for Whittier Boulevard was serious.

The old-timer Marcos: "Ah man, you iron and starch your pants. Iron shirts. Some would iron their boxers and socks. I say, man, it took me a good hour to get ready, put my cologne on and shower, shave, and all that good stuff. Put on my clothes nice and slow, try not to dent the crease. Buckle up, put on socks and calcos [shoes], T-shirt, and then my Pendleton [wool shirt]. Get my shades. Make the phone calls, see if the homeboy's ready. Pick him up, or he'll pick you up, whatever it may be. Pick three or four homeboys up and take off. Hit the store about six o'clock, hit the beers on the way. Get there—Oh, man! That was the place, the party place. People show off who they were, kind of like stardom, man. Like in Hollywood, they have stardom. That was our stardom."

Living Whittier Boulevard was a blast.

The old-timer Giant: "You kick it out there with a [Chevrolet] '52 Deluxe with hydraulic lifts. You got all the attention drawn to you. 'Look at that car!' You'll see the lowriders with hydraulic lifts, going up and down, dropping its lifts. They'll say, 'Hey, man, look at the car. I would like to get to know that dude,' you understand what I'm sa-a-aying?"

The old-timer Nando: "Híjole, it was fun. Aye, jainas [girls] walking on the Boulevard. I'm talking about chingo de [a lot of fucking] jainas. Cholitas [gang girls], homie, walking on the Boulevard. And then you're in your fucking ranfla [car], homie. 'Hey girl, what's up?' Those days were bad, homes."

The old-timer Emilio: "You could go down the Boulevard on New Year's Eve and you could just stop your car and you could kiss almost any girl you wanted to."

The old-timer Nando: "That was your girl for the whole night. For the whole night on New Year's Eve. That was a trip. Back in the day, when the Boulevard was right here, homie."

Beautiful nostalgia, beautiful remembrances, memories that enchanted the much older drivers, passengers, and crowd. And the people were everywhere. They lined the boulevard from Ford Avenue to Atlantic Avenue, mostly gathered between Arizona Avenue and the Whittier Boulevard arch. They stood on the sidewalk or sat in chairs, chatting, eating, and drinking in front of stores, loving the lowrider cars that cruised down the street. Most of the men wore *tando* hats and Pendleton shirts. Most of the women, young and old, wore some retro clothing from the 1960s and 1970s, or teased their hair high above thinned eyebrows. It was magical.

The old-timer Chico: He was in a dream. We drove to Whittier Boulevard in my car—a Subaru hatchback, the antithesis of a lowrider—wearing *tando* hats, old-school style. I had the windows rolled down and blasted oldies music.

♪

Are you angry with me darling,
With me darling, with me darling
Are you sorry that we met,
That we met, that we met
Have you learned to love another,
Love another, love another
Has he taught you to forget,
To forget, to forget . . .

♪

He loved it. "Randy, there were so many jainas [girls] walking out on Whittier when I used to come here. They were everywhere. We had a good ol' time. Man, Randy, this reminds me of riding around with my homeboys!" Later, as we walked through the crowd and reached the Whittier Boulevard arch, he became so energized that he remarked, "Man, Randy, back then, when I was a dopefiend, if I would'a seen you walking around with that camera out here, I would'a just taken it from you, hahaha!"

A couple of blocks away there was Antonio. All smiles. He loved lowrider cars, the old-school gangster clothes, the beautiful cholas who wore their hair about six inches high but combed down long on the back and sides. Look at him: he grinned as he spoke with old-timers about the cars he had seen today. Then he spoke with a *veterana* dressed old-school, with the high hair and all. She greeted me like she knew me, perhaps because I wore a *tando* hat. After she departed Antonio told me that back in the day she was something else, the beauty queen of the neighborhood. But, unfortunately, she got along too well with the neighborhood homeboys.

The festivity of Whittier Boulevard brought joy to Maravilla old-timers. It made them friendly and gracious. It made them feel young. I drove back home just as energized, playing the oldies full blast.

♪
Many hearts may learn to love you,
Girl, and many hearts may be kind
But there's no broken heart
Like this broken heart of *m-i-i-i-i-ne* . . .

So *I-I-I, I-I-I, I-I-I, I-I-I* just want to know,
Girl before you grab your hat and walk up on out the door,
What did *I-I-I, I-I-I, I-I-I, I-I-I* do to make you blue,
Don't you know I tried so hard to be true to you

Are you angry with me darling,
With me darling, with me darling
Are you sorry that we met,
That we met, that we met . . .
♪

Race, Space, and Representation

I almost never learned about the old-school Maravillas. As a new-comer to LA I learned that "getting in" gang research was hard. For two years I met with more than a dozen gang-affiliated people for a chance to study their neighborhoods. All my attempts failed. No one knew me. *Coño!* No one trusted me. *Carajo!* Gang members thought that I was an undercover cop since I claimed no LA past.[13] *Who is this fool?*

Then I got lucky: A French researcher who had studied Compton gangs learned of my interest. He connected me to the director of the Maravilla Historical Society in East LA, whom I later met at the Maravilla Handball Court. Between the 1930s and 1970s this open-air court offered recreation for East LA residents, especially for neighborhood gangs. There they played *rebote*, or handball, and used it as neutral turf to settle problems. In the 1980s, however, the handball court became a drug den where drug deals and violence happened. Residents were scared of the court, which now carried a terrible stigma. By the 2000s the drug dealers and users had disappeared, but the court was still old and rundown. Metal appliances crowded some spots; cracks split open the court's concrete; and rot ate its wood. To restore it, the Maravilla Historical Society held fundraisers that featured handball events and Mexican holiday celebrations.

I learned this from the director, a streetwise *veterana* who was once active with El Hoyo–Maravilla. In her late fifties, she loved East LA and distrusted outsiders. Since the 1970s, she explained, researchers have visited East LA to collect data, only to disappear. She was tired of East LA residents getting nothing in return.

I understood her frustration. I always get uncomfortable when ethnographers claim that participants benefit immensely by having their stories told. But revealing participants' stories does not help pay their rent, mortgage, or utilities; purchase or fix the car needed to commute to work; pay for emergency medical bills; buy them nutritious food and quality clothes; or help them move to a better neighborhood for safety and superior schools. The research product, though, could help ethnographers get promotions and raise their professional standing. At that time, though, I was at Cal State Fullerton, with no research funds, a low salary, and no pay raise in sight. I could only offer my physical labor to help restore the handball court and recruit student volunteers. After hearing me out, the director seemed unsure, but she agreed to let me hang out for a probationary period. *Yes!*

Not so fast. She wanted no depictions of crime and violence, only stories about Chicano empowerment. I became alarmed. As an ethnographer I have always depicted the good and the bad, the victories and defeats, and the happiness, misery, glory, and pain. It would be an intellectual distortion if I focused only on either the beauty or the ugliness of humanity. I had to cover it all. Clearly, I understood her. Especially since I was an outsider, a Dominican Afro-Latino who grew up in the Bronx. The following are some examples of our differences:

As for looks, Mexicans are mostly indigenous and European; I'm a mixture of African and European. So I stood out in East LA, with its residents thinking that I was African American (I have puffy, curly hair).

As for language, I often removed the beginning and ends of Spanish words and skipped the letter *s* (*Cómo e'tá* rather than *Cómo estás*, and *'ta to' bien* rather than *Está todo bien*). Mexicans pronounced almost every syllable of a word, which made me feel self-conscious (Mexican students giggled at my Spanish pronunciations).

As for the rest, I came from New York City, where people speak and act differently and experience their own territorial pride. I spoke in a staccato manner; Mexicans lengthened their words. I slung my shoulders low; Mexicans stood upright. I favored the Knicks, Mets, and Yankees; Mexicans cheered the Dodgers and Lakers. I enjoyed crowds and dense, diverse neighborhoods. Los Angelenos seemed fine driving everywhere and living segregated, suburban lives. Once, while talking with a middle-aged Mexican, he suddenly asked where

I was from. *New York City*, I answered. *No wonder*, he said with a laugh, referring to my manner of speech. I was that different. Racially. Spatially. Ethnically. I could not write from a Mexican standpoint. I knew nothing of Mexican culture, community, or life.

That said, I knew that writing about the Maravillas (or any LA gang) meant that I had to cover violence and crime. Otherwise I would misrepresent them. I told this to the director. She paused and then hesitantly told me that we would play everything by ear. With that matter settled, I did whatever she asked of me. I printed out event flyers. I brought in student volunteers. I unpacked boxes of donated food and household products. I hosed down the court. I drove people home when they had no bus fare. I opened the handball court three days a week. I instructed curious residents on how to play handball. I played with Maravilla old-timers who reminisced about the handball court's heyday.

I eventually met Maravillas from different neighborhoods. They were mainly over forty years old and suffered from poor health. They were usually reserved with me. When I approached them, they hesitated to speak to me and avoided eye contact. They also politely excused themselves from our conversation, saying that they had to do something (which was often to go outside and joke with friends).

I told the director about my troubles. She felt that my signs of Blackness could be the cause. Like most Mexican gangs, the Maravillas took part in the racism that structured LA gang politics. But the director was savvy: she stopped introducing me to everyone as "Randy" and instead pronounced my full name in Spanish, with a strong roll of the letter R. "This is R-R-R-andol Contr-r-e-r-r-as," she would say.

It worked. Conversations lasted longer and the Maravillas started including me in their jokes. Yet when new gang members arrived, many of them appeared uncomfortable around me, so I searched for a way to blend in. My solution came from my observation of gang members in their twenties and thirties, who often had closely shaven heads or were bald. I cut my curly, puffy hair short to conceal its texture.

That worked too. Maravillas relaxed and maintained eye contact with me. Not that everyone saw me as Mexican. They saw me as some type of Latino, such as a Cuban or Puerto Rican, two ethnic groups with small communities in LA. Eventually the old-timers warmed up to me, revealing stories usually reserved for their "homies," or close friends. They recounted heroic tales, revealed family problems, and admitted drug and alcohol abuse. They accepted me.

Then it ended. The Maravillas stopped talking. Now, when I asked Maravilla-related questions, they changed the topic. When I started conversations, the director found things for me to do alone. *¿Qué pasó?*

I found out what happened. One evening I asked an old-timer about gang boundaries in East LA. Under a heroin high, he slurred his answer. Then he stopped, saying he could not speak with me. *Why?* I asked. The director, he said, told everyone to stop helping me because once I got enough data, I would leave and never return. I was shocked. I had shown my commitment by volunteering at the handball court. I kept it cool, though, not showing my hurt. I respectfully turned in my keys and left.

I kept in contact with a few Maravillas, who later found a neighborhood, or gang, willing to work with me. There the research got complicated: a few members disagreed with me and among themselves about what I should write about. I felt vulnerable amid the neighborhood politics and I walked away.[14]

A few Maravillas, though, intervened. They felt that I had shown honor and commitment and asked me to write about them. And they wanted their stories of drugs and violence told. Only then, they argued, would readers learn about what it means to be a Maravilla. I was moved by their trust and restarted the project. I began interviewing Maravilla old-timers in other East LA neighborhoods.

In all, I interviewed thirty-eight Maravillas who came of age between the 1970s and 1990s. I also followed four male old-timers in their late forties to mid-fifties. For two to three days a week I observed their drug and alcohol addictions, their refuge in methadone clinics, their involvement in Christianity, and their experiences with homelessness.

I started my field research in April 2012. After I got a job at the University of Toronto in the fall of 2014, I reduced my field visits to about one week per month during the term sessions and then resumed field research during the winter and summer breaks. After returning to California permanently, I collected more interviews and observation data. Soon I returned to the field only to clarify stories and accounts.

I must be clear. Since my Maravilla research did not begin until April 2012, I never observed or spoke to participants before then. However, the Maravillas recounted important past events. In such cases I verified the data through other Maravillas, family members, and friends. I sometimes asked for proof from gang members outside East LA who fought against them in prison. When I could not access corroborators or find similar experiences, I did not write about the topic.

As in my previous work, I place digitally recorded dialogue in quotes; and, like sociologist Mitchell Duneier, I place dialogue from field notes in italics.[15] This lets readers know whether the words are verbatim. I also edited dialogue, removing extra words and phrases such as "um" and "you feel me" to avoid distracting from an account's meaning. I kept terms such as *órale* (an expression of approval), *chale* (an expression of disapproval) and *simón* (a firm expression of approval) since they capture the richness of the participants' speech and give their language a unique rhythm.

Finally, the participants often referred to anyone of Mexican descent as "Mexican." They used this term even when speaking about Mexican Americans. When they wanted to make intraethnic distinctions, they referred to Mexicans from Mexico as "immigrants" or "*paisas*" and to those born in the United States as "Chicanos." Since they used the term "Mexican" mostly to describe Mexican Americans, I do the same throughout the book.

Lost Participants

When I walked away from the handball court, I lost important participants: women. At the handball court I had interviewed three women (one of whom was not from Maravilla). Once I left, they no longer spoke to me. I also had a phone conversation with a middle-aged Maravilla woman still on the streets. However, as we discussed a way to meet up, she kept mentioning that she did not want her "old man" (husband or boyfriend) to get upset. Since I did not want to cause a rift or violence in their relationship, I never followed up with her. Later, I met and spoke with the wives, girlfriends, and daughters of some of the participants, but none of them wanted to be in this book.

I kept trying. I contacted a woman who created a wonderful video on YouTube that honored her dead Maravilla homies. We spoke over the phone and I learned that she was once active in the women's clique of a particular neighborhood. She had to consult with her "older homies," though, to see if she and her homegirls, who were in their fifties, would participate. She later gave me bad news: the older homies told her not to do it. In the end, I could not include women as main participants. I also did not want to misrepresent the few interviews I did with women as "fieldwork."

I lost other important participants: stable, working Maravillas who had escaped the streets. I had met them in the neighborhood that I walked away from. They had never done hard drugs or committed serious violence. They also matured out of their gangs into mainstream jobs. Some of them even had classic lowrider cars from the 1940s, 1950s, and 1960s. They worked on them on the weekends and drove them on evenings. *Beautiful.* But once my research failed in their neighborhood, I lost them as participants. Later I contacted the older homies in one Maravilla neighborhood to see if I could just include their lowriders in my research. They never answered my text messages or calls. They were friendly, though, when we later saw each other on the street.

I met other stable Maravillas from different neighborhoods. They worked full-time, lived typical family lives, and spoke enthusiastically about their Maravilla heyday. After one or two conversations, though, they seemed unwilling to speak or hang out with me. I later learned that they thought their words might drag them back into gang politics, or away from their hard-won conventional lives.

In the end I studied Maravillas that kept their ties to the streets. They were either homeless or helped the homeless; had drug addictions or helped the drug addicted; did jail and prison time or helped friends transition from confinement to conventional life. Overall, they had a strong presence in East LA, which reinforced their Maravilla identity. More important, they wanted their stories told to document their existence and reinforce their legendary status. Despite their marginality, they wanted to matter to the world.

Protection

Over the last several years I have spoken to many LA gang members. They always proudly claim that their neighborhood is the most violent. I hear stories involving gunplay, knifings, and beatings with crowbars, baseball bats, and fists. Some gang members have scars as proof. Others claim to have metal plates protecting their skulls. Yet when I ask about their jail and prison experiences, they slow down. California prison politics loom large.

An informal rule exists among California prisoners: what happens in prison stays in prison. Only the homies, or fellow gang members, get reports of what goes on. Inmates protect prison information since prison politics guide the underground economy, maintain social order, and provide power, status, and meaning. Outsiders, such as journalists, must never know the details. If an inmate discloses specifics, they can get killed.[16]

However, I must discuss incarceration. Many Maravillas have spent about a quarter of their lives in juvenile facilities, jails, and prisons. Except for one person, the Maravillas wanted their prison stories told. But spending time with them did not make me an honorific member of their gang. I was not Mexican and never defended a Maravilla neighborhood. So, when they discussed prison events, they rarely mentioned names. Such information was considered a "religious matter," a phrase used to let outsiders know that sensitive information would not be shared. For instance, when two Maravillas I had just met discussed their greenlight experience, the following occurred:

"We were getting hit all the time by the Sureños [La Eme's fighters] up in —— prison," John remembered.

"Yeah, I heard about that," said Waldo. "I heard that we were getting hit hard everywhere there. Is that when the guys from [looking over at me], you know the guys got together from . . . [looking at me again and never mentioning the specific Maravilla neighborhood]."

"That's right," John said, hesitant. "They got together to talk about religious matters."

Over time, such smoke screens were used less often. When they were used, I was unbothered. My book was not about who said exactly what, when, and where in the gang world. I also did not want La

Eme's attention. Thus, for their protection, I gave participants pseudonyms (one participant chose "Chico" as their own fake name). I also did not discuss their informal money-making strategies since their specific labor would reveal their identities. Last, I obscured their specific Maravilla neighborhood or gang. The participants and I did not want the book to worsen tensions between Maravilla neighborhoods and La Eme.

Yet I still situated them in East LA and referred to them as Maravillas. First, the term *Maravilla* has special historical and spatial meaning for participants. In fact, they would not let me write this book unless I referred to them as such. Second, using the term eases the work of readers who want to research or challenge my depictions of the people and place.[17] I just hope that readers do not become what I call "rogue unmaskers," who decide to reveal participants without invitation or permission.[18] This is not the time to be smart or cute. This is not a game. People's lives are at risk.

Fear

I must remove all masculine pretensions and admit the following: this research made me afraid. I am not ashamed of admitting this. In my first book I coined the term "cowboy ethnographer" to describe researchers who purposely portray themselves as fearless in the field.[19] That is not me. Deep reflection made me realize how masculinity can influence ethnographers to present themselves as daring and brave. This masculine preoccupation impacts how both men and women represent themselves in their work. In their book *Harassed*, sociologists Rebecca Hanson and Patricia Richards show how danger for women ethnographers increases because of their risk of sexual harassment and assault at any time and place.[20] Yet women rarely reveal such matters. They want to appear strong like the men who dominate ethnography and can make or break careers.

Thus, I cannot contribute to the ethnographer as hero or cowboy. Such images distort field research, especially when studying violence. I research men who have violent pasts, some of whom have been convicted of murder and speak freely of it to remind others not to cross them. So, I am uneasy when participants ask me if I am an undercover cop or federal agent; or what type of car my wife drives; or what my wife's working hours are and if she spends time alone at home.

I felt even more uneasy when participants repeatedly asked me how much money I made from the film *The Stickup Kids*. No matter how many times I explained that I had no role in the film—that the film was produced five years before my book with the same title was published; that the film was based on African Americans in Harlem, not Dominicans in the South Bronx; and that I have never seen the film—they continued to ask me. It seemed like they speculated about my finances when I was not around. It seemed like they saw me as a hustler, a liar who wanted to profit from their stories alone. *Que peligro!*

For safety, I never shared my home address. In fact, most Maravillas who now live outside East LA rarely do. A well-respected old-timer once shared the following with me:

"I'm going to tell you right now," he said, "don't tell any of these vatos [guys] where you live."

"Why not?" I asked.

"Because a lot these vatos around here," he answered, "todavía están locos [they're still crazy]. They're still drinking, slamming [heroin], doing all sorts of stuff on the streets. You don't know what they're thinking. They could show up to your house acting like, 'Órale, homes, let's just kick back. Let's drink some beers.' But they're really there to ask for money. They're really there to see what you got."

"Do you tell people where you live?" I asked.

"Chale, homes," he responded. "None of these vatos know where I live. I don't want them thinking that they could just stop by whenever they want. Then they start asking for favors that I can't do. They get mad, [saying], 'Who does this vato think he is now just because he got a house? He thinks he's better than me?' That's when the problems start. I have a job and family now and need to avoid problems."

Other Maravillas also avoided sharing their new city of residence. I observed them tell others that they lived in the city of Whittier despite telling me when alone that they lived in Ontario, San Bernardino, or Pomona. I even saw a Maravilla abruptly cut off their teenage nephew in a group conversation after he named the area where he lived. Later I was present for the scolding: *Don't tell anybody here where you live! How many times am I going to tell you? You have to be careful with that information!* Such observations made me uncertain.

Perhaps I was wrong for being distrustful. Perhaps the participants just wanted to know more about my personal life to ensure that I was not law enforcement. Perhaps they wanted to know just as much about me as I did about them, which included where I lived. Perhaps they felt disrespected since I had never invited them to my home. Perhaps they did not want a lopsided relationship, where I had the power to show up and disappear—forever, if I wished—and they could still be found. Perhaps they wanted a real relationship based on trust.

Perhaps.

To the participants: I apologize if this makes you feel insulted or disrespected. I know that most of you would not harm me. Most of you have only been generous with your thoughts and time. Some of you have even gently placed your hand on my head and prayed for me after I acquired a chronic illness. But there might be a few who would cause pain. I must protect not only me, but also my family. In doing so, I protect us all.

Race, Presence, and Uncomfortable Truths

In his Pulitzer Prize–winning ethnography *Evicted*, sociologist Matthew Desmond contends that ethnographers write too much in the "I," or the first person.[21] This makes the text more about the researcher than the participants, which can hinder social policy that helps, in his case, the poor. So, Desmond removes himself from the text, only providing snapshots of poor Black people facing eviction. He tells readers that when he does appear, it is in the guise of a character called, "John," which he created to keep attention away from himself.

Despite his great intentions, I disagree with Desmond. Scholars like Nancy Scheper-Hughes, Ranita Ray, Philippe Bourgois, Teresa Gowan, and others have written in the first person and brilliantly brought attention to the plight of the poor.[22] When reading their works I never lost focus on their impoverished minority participants. In fact, I learned more about them through their relationship with the privileged researcher. Because once you enter the lives of participants—once you speak with them, stand with them, walk with them, drive with them, eat with them, drink with them, and share problems with them—you have impacted the research. Now you have a place on the corner, at the bar, in the gym, at the vending table, in the school, on the rooftop, and so forth. Ethnographers, whether they want to or not, become a part of the story. They should then be transparent about how they shaped or influenced situations.

Perhaps my positionality influences my stance. As a person of color, I find it hard to disappear. This includes in the research space. As I mentioned earlier, with my hair cut almost bald, the Maravillas categorized me as some type of Latino. But my Blackness returned whenever my hair grew. One of the Maravillas, whom I call Emilio, worried that my signs of Blackness might offend his racist peers. He then reshaped my ethno-racial identity. In a drunken state—he was an alcoholic and heroin addict—Emilio introduced me to everyone as his cousin *de sangre*, or blood cousin, and claimed that I was a family member of Mexican and Puerto Rican descent. He felt that the Puerto Rican angle would explain my Blackness, which his peers would accept since a few Puerto Ricans were members of Maravilla.

Then he started calling me "Rico from Puerto Rico," the cousin who wanted to write about Maravilla culture. I pleaded for him to stop saying that I was "Rico from Puerto Rico," that it was putting both him and me in danger. But he felt that it was the only way to get some Maravillas to talk to me. Most of the people I met through him, though, knew that he lied. For instance, after one introduction one of his homeboys asked him, *No, tell me really, where did you find this guy?* But Emilio swore that I was his *primo* who was half Mexican and half Puerto Rican.

After another introduction, he left me alone with a highly respected Maravilla to go drink a beer. The Maravilla then quizzed me about other Maravillas I had met, asking how I got to know them. He seemed like a customs officer at an international airport, asking quick questions to trip me up. Then he quickly asked: *What's your nationality?* I could not lie. *I'm Dominican.* Then he asked, *Do you speak Spanish?* I answered: *Claro que sí* (of course). He paused.

Then, to my relief, he spoke about how he wanted to write a book about everything that led up to him doing time in prison. He wanted to know if I could help him with it. I told him that I would. In this case, everything ended safely, but it could have ended badly. I then enlisted the help of another participant, Chico, to tell everyone who I really was and my research intentions. He used my real information: "This is Randy Contr-r-r-reras from the Bronx."

Such experiences gave me great insight into how the Maravilla participants constructed Blackness. Later I met Maravillas who became comfortable enough to discuss their anti-Blackness with me. Some of them, though, were still unsure of my ethnicity. I found out that one Maravilla called me a "biracial mutt" behind my back, insisting that I was half African American. Also, before discussing Black people, some Maravillas still asked me, "Are you Black?" or "Are you half Black?" I always answered that I was Dominican. They followed up with, "Do you speak Spanish?" I answered, "Yeah, I speak Spanish." Then they freely told me about a negative experience with a Black person or their folk analysis of the Black community. The Spanish language seemed to set the Maravillas at ease with me. It allowed them to reshape my Blackness to their liking—or perhaps cleanse it enough to justify my presence. How they categorized me shaped what they said or did around me. This was invaluable data.

The data, though, revealed an uncomfortable truth: Mexican racism toward Blacks. As critical law scholar Tanya Hernandez reveals, African Americans and Afro-Latinos often suffer from racism at the hands of Latinos.[23] Yet while Latino anti-Blackness remains invisible in public discourse, it is visible in everyday life. I saw it in the Dominican community that I grew up in and later researched: Dominicans tried to whiten themselves by denigrating Black Dominican women and African Americans.[24] Now I saw this in East LA. Some Maravillas equated Blacks with monkeys and angrily claimed that society provided Blacks with more political rights and civil liberties than Mexicans. I began to feel like an outsider even as they welcomed my "Latino-ness."

Not all of them were openly racist. But there were some I considered friends who were the greatest offenders. In fact, there was an incident that made me question my friendship with a participant I call Juano. One day we were organizing some merchandise that had been donated to the Maravilla Historical Society. Suddenly, Juano said:

Oh, what's that? Is that a monkey? Look at that little monkey over there. Is that a little monkey? It's a cute little monkey.

Another Maravilla and I started looking around, scanning the ground and the area behind the boxes.

Don't you see it? he asked.

We continued looking, but I still could not determine what he spoke about.

Oh, my mistake, he finally said. *It's a baby. I thought it was a monkey.*

I then realized that he was referring to a box of diapers with an illustration of a Black infant. My son, and other family members, looked like that illustration as babies. I became disgusted and said nothing. Juano thought that I had not heard him and repeated the joke. The other Maravilla finally got it, chuckled, and resumed his work. I left the area, finding something to do a good distance away. This moment, and other such moments, hurt me. The hurt clarified that I could not take Maravillas' racism for granted. Being Brown did not disqualify them from being racists that caused pain. And I kept their offensive, racist words in this book since it reflected how participants viewed their place in the racial hierarchy and resisted a changing world.

In short, we have yet to reach the historical moment when social categories no longer matter. Thus, I cannot disappear, not even from an ethnographic text. My race, class, gender, ethnicity, and other categories influence my participants to say and do certain things. This provides tremendous insight into their lives. I am disappointed, then, when ethnographers pretend not to be "there," even though we all know—and they tell us—that they were. As a progressive Afro-Latino scholar, I have shaped many interactions with my Chicano participants. It is only fair to acknowledge my presence and show how it influenced my data.

I *Becoming Greenlighters*

1   *The Birth of East LA*

East Los Angeles is a poor and working-class unincorporated area, distinct from the city of Los Angeles. It depends on Los Angeles County for its public services, such as the LA Sheriff's Department for its police. Its steep hills are mostly found to the north, in the City Terrace area, an elevation many East LA residents see as another world. Overall, East LA is bordered by Boyle Heights (Los Angeles) to its northwest; by the mostly Asian and middle-class Monterey Park to its northeast; by the modest city of Montebello to its east; and by the small industrial city of Commerce to its south. East LA also holds a dubious distinction: it is the least diverse area in LA County, with a population of over 95 percent Latino residents.[1]

Longtime East LA residents remember Maravilla gangs ruling the streets between the 1970s and early 2000s. They hung out in alleys, sidewalks, and public parks, and fought with fists, bats, tire irons, knives, and guns. *Tecatos*, or heroin users, enhanced the menacing imagery as they committed crimes to support drug addictions. The Maravilla participants came of age in the early 1970s, when they lived *la vida loca*, or a violent, drug-induced life. And certain historical factors set the stage for their dramatic lives.

Admittedly, it is hard to incorporate history into ethnography. Where one starts, where one ends, what one keeps, what one sheds—

all pose a problem. Like a Russian doll to infinity, one moment begets another, which then begets another, which then begets another until it reaches a point that seems too far gone. Hence, I cannot cover it all. Rather I cover key historical periods to show how a history of political, economic, and geographic racism and violence made the Maravillas. They later picked up the baton to extend that history themselves.

Racism and Resistance in LA

LA was no Eden for Mexicans.

During the early twentieth century, Mexican migrants settled in the United States to escape Mexican policies that took land and farm work from peasants.[2] They also fled the bloody Mexican Revolution, during which men and boys were forced to enlist in the military and women experienced wartime rape.[3] LA's white Anglo nativists immediately took the stage. They already blamed Chinese immigrants for LA's crime and labor shortages.[4] Now they created what historian Richard Romo calls a "Brown Scare."[5] Nativists claimed that Mexicans, who were recruited during labor strikes, caused labor disruptions and violence; that Mexicans colluded with Germany against the United States and aimed to retake California; and that Mexicans were criminal, immoral, and carried deadly diseases.

An Americanization movement also emerged.[6] White reformers bombarded immigrants with the so-called high ideals of Anglo-Saxon morality and government.[7] They visited Mexicans at job sites, schools, community centers, and homes to teach them hygiene, work ethic, English, and American cuisine. However, the Great Depression (1929–39) halted Americanization efforts. Contempt for Mexicans grew. Public officials who once embraced cheap Mexican labor now framed it as a threat to white employment.[8] They then prioritized whites for jobs and welfare relief, and prohibited Mexicans from work on government projects.[9]

Yet some Mexicans resisted injustice through a new aesthetic. Enter the pachucos.

The pachucos had started in Mexico's underworld. Their members often traveled between the border cities of Ciudad Juárez in Mexico and El Paso in Texas. Their cool manner was enhanced by their long hair, combed back high, and by their use of a mix of Spanish and Roma phrases known as Caló.[10] Their style spread within the Mexican community of El Paso, a city also known as "El Chuco" and its residents as "pachucos."[11] In the 1920s pachucos migrated to Arizona and California, where middle-class Mexican Americans despised their boldness and looks. Some Mexican youths emulated them, becoming pachucos to enhance their self-worth.

In LA the pachuco and pachuca emerged as resistance to white racism and discrimination. For instance, Mexican children were often enrolled in poor and segregated public schools; they were banned from swimming in public pools with white children; and, at the beach, whites verbally and physically harassed them.[12] Law enforcement also falsely accused them of crimes.[13] And they were often denied work because of their ethnicity. Mexican youths had little hope in an LA that was dominated by white Americans. Style became their vehicle for meaning and change.

They wore zoot suits, a fashion started in Harlem's Black community. It is unknown how the style reached the Southwest, but most accounts claim that it migrated with jazz and swing bands, whose performers wore them as they toured.[14] What is known is that its style was loose and easy.

Suit jackets: Exaggerated. They had wide, padded shoulders and a robe-like length that reached the knees.
Pants: Baggy. They started right below the chest, then ballooned at the knees, then tapered tight at the ankles.

Hats: Wide. The brim was often turned up all around or only at its front or sides.

Colors: Loud. The suits sported bright colors that popped.

Shoes: Pointy. They were thin, sharp, and shiny, either two-toned or in a solid color.

In East LA Mexican pachucos donned the look, but with less exaggeration. They wore wide-brimmed *tandos*, or hats. They wore baggy slacks that started at the navel, with a modest balloon at the knee. They wore *tacuches*, or long suit jackets, which ended at mid-thigh. They walked and danced in their *calcos*, or thick-soled shoes. They combed their long hair up high, in a pompadour that ended in an inward taper behind the head that resembled a ducktail or "duck's ass" (later called the DA).[15]

Pachucas gave the style a feminine and masculine blend.[16] They wore heavy makeup and plucked their eyebrows into thin, barely visible arcs. Their hair was larger than the pachuco's pompadour but settled lower, onto their shoulders. Sweaters were tight and skirts were high. Some even wore the *tacuche*, or suit jacket, along with pleated skirts or baggy slacks that tapered at the ankle to reveal huaraches, or partly open sandals.

They all spoke Caló. When they departed from nightclubs, dances, pool halls, and street corners, they repeated the rhyme *Al rato, vato*. If they wanted to clarify a point, they punctuated it with the rhyme *¿Me comprendes, Mendez?* When they referred to someone, they appended their sentences with *esa* (woman) or *ese* (man). When they disagreed or rejected an idea, they said "chale!" When they agreed with or wanted to emphasize something, they said, "órale," "simón," or an excited "simón que si!"

In all, they exuded coolness and confidence, demonstrated resistance and rebellion, and challenged mainstream culture through their dress, makeup, slick hair, and wit. They could not be missed.

Whites took notice. In LA youths who wore *drapes* (as the zoot suit style was called there) were falsely tied to criminality.[17] And whites disliked the pachuco's cool manners, hip language, and exaggerated clothes, which were a challenge to white power in LA.[18] The onset of World War II further raised white resentment. Mexicans joined the booming war economy and began earning good wages.[19] Like other ethnic groups that suffered through the Great Depression, young Mexicans now indulged themselves by buying pricey *drapes* and enjoying nightlife. Whites, though, saw them as living above their social position and selfishly wearing large clothes despite government rations placed on clothing material. They also viewed them as anti-American since their long hair and baggy clothes were the antithesis of the military buzz cut and uniform.[20]

Violence exploded. The military, police, Mexican youths, and white citizens were all involved. The violence was referred to as the Zoot Suit Riots, even though it involved a white military attack on young minority men.

The conflict's origin started near a large naval facility in the Chavez Ravine neighborhood, just north of downtown LA. Its white sailors would leave their quarters to go to bars, restaurants, and movie theaters and often returned drunk, acting rude as they walked through Mexican neighborhoods. They taunted Mexicans wearing *drapes* and approached Mexican women like sexual objects.[21] The younger Mexicans, those born in the United States and who felt no need to act deferential, saw the streets as their own and retaliated.

When white sailors walked toward them, some young Mexican men locked arms and spread across the sidewalk, forcing whites to walk on the street. It was their public space. When white sailors strolled by, young Mexican men in cars yelled at them, spat on them, and called them "sons of bitches" and "bastards." It was their public space. When white sailors wanted entry into dance halls, movie theaters, and restaurants, young Mexican men blocked them from entering. It was their public space. When white sailors went any-where, they heard young Mexican men ridicule them for enlisting in the navy, which they considered feminine. It was their public space. A space for *real* men.

It became a tit for tat: white sailors disrespected Mexican men and women, and young Mexican men disrespected white sailors and their girlfriends. Once again the image of the pachuco—an arrogant and flamboyant criminal—rose to the fore. But another dimension was added: the idea of the unpatriotic pachuco, who stayed home rather than fight in the war.[22] This, of course, was untrue. Pachucos and non-pachucos who wore *drapes* were serving in the military, and many of those now wearing *drapes* had plans of enlisting.[23] Neverthe-less, conservative newspapers and law enforcement sensationalized the pachuco as relishing violence, insulting the country, and sexually assaulting white women.

The public's conclusion: the pachuco had to be caged.

The white sailors' conclusion: they would squash pachucos.

During an infamous five days in June 1943, thousands of sailors and soldiers flooded the city, arriving from all parts of Southern Cal-ifornia. White civilians joined them. They marched the streets of LA, going deep into the Black and Mexican neighborhoods. The soldiers overtook the streets with bottles, belts, and pipes, setting upon mi-nority men. The scene was a blur of shouting and screaming and kicking and punching and running, of beaten and defeated young men of color absorbing blows and being stripped of their clothes. Po-lice clubbed and arrested minority victims. Soldiers stopped street cars and burst into businesses to drag out minority victims. Worse, soldiers crossed the sacred line between the hearth and the street by barging into Mexican homes to look for targets, and beating up moth-ers and fathers who protected their children.[24]

Young minority men did resist.[25] Black and Mexican boys teamed up to confront soldiers with homemade weapons. They also staged sniper attacks that entailed throwing bottles and rocks at sailors and soldiers from afar. But they were outmaneuvered, overpowered, and outnumbered: white military men used army jeeps to race from skirmish to skirmish and received physical and emotional support from white citizens and police.

The military won. It was their public space. The city belonged to white men.[26]

Eventually, the pachuco became public enemy number one. Even middle-class Mexican Americans, who used the violent episode to rally politically, distanced themselves from pachucos. In fact, they blamed them for white violence against LA Mexicans.[27] They also portrayed pachucas as dangerous to traditional Mexican values because of their alleged cruelty and loose sexuality.[28] Pachucos and pachucas now became *the* reason for the Mexican community's low status.

The Start of East LA

Let us now go back a few decades to situate the formation of East LA. Before the Zoot Suit Riots, marginalized Mexicans often lived in the impoverished north part of downtown LA. Whites derisively called this area "Sonoratown" despite its residents being mostly Mexican Americans and not from Sonora, Mexico.[29] Here Mexicans rented beds in rundown boarding houses or lived in employer-provided housing (companies figured out that the squalid shacks cost less than a slight raise in wages).[30] Mexican families also resided in "Cholo courts," or cramped housing compounds with shared outdoor faucets and toilets.[31]

World War I, though, proved a boon for the city. LA's core (or downtown) area expanded its railroad depots, food companies, breweries, lumberyards, metal factories, and oil refineries. The growth raised rents into the 1920s, which pushed poor Mexicans out. Moving west was not an option: housing was not sold or rented to minorities.[32] Moving east to Boyle Heights was better, but it was a working- and middle-class Jewish community with pockets of Italians and Russians.[33] Mexicans would settle further east, in Belvedere, which later became East Los Angeles.[34]

Belvedere resembled a shantytown. It lacked paved roads, sidewalks, and sewer systems, which created floods and standing pools of putrid water.[35] Its housing was a line of flimsy shacks that were rarely built to code. The poverty worsened in its east section (which ironically was called Maravilla, meaning *marvelous*), where residents often starved. Overall, however, Belvedere provided cheap homes and rentals, which gave residents a sense of permanency and upward mobility. They also spoke Spanish, practiced Mexican culture, and started businesses with less Anglo interference. It was a place to call home.

As electric trolleys expanded eastward, more Mexican residents moved to Belvedere. The trolleys offered cheap commutes to LA's work districts. By 1930 Belvedere had about thirty thousand residents of Mexican descent—the largest concentration of Mexicans in LA County. By 1960 the area of about eight square miles had become known as "East Los Angeles" and had a population of about 105,000.[36] Yet it stayed unincorporated, which meant that it was not a city. The city of LA had also refused to annex it because of its weak tax base.[37] East LA thus relied on LA County for its needs. Schools were bad; police were unjust and limited in number; and the infrastructure and available social services were horrible.

During the 1960s, local politicians and community groups tried to turn East LA into a city, but labor unions, business interests, and property owners blocked them. They feared that a new political system would raise taxes and reduce profits, wages, and jobs.[38] Worse, East LA became a victim of LA County's freeway construction. The Long Beach, Pomona, San Bernardino, and Golden State Freeways all cut through East LA. These monstrous constructions destroyed between 25 to 43 percent of owner-occupied homes, and intersected hundreds of feet aboveground, creating gray, ghastly structures that deadened streets.[39]

East LA's housing stock also crumbled. Except for two census tracts that bordered the city of Montebello to the east, only 27 percent of its housing was considered "sound" in 1968.[40] For relief, a public housing project was built in the Maravilla section, which already held the area's poorest and least educated homeowners and renters. The new public housing residents were worse off and less politically inclined.[41] East LA sunk deeper into misery.

Resistance in East LA

East LA residents fought back. Throughout the 1960s and 1970s, Mexican college and high school students took to the streets. They protested racism, discrimination, sexism, and the Vietnam War. Mainly, they criticized LA's public school system, which still featured Anglo curriculums, overcrowded classrooms, and racist teachers. Worse, it placed large numbers of Mexican students in special education and had a Mexican dropout rate of over 50 percent.[42]

At first the students were ignored, but through the leadership of a Chicano high school teacher, Sal Castro, more than ten thousand Mexican students took part in the 1968 East Los Angeles Blowouts.[43] For over a week, Mexican students, mostly those living east of downtown LA, walked out of their classrooms.[44] They marched. They picketed. They chanted. They made demands. *Smaller classes! Better bilingual education! Chicano history courses! Community control of public schools!* Most rallies were peaceful. A few, though, became violent after riot police attacked students. As the East LA Blowouts gained national attention, thirteen students were charged with conspiracy.

After two years of student rallies and community and legal support, the charges were dropped. Young people continued the fight.

August 29, 1970. About twenty thousand protesters gathered against the Vietnam War in an event known as the National Chicano Moratorium.[45] The Brown Berets, a group of militant Mexican youths, marched stone-faced and in steady cadence, *tit-tat, tit-tat, tit-tat.* Activists with bullhorns yelled out, *We want justice! Brown pride!* Elderly ladies walked in their Sunday best and toddlers wore sombreros. Órale! Young people chanted and waved large signs: *Queremos Justicia. Be Brown & Be Proud. Chale con Nixon!*

The marchers eventually arrived at Laguna Park, near the western border of East LA. There, they listened to peace activists call for a rise in ethnic pride and an end to the Vietnam War. They spoke about how Mexicans still experienced racism and discrimination despite fighting honorably and having a high proportion of war casualties and deaths relative to their numbers. The crowd also listened to bands that played protest songs to traditional Mexican music, songs that emphasized brown unity and social justice. Children in traditional Mexican dress danced in choreographed circles, with girls holding up the hems of their long, colorful dresses to step and dip from side to side. The peaceful crowd, which included grandparents, parents, and children, picnicked on the grass to enjoy the show.

Suddenly, a fight broke out. A few mischief-makers had stolen soft drinks from a crowded liquor store, claiming that the items were supposed to be free. The police intervened and then used the incident to end the event.[46] In riot gear, they lined up as if preparing for battle against the peaceful protesters. Words were exchanged. Then:

Disperse, disperse! demanded the police, suddenly defining the event as an unlawful assembly. Confused participants scattered, with many unsure of what was happening. Their slow movement frustrated police. Then war: The police crashed into the crowd, swung their nightsticks, and caused panic as they wildly beat people on their arms, legs, and heads. Helicopters appeared overhead, *chop, chop, chop*, and dropped canisters of tear gas onto the people. More police appeared in riot gear, *move, move, move!* and shot canisters of tear gas at the people. Shrieks cascaded through the crowd. Some people ran this way, others ran that way; some created a stampede, which crushed others against buses and park fences. Some fell to the ground and balled up for protection; others raised their arms in surrender, only to be beaten to a pulp. Hundreds of youths fled into the neighborhoods, with police officers hot on their tracks.

Then the people fought back. With an emotional surge, they threw bottles and rocks at police officers, then charged into the helmets and nightsticks, punching and kicking and shoving despite choking and tearing up from the gas. They gave blows; received blows. Became bloody; made others bloody. They spilled onto Whittier Boulevard and attacked patrol cars, broke store windows, and set fire to those patrol cars and stores. It was mayhem. Sirens. Shouting. Screaming. Running. Shooting. Shattered glass. Flames. Smoke billowing in the sky above East LA. In the aftermath, about a million dollars' worth of property was destroyed; 250 people were arrested; and four people were killed.[47]

The clashes with police continued. A few months later, during the 1971 March for Justice in East LA, one person was killed, around fifty injured (all by police), and eighty-eight arrested. The police justified their violence by claiming that antipolice demonstrators were lawless and brainwashed by communist agents.[48] Major LA newspapers supported the police. East LA residents stood alone, receiving assaults from all sides.

East LA's Mexican boys and girls continued to experience racism, discrimination, and police brutality. They felt like disrespected Americans. As early as the 1920s, they had formed the Maravilla gangs for meaning and status. According to sociologist Joan Moore, the Maravilla gangs started as friends who identified with a street, such as Ford, Lopez, Kern, Arizona, and so forth.[49] They attended dances and parties and sometimes competed in sporting events. Later they matured out of the neighborhood as they found work, started families, and hung out in adult spaces, such as cantinas or bars.

But by the 1950s, the Maravillas—who wore *drapes* and spoke Caló—were likened to animals by their own East LA community.[50] Thus, the youths faced both poor barrio conditions and a criminal stigma. The gang then became what Moore calls a "quasi-institution."[51] As a neighborhood fixture, it socialized members, providing them with rules, norms, and roles that gave them structure and meaning. It also provided a space for defiance. Gang members challenged the community, school, and police authorities—Chale! Challenged conventions in dress, talk, and attitude—Órale! Showcased their smarts, courage, and independence, and an ingenuity and seriousness beyond their years. Simón que si!

By the 1960s, however, many Maravillas were no longer maturing out of gangs into conventional life. A disastrous economy, racist politics, and a mighty drug all played important roles.

East LA Pushed Underwater

While East LA residents resisted, economic conditions worsened. Minor recessions occurred here and there, and in 1958 a major one hit, which led to layoffs of blue-collar workers.[52] Later, the turbulent 1960s saw more job losses in the auto, manufacturing, and aerospace industries, which closed or relocated for greener tax pastures. Now more Black and Mexican workers lost stable middle- and working-class jobs.[53]

As historian Rodolfo Acuña notes, by the 1970s, the US economy was a mess.[54] Unemployment was high. Home interest rates rose by about 150 percent. Food prices rose by about 15 percent. Oil-exporting nations cut supplies to the United States, which raised oil prices by more than 100 percent. Inflation rose to a height of about 9 percent before leveling out to about 6 percent, which was still two or three points above the 1960s average. LA's minority communities became poorer. Whites, the great benefactors of California's earlier industrial booms, felt insecure. They wanted answers.

White politicians gave them racist answers. They claimed that lawless minorities stole white jobs, wallets, purses, and tax dollars. "Get Tough on Crime" became a popular slogan, which deflected attention from how countries like Japan and Germany had rebuilt themselves after World War II and now competed globally with cheaper and more efficient products. "Socialism is evil" became a popular battle cry, a call to reduce welfare programs and raise resources for law enforcement.

The governor of California, Ronald Reagan, provided subtle racially coded answers. With his charismatic voice and aging movie star face, he blamed the poor for being poor and accused them of welfare dependence. He assured his white voting base that limited government solved all problems, including poverty. He then drastically cut funds for public schools, welfare, and Medi-Cal. He even tried to raise university and college tuition, which would have hurt minorities seeking managerial and public sector jobs.[55] The political and social gains made through protests, walkouts, and rebellions now seemed small. The economy was in a rut.

East LA had put up its political fists but was now exhausted, breathing hard, unable to dodge the economic blows. Poverty increased. Unemployment rose. Union jobs declined. And in the late 1970s, poor and unskilled Mexican immigrants—who did not vote, who earned miserable wages, and who stayed under the radar—settled in East LA in larger numbers. But the strength in numbers did not translate into political and economic might. East LA was on the canvas, down for the count. Then a mighty drug stepped into ring to ensure that it never got up.

Heroin.

American Dopefiend

During the 1960s and 1970s, heroin addictions rose in East LA. This period became the backdrop for the Maravilla participants. But Maravilla heroin users descend from a long line of American dope-fiends. Drug addicts were found in other ethnic groups before them and alongside them, which devastated communities across the US.

For instance, during the latter half of the 1800s combat veterans from the American Civil War (1861–65) had fallen to morphine addictions. These addicted white war veterans no longer worked or contributed to families, spending their days in a euphoric stupor. Syringe injections pockmarked their torsos and limbs, and their reduced appetite produced emaciated figures that lay about.[56] During the same period southern upper- and middle-class white women also suffered from opium and morphine use. In fact, these high-society women statistically made up most of the opiate-related addictions.[57] True, their male counterparts, such as novelists, senators, and lawyers, also consumed opiates (for instance, 5 to 25 percent of US physicians during the early 1900s had opiate addictions).[58] But sexist doctors treated women's afflictions, such as menstrual cramps, uterine infections, and discrimination-related frustration, with morphine.[59]

When the medical establishment no longer approved of heroin as a medicine (it was addictive), the drug hit the streets during the early 1900s. Heroin addicts were usually young, poor white men in urban areas, often born in the US to European immigrant families.[60] Some were gang members who did recreational drugs for kicks, thrills, and risk-taking. They placed the powdery substance on a kitchen spoon holding water, then they heated the spoon until the liquid bubbled and the heroin dissolved. To filter out debris or impurities, they placed a cotton ball or cigarette filter in the solution. Then they safely withdrew the liquid into a syringe, injected it into a vein, and waited several seconds for the euphoria. The withdrawal, or aftereffect, was awful. Unbearable bone aches, stomach cramps, headaches, fevers, chills, diarrhea, and more forced a user to chase the drug for life. Several of these young men eventually took to the streets for the long haul, untidy, unhygienic, and on the fringes of the underworld.[61]

Poor white women, especially sex workers, also became heroin addicts. For instance, in New York City the Mafia gangster Luciano organized a prostitution ring in which he controlled thousands of brothels. In a diabolical pursuit of profit, he purposely addicted sex workers to heroin. He wanted them pliable and compliant as well as dependent on sex work to secure the drug. In doing so, the prostitution racket earned him about ten million dollars a year.[62]

After a lull in heroin addictions during World War II, Blacks and Latinos replaced whites as the main American dopefiend. As historian Eric Schneider notes, after the war, many whites fled inner cities to the suburbs, which decreased their contact with the drug.[63] At the same time, heroin made the rounds among the coolest and hippest Americans: the Black jazz players and singers like Charlie Parker, Miles Davis, Billie Holiday, and John Coltrane. Aspiring Black musicians wanted to be just like their heroes, who performed brilliantly under a heroin nod. Jazz and bebop fans wanted to be just as hip as their idols who acted so cool. Many of these Black and Latino admirers experienced racism, resided in slums, and searched for respect by being a part of the cultural elite. All increased their chances of using heroin.[64]

Heroin use then spread through poor minority neighborhoods in cities across the country. LA, though, was unique in its heroin experience. The limited historical research finds that LA Mexicans mainly relied on the gummy unrefined black tar heroin from Mexico.[65] Barrio gangsters used family ties to do business with Mexican heroin dealers, often trading stolen goods, such as cars, for heroin.[66] LA's Mexican hustlers and pimps were the first to brazenly use heroin, cultivating an aura of coolness. Barrio gang members followed rapidly, falling victim to heroin as they emulated their street idols. East LA suffered. It was already the center of Mexican gang life. Now it became the heart of Mexican heroin use.[67]

Fortunately, US heroin use dropped across the nation after 1951. The younger generation had witnessed the ill effects of heroin and stayed away from it. The drug rejection was short-lived. By the early 1960s heroin use was up again. Demographically, the number of young minorities—the ones most likely to experiment with drugs, live in wretched poverty, and have little memory of heroin's past harm—had grown.[68] The counterculture movement also expanded. White middle-class folks became beatniks and hippies who embraced drug use for otherworldly experiences. Some of them became addicted to heroin.[69] Heroin was everywhere.

Especially in East LA.

Sociologist Joan Moore documents how Maravilla gang members increased their drug use during this period.[70] Their heroin addictions kept them on the streets into adulthood and often landed them in prison. By the mid-1970s East LA had an established heroin subculture with consistent dealers and users. Treatment centers, such as methadone clinics, also became commonplace, which proved that a heroin problem existed. Moore concludes that heroin use in East LA had become institutionalized. It was an ordinary part of gang life.

The Stage Is Set

At the start of the 1970s the Maravilla participants were in their early teens, and in trouble. They still faced police brutality and poor public schools and had few community resources. And they did not know it. They were too young to know (and perhaps to care about) the history that set the stage for their lives. They knew nothing about how white nativists, politicians, media, and law enforcement portrayed their parents and grandparents as communists, job stealers, welfare cheats, and predators. They knew nothing about how earlier generations of LA Mexicans were attacked with impunity by the police, the military, and white citizens. They knew nothing about how East LA was considered the region's gutter. Or why this stigmatized area became a space of protest and resistance. They knew nothing about how all these social and political factors converged to shape the course of their lives.

They did know one thing: how to show smarts, defiance, and independence. And they would follow right behind the earlier East LA youngsters who joined the Maravilla gangs. Tragically, many of them became violent and succumbed to heroin.[71] The powerful drug made them dismiss their families, commit crimes, and spend long periods in jail and prison. Gangs, violence, and chasing *carga* (heroin) became their *vida*, or life.

2   *La Vida Loca*

There are many reasons someone became a Maravilla. Every reason did not apply to all. Some Maravillas came from nuclear families; others came from single-parent families. Some Maravillas came from families with generational gang membership; others came from immigrant families with no Maravilla ties. But they all grew up poor and experienced what anthropologist James Diego Vigil calls "multiple marginality," or marginal neighborhoods, schools, families, and overall community. And they tried to prevail through autonomy, or what sociologist Martín Sánchez Jankowski calls a defiant individualism.[1] As children, many of them showed maturity, drive, and intelligence. In a privileged context, this might be seen as a strong faith in the American achievement ideology.[2] In their unprivileged context, it led to drug- and violence-related traumas that haunted them for life.

Early Exposure to Crime

August 1970. Out of curiosity, an eleven-year-old Emilio joined the thousands of people marching down Whittier Boulevard for the National Chicano Moratorium. He tagged along with some teenagers looking for something to do. They did not understand the politics that swept them to Laguna Park, nor the cries for Brown power and unity. Or why violence suddenly erupted. "Everything just went haywire," Emilio recalled. "Everybody started running east towards Whittier Boulevard where they were looting. At that time, they didn't have the wrought iron gates on the [store] windows. It used to be just windows and the merchandise used to be in there. They never used to put it [the merchandise] away. So, it was a day of opportunity. People just started looting, breaking windows."

Emilio became frightened. "People were just running from the police. The police were shooting their tear gas canisters. I mean, you could see the cops literally beating people down with their clubs. And I remember that. That scared me. People were screaming, crying. It was crazy."

Emilio scampered home, dodging the police and weaving around looters, who carried televisions, radios, and clothes. Back at the run-down two-bedroom apartment his family rented, he found his teenaged sister in high spirits. She had looted a jewelry store and showed him the diamond rings and gold chains. Emilio now wanted to return to the smoking madness for sparkles of his own, but his mother demanded that he stay home for his safety. Such parental worry seemed odd coming from her. She and her husband already endangered their children in the drug world's chaos, which accounted for Emilio's adulthood suffering and pain.

Emilio's mother and father were heroin users who shoplifted, burglarized, and dealt drugs from home. Emilio often heard their crime plots and saw them exchange money and drugs with strangers. One incident impacted Emilio forever. It happened on his birthday when he turned eight years old. While his father was in prison, his mother did a drug transaction with a male partner, who was an undercover police informant. While they cut the heroin, Emilio nagged his mother about wanting a kite for his birthday. After the drug deal, she hid the drugs on her and took him to purchase the kite.

"My mom said, 'Let's go,'" Emilio remembered. "We jumped in the car. As soon as we pulled in the market, the cops came—Wooo! Wooo! Wooo!—from all sides. I remember my mom grabbed me and she held me. And the doors came open and this officer, I'll never forget him. He had a reputation out here in East LA. He started socking my mom. Started beating her. [The officer yelled:] 'Spit it out! Spit it, bitch! Spit it out!' He was just hitting her. And I'm eight years old, and I remember my mom, she was putting her hands down my pants, man. And I didn't know what was going on. And it went on for a few minutes, and he was just hitting her, hitting her bad. And then she finally just surrendered. And amazingly they let me go."

Emilio walked to his grandmother and aunt's home. His aunt then took him to the bathroom for a wash. "And when she took off my clothes," he remembered, "all these big ol' balloons full of heroin fell out. My mom was stashing [it in my clothes]. And once she got rid of what she had to get rid of, that's when she surrendered [to the officer]. He broke her jaw. He broke her nose. He beat her like a man. And I didn't see my mom for a couple of years after that."

While his mother was incarcerated, Emilio and his siblings lived with extended family members for one or two months at a time. After his mother's release, they reunited and returned to their former apartment. She started using heroin again. As he got older, he returned from school to find his mother, father, uncles, and aunts sitting around silently, with their eyes shut and heads slowly nodding. Sometimes he saw them overdose and his mother come to the rescue with homespun remedies. Emilio wanted to know why his family members chased that drug. His mother, in her warped way of nurturing, provided guidance that caused permanent harm.

"I got curious at the age of thirteen years old," Emilio recalled, "and I told my mom, 'I want to do that [heroin].' And she goes, 'What?' I said, 'I want to know what you guys feel.' And she cried and she cried and she cried. She says, 'Why would you want to do something like that? Haven't you seen what it's done to us?' And I said, 'That's why I want to know.' And my mom was the first person to put a needle in my arm. She knew that I was going to do it [eventually]. And a mother's instincts is to take care of her kids. They want to protect them. Although it was against the law of the land—the law of the Lord—she went on and did that. I got my first taste of heroin when I was thirteen years old."

Other Maravillas grew up in more stable environments. Chico, for instance, was raised in what seemed a typical East LA family in the Maravilla projects. His father had first tailored clothes in downtown LA and later got a stable state job working with juvenile delinquents. His mother, a devout Pentecostal, devoted herself to raising a God-fearing family. His father showed less religion: he sold marijuana from home. It was the 1960s, when peace and love became movements, and marijuana became the recreational drug of choice. Chico's father, who had marijuana connections in Mexico, dealt the drug in wholesale quantities.

Chico remembered being about four years old and running to his father for a whiff of his fingers. The burnt popcorn smell intrigued him. His father laughed at Chico's fascination with his fingers that smelled of marijuana and, as a game, gave him roaches, or the small remains of a marijuana joint. Little Chico chewed on them, acquiring a taste for the marijuana's flavor. By eight years old he smoked joints with his father's knowledge. In fact, his father included him on drug runs.

"He would take me in the car for a ride with him," Chico recalled. "He would put these baggies, sandwich bags full of pot, stick them down my drawers, my little underwear. He would put it in my little crotch area. And I would sit in the front [of the car] and we would drive around. And I realized what he was doing. He was using me to deal marijuana to his customers."

Later his father had customers come to the home. Perhaps because of his desire to enhance Chico's manhood, his father made a move that damaged Chico for life. He included his eight-year-old son in his drug business. "He'll tell me, 'Take the money, and take them [the customer] this, an ounce of weed,'" Chico remembered. "So, I would get the money and hand them the ounce of weed. He put me in the middle of it. After a while, after running back and forth so many times, he told me, 'For every ten [ounces] that you sell, I'll give you one. You can either have an ounce of your own or ten dollars. Which one do you want?' I told him I'll take the ounce and I can roll joints and sell them for fifty joints and make twenty [dollars]."

By the age of thirteen Chico had a weed business. He had saved enough money to buy a kilo from his father and expanded his sales to other neighborhoods. His older brothers, whom his father had dismissed as unambitious, long-haired, peace-loving hippies, introduced Chico to other customers within the counterculture. He earned the nickname Chico Clavo (Stash), which swelled his pride.

Risk-Taking Masculinity

Sociologist Adam Reich describes how some young marginal men develop an *outsider masculinity* in which they construct their manhood outside the law. The young men then turn their pursuit of crime into a *game of outlaw* in which they show courage, take risks, and do violence to outdo like-minded peers.[3] They learn how to make meaning of such risks through what anthropologist James Diego Vigil calls "street socialization." In this case, gang peers prevail over the family and school as social influences, especially when the latter fail to provide support or resources. For Emilio and Chico, the streets would play a large role in socializing them. They would join gangs to earn respect through manly risk-taking.[4]

For Emilio, it started with his run-ins with the neighborhood youth gang. It was made of boys no older than fourteen years old and was not an official Maravilla gang. Once in their group he spray-painted graffiti, fought with rivals, drank beer, inhaled paint fumes, threw rocks at buses, and shattered car windows. He also broke into his middle school, which he did for both thrills and much-needed food.

"We had A-keys," Emilio explained. "The A-keys opened all the doors in the school. We would burglarize the school and spend the weekend in there. We'll go in the auditorium, put movies on. We'll go in the cafeteria and eat. Me, I'll be coming home with crates of the little carton milks and the baloney sandwiches because I didn't have food in my house. And I didn't have milk in my house all the time. So my thing was always trying to give to my house. So it was survival."

As the gang gained status, Emilio helped transform it into a Maravilla gang. In fact, it was a revival of the neighborhood's old Maravilla gang that had disappeared during the early 1960s. "The neighborhood didn't exist anymore," Emilio explained, "so we just brought it back to life again. And what we did was we walked each other in [initiation by beating]. 'Alright,' boom, boom, boom."

Chico also relished his reputation as a risk-taker. "I was the daring guy, the smart guy, the first guy to do everything. I was one of them kids. The first guy to punch somebody out. The first one to smoke weed. The first one to sniff glue, to pop a pill. I wouldn't hesitate when it came to climbing through someone's window to steal something. I didn't hesitate, especially to fight. And I wasn't a big guy. I was a skinny, wiry kid. But I guess I had the balls of a Chihuahua, so my peers looked up to me."

At about twelve years old, the precocious Chico started a crew modeled after the Brown Berets, a Chicano militant group that started in the 1960s to resist white racism, police brutality, and inequality in healthcare and education. "So my little posse," he recalled, "ten-, eleven-year-old youngsters—we went and got Brown Beret hats from one of the Whittier Boulevard clothing stores. We might not have even bought them; we might have stolen them. But we got them and we started wearing them. So I started a little clique called the Brown Berets de Maravilla. And there was only like ten of us. We wore our brown berets and walked around real tough, no-nonsense. We wanted to let everyone know that we were important, just like the real Brown Berets."

The baby Brown Berets, though, soon bored of strutting around. The neighborhood's Maravilla gang had caught their attention. With about a dozen other preteen boys, Chico started a *clica*, or sub-group, called Los Chicos. The older homies, who were in their late teens, sent Los Chicos on "missions" to hurt rival neighborhoods by shattering windows, crossing out graffiti, and stealing and vandalizing cars. Los Chicos put in a lot of work, making Chico felt that the older homies took advantage of them. He wanted to quit. The other members wanted to leave too, but when a member left a gang they got "beat out," or physically punished. As budding gangsters, Los Chicos wanted to follow the adult rules. Chico led the way.

"So we said," Chico recalled, "'if everybody wants to get out, let's have a free-for-all.' So, we started boxing with each other. We were fighting, cracking each other, busting this guy's eye over here, busting another guy's lip over there, cracking each other's ribs, swinging at each other for a good two or three minutes. Then it was over. We were out of [the gang]."

Later Chico partied with different Maravilla neighborhoods. When he found a summer job at a community resource center, he spent time with the boys from that area. They befriended him and invited him to hang out. After several months of drinking, drugging, and having laughs, he joined them.

A gangster was born.

Necro-Living: The Vatos Locos

Living *la vida loca*, or the crazy life, was a phase that characterized early gang experiences. It was a period when participants seemed to care little if they lived or died. The vatos locos (crazy ones) became neighborhood fanatics who obsessed over enemies. If they had a *cuete*, or gun, they shot it. If they had a *filero*, or knife, they stabbed with it. If they only had their *puños*, or fists, they swung hard. Like courageous men, they headed into danger, daring death to snatch their lives. Historian Deborah Levenson refers to this lifestyle as necro-living, or a life in which dying or killing guides behavior.[5]

Most Maravillas became vato locos after dropping out of high school. For these bright and independent youths, the classroom was a boring space where they needed to get high to relieve the monotony. Yet they felt alive in schoolyards, hallways, and lunchrooms, the battlegrounds where they fought neighborhood rivals. Thus, many of them got multiple suspensions and expulsions. Emilio's gang violence, for example, got him expelled from middle school and placed at Andrew Jackson High School. Jackson High was a trade school that delinquent and violent boys attended from the seventh to twelfth grades.[6] As a youth, Emilio framed this experience positively, making it seem as if this school with a dead-end reputation increased his masculinity.

"Because when you went to Jackson High," Emilio explained, "you were making a statement: 'I'm a bad dude, man. I'm going to a boy's school.' And people respected that. They respected that. Because it's like if you went to juvenile hall, you come out and it's, 'Órale!' You get that much more respect. You go to Jackson and it's the same thing."

Emilio often attended class in a daze since he found his teachers uninspiring. In fact, he would recreate a party atmosphere at school to make the experience enjoyable. "When I went to Jackson [High

School] I was into sniffing paint, or inhaling paint. And there was a hardware store where they had the best paint, the 5 Star Clear Plastic. I would sniff the paint, get high, hang out with the homies, and be zoned out in class. So that was just another party I went to, man. Just in a different part of town."

Juano, who was Chico's younger homeboy, experienced rougher school transitions. He claimed that after his beloved older cousin was killed in gang warfare, he joined a gang to relieve his rage. He did violence so well that he got expelled from East LA's Garfield High School.

"There was this guy in two of my classes," Juano recalled, "he was always talking shit. So, one day, I got pissed off. I don't remember what he said, I just go up to him and I just started bombing [hitting] him, started beating him up. So they took us to the dean's office and, believe it or not, I was more scared of my mom coming to the office than the principal or the dean. He [the rival] was there [sitting] across from me. He was busted up pretty bad. His dad and mom got there, and they were like, 'Why did you did this?' So I was getting kinda scared. His dad was like this older cholo [gangster]. And my mom walks in, 'Qué pasó?' What happened? And I lied. I told her, 'Mom, this fuckin' guy over there was talking about you, saying bad things about you.' She said, 'Qué?' I said, 'That fuckin' guy over there, cabrón [bastard].' So we talked to the dean, whatever, and he expelled me and shit."

Juano then enrolled in a degree-granting occupational center in Monterey Park. However, he and four other homeboys were kicked out for skipping school. He then tried to enroll in Woodrow Wilson Senior High, about four miles north, in El Sereno. Afraid to tell his parents of his new expulsion—his parents often beat him and made him kneel on raw beans for punishment—he convinced an older homeboy to act like an uncle who wanted to enroll him at the school.

"I'm telling him, 'Take a long-sleeve shirt so you could pass for my uncle,'" Juano recalled. "And he's like, 'Alright, homie,' but then picks me up the next morning and he had a short-sleeve, all these tattoos, thick mustache, he got his hair short, you know. He looked like a fuckin' gangbanger. I was like, 'Fuck, man.' So we get there, and I don't know how we did it, Randy, but they let me in the school."

Juano, however, was a gang member. After two days of attendance, a few guys "hit him up," or asked about his gang affiliation. "They were all these guys from those neighborhoods [gangs] up there, like from Hazard and Sereno," Juano explained. "So I was there for two days, and on Friday I got hit up by a couple of guys and I told them 'Soy de Maravilla.' And they said their neighborhood and one fucking dummy says, 'Fuck your neighborhood.' I say, 'Fuck your neighborhood!' So it started. We got down [fighting]. I got fucking kicked out [of school] again."

After the expulsion Juano attended another occupational center. This one was above Boyle Heights by the Los Angeles County General Hospital, about four miles away. He ran into problems again since local gangs controlled the school grounds. Worse, gang members from different parts of LA were bussed in, creating a chaotic, adrenaline-filled environment. Soon he got into conflicts with gangs from Boyle Heights and 18th Street. He was expelled one more time.

"'Cause I was an outsider again," Juano explained. "So when I went to another school, it was like, 'Hey, who's that new dude over there? Where he's from?' I'm by myself now, so they was like, 'Hey homie, when you're gonna get into our barrio [gang]?' I'm like, 'Nah, homie, I just kick it with you guys.' When other guys hit me up, I would say, 'I'm from Maravilla.' They were like, 'Fuck your neighborhood.' And I was already looking for an excuse to fight. I was full of rage, Randy. I was full of anger."

Having nowhere else to turn, he dropped out of school and put his boxing aspirations aside. "I was getting really good at boxing," Juano explained. "I boxed for the [LA County] sheriff's department, where they taught us how to box and took us to competitions. I let that go to fight in the streets. What I learned in boxing, I kind of combined it and just made ugly ass fights in the streets. I used to go to the gym a little bit, but they weren't training me like the way they were before. They were like, 'He ain't gonna go nowhere no more. He's just here to mess around.'"

Juano now immersed himself in necro-living. In fact, he viewed gangsterism as a job.[7] Just like a sports scout, Juano recruited and studied potential members during their neighborhood visits. He specifically evaluated their potential to deal with violence. "If I knew that the gang wasn't for somebody, I let 'em know," he explained. "There were a few friends of ours that were my carnales [best friends] that didn't get into the gang 'cause I let them know that this wasn't for them. They didn't have it in them. And you know, they should be thankful today. The gang life wasn't for them. And it was for other people. You could tell who could handle it and who couldn't handle it."

Juano also expected new members to drop everything for the gang. For instance, when a homie got a girlfriend, Juano questioned their loyalty. "If I saw someone already with a girlfriend, and I knew that he really wasn't like down or like he didn't put in work for the 'hood, I was like, 'Look at this fuckin' guy. He already fuckin' got a girl and he's settling down, already talking about "*Yeah, homie, that's it for me, the barrio life.*"' I would tell them, 'You never did shit for the barrio.' And when I got a [serious] girlfriend at fifteen years old, I said to myself, 'If I ain't out here, then nobody'll be out here.' Those thoughts was running through my head. That's when you make your decision. 'Do I want to be a family man or do I want to be from the 'hood?' I decided that I was from the 'hood before anything."

His high drive and ambition, though, often brought him close to death. For instance, after partially recuperating from a gunshot wound to his neck, he went to a neighborhood bar for some drinks.

He was only sixteen years old, but the bar owner relaxed the rules for his neighborhood since its members were steady customers. After settling down for a beer, Juano saw an older guy yelling at his girlfriend.

"But there goes Juano," he recalled, referring to himself. "I say, 'Ay, man, I want you to stop that shit. Be cool, homie, or take that somewhere else, ese.' And he goes, 'Ese, who the fuck [is] talkin' to you?' I'm like, 'Hey homie, I'm just sayin' you don't have to make a big fuckin' escandalo [scene] right here.' And she goes, 'Ay, what's your name?' And I go, 'Juano.' And this fucker says, 'Is that him?' And I say, 'Is that him, who? What the fuck's going on?' He says, 'Come on, bitch!' And my homeboy's like, 'Ay, fuck that pedo [problem], let them go outside.'"

As the couple exited, the guy slapped the young woman. Juano followed them out. "Fuckin' Mister-Get-Involved, I go outside," he recalled. "I say, 'Hey man, why don't you fucking leave her alone?' He said, 'What? Who the fuck are you?' I say, 'I'm Juano from . . .' He says, 'I'm so and so from this neighborhood.' We already had pedo [problems] with them. And he's this older guy, so, I say, 'What's up, ese?' We take a walk to the parking lot. I fucked him u-u-up. I dropped him. Poom! I say, 'Get up ese! Get out of here!'"

The bouncer, who was Juano's friend, escorted the beaten guy off the premises. Juano walked back into the bar, washed his hands in the restroom, and came out to find the young woman waiting for him. They decided to attend an after-hours party. She and her friend rode with Juano and his homeboy to a convenience store to buy beer. After the purchase they tried to drive out of the parking lot, but a car blocked their path. They drove the other way, only to find the same car following and eventually pulling up to them.

"My homeboy's in the front, and I'm in the back," Juano recalled. "So fuckin' the girl, her friend was driving. My homeboy started saying, 'You better punch it [accelerate]. Get the fuck outta here.' She's driving away and I say, 'Turn right here, turn right here!' She's turning in one block [and] while she's turning, she kind of left them behind. But then she turns another corner, and another corner, and they end up right in front of us. I jump out the back seat. I got right in front of them, and I'm like, 'Wassup, ese! Get off [the car] or what!' I had that stupid-ass problem that I used to walk up to cars. And they didn't get out. The fool in the front just said, 'What?' I said, 'You gonna get off or what, ese!' And when they started pullin' the gun, I turned and tried to run. So I went like this [makes a sideways movement] and he shoots me right here [side of the stomach] and it came out the side. He got me right there—poom! So I fall on one knee, and I could hear pah! pah! pah! And then they fuckin' leave.

"But I was on PCP. Before we left the bar, we smoked some PCP. So I got shot and fell on my knee. I remember I wanted to get up and my homeboy's like, 'Jay, sit down, sit down.' And I sit on the sidewalk and I'm just in a white shirt, you know, and some basic fuckin' khakis. And I'm sitting there, and I'm stuttering like, 'Where the fuck were you guys?' And the girl starts screaming, 'He's fuckin' shot! He's fuckin' shot!' And I remember I get up against the car slowly. I don't remember getting shot or nothing. I remember being in the hospital. They put some injections to take away the fuckin' drugs [out of my system] and all that. And all of sudden, I'm like, 'Ahhhh!' I got a cramp, like when you gotta go to the restroom, but ten times that, like 'ARRRRGH!'"

Later in life Juano got stabbed once, and then he was shot two times in separate encounters. His loved ones often asked him, *Who do you think you are?* His response was, "If you gonna be a gang member, fuckin' be the best fuckin' gang member you could be. If you can't do that, get the fuck out. What's the fuckin' point?"

Juano also viewed street fighting in stark terms. His goal was both physical and psychological domination within the gang world. "Let me tell you something, Randy," he explained, "there's something that

I learned a long time ago. It was this: if you gonna get in a conflict with somebody, make sure you fuckin' beat his ass so bad that he don't think of coming back. That's the answer to what the fuckin' game's all about. If I beat somebody down, and let's say that's it, he gets up [and says], 'Fuckin' watch. I'ma get that fucker later.' He's carrying that with him, 'I'ma get him back.' But if you keep fuckin' pounding on him, fuckin' pounding on him, like I do, or like I did, you know, out of their misery, 'Damn, dog, no more, no more!' [I say] 'Don't tell me no more, motherfucker! I'll tell you when it'll stop.' By that time, the next time you see this person, if you come across them, they're gonna look at you and do like a glance and walk the fuck away. Or, if anything, they'll walk by and be like, 'Wassup, man. Everything firme [alright]?' The only thing they think is, 'Fuck that. I don't want to be on the fool's bad side.'"

Juano's younger brother, Tito, who later joined the neighborhood, marveled at his brother's violence. He also noted that Juano brutalized even his own homeboys. "He was the type that if he sees any homeboy late at night walking around two, three in the morning—they're just lookin' for a hustle to get high, or up to no good—he would beat 'em up. As strong as they were, he would beat them up. He'll beat up the guys that you seen them all cracked [drugged] out. Because in our neighborhood people used to be able to leave their cars open [unlocked]. There was rules, like that nobody's gonna steal nothing. If somebody steals something, we knew that it was a homeboy. So we'll get to the bottom of it. And my brother used to come out, I ain't lying, he used to beat up a lot of homies. I say beat up because he beat 'em up bad. The next thing you know, everybody hated him. But to this day they won't say nothin' to him. He's still the same."

Life as a Dopefiend

Even more tragic was how many Maravillas, once they passed the vato loco stage, became *tecatos*, or dopefiends. During their teens they often graduated from beer, to marijuana, to uppers and downers, and then to PCP. Their lives then became a big blur, a spacey existence that impaired their judgment and enhanced their violence. Later some of them framed heroin users as weak individuals unable to handle hard drugs. Feeling invincible, they tried heroin as well. The first or second hit got them hooked. They then lived a fast-paced life of earning drug money against a ticking time bomb: the onset of heroin withdrawal. They then showed the heroin addict's version of hypermasculinity. They did not beg or panhandle. They did not offer to work for food. Instead they took thrilling risks to get money, which Philippe Bourgois and Jeff Schonberg refer to as an "outlaw masculinity" among heroin users.[8] The participants committed burglaries and robberies and sold drugs. Such activities announced that they were still daring and violent men.

Chico Slips into Darkness

Like many of his Maravilla peers, Chico lived his teen years on a roller coaster of barbiturates, marijuana, and liquor. He believed that drugs could never bring him down. That delusion led to a costly error. "I just thought these guys [heroin addicts] were just weak. They just didn't know how to control it [heroin use]. I thought I could outwit the drug. 'Cause I was curious. I wondered why this drug had these guys like that. And by that time I wanted to try something different. I was already tired of the pot [marijuana], the pills, and alcohol. . . . I would see these guys [heroin users] and how they carried themselves. These were the guys I looked up to. They were hustlers. They were convicts already. Been to the joint [prison] two or three times and they were still in their early twenties. I would see some of them get sick too. And then I would see them get well like that [snaps his fingers]. They go from being tore-up to being superhuman, happy, and nodding out. It was time for me to find out."

At that point the twenty-year-old Chico was married with a couple of children. He even had a steady job at a nearby hospital, which he balanced with his gang life. But he had made up his mind. "I went to someone in a different neighborhood," Chico remembered. "I asked him if he knew where I could get some carga [heroin] and he got some for me. And when I first tried it, it must'a not been that strong or I must have done it wrong 'cause it didn't have that strong effect on me. So I tried it again. I did it right that time and it did the effect that I was looking for."

Chico experienced bliss . . . then heroin withdrawal. Several weeks later he was on the street. "I lost everything," he explains. "Gave up everything: my wife at the time, our kids together—I gave up that life, the family life, to pursue the criminal life. After that I went from ten miles per hour to sixty miles per hour, and just running, just running hard. 'Up and running'—that's what we called it. Always looking for the drugs, always looking for the money to score."

Up and running, he checked cars for unlocked doors; he cased houses that appeared to have no one home; he scanned sidewalks and checked pay phones for change; he searched for victims to mug or rob. He lived an uncertain life in which he pressed the pedal to the metal until he finally injected the *carga* into his vein.

"Every now and then," Chico recalled, "I would run into a 'stuck' where I didn't have anything going on and I would be up *caca* [shit] creek. So it got to the point where I would call the [drug] connection up and say, 'I want a fifty-dollar bag.' And I didn't even have two dollars. And I'd rob him. He would show up and I would take what he had. I remember I was short one time and I called the connection for a large quantity [of heroin] and I took his stuff with a knife. It was in a supermarket parking lot and daytime. People were there and watching this happen. I made him look like the bad guy. People started coming around and I said, 'This guy tried to rob me.' So I kind of put them at ease for little bit. By the time they figured it out and put two and two together, I was gone. And back then, I didn't think about re-taliation. You catch me when you can—if you can."

Soon Chico's new identity as a *tecato* overtook his identity as homeboy. But gang members understood heroin's demands, so they no longer depended on addicted homies. "Being an active gang member," Chico explained, "and getting involved in all the violence, the retaliation, all of the divine aspects of gang activity—it takes a back seat because you're using [heroin]. You're on a different mis-sion. You're still from the neighborhood [gang], but you're not ex-pected to be at the front, to be a frontline soldier."

Another rule related to heroin use involved the politics of neigh-borhood boundaries. If gang members were known to be a *tecatos*, they were allowed to purchase heroin in a rival neighborhood. This came with a demotion in gang status, a stigma that made them less meaningful men. "I even started buying drugs in neighborhoods that my neighborhood didn't quite get along with," Chico recalled. "And they would actually come to our neighborhood if it was drug related. Dopefiends kind of got a pass. People understand that they're not here for any reason other than to score their dope. They would come into our neighborhood depending on who they were and who allowed them to come in. I went to another neighborhood, into El Hoyo, to score. I wasn't with anyone. I just happened to go in there. And I felt like I put myself in jeopardy. I felt like sharks were circling me when I went in there. But nothing happened. I bought my drugs and left."

Later Chico became a dealer to ensure a steady supply of money and heroin, but his days remained uncertain. He had good days, when he sold lots of heroin and could slam up to six times. He had bad days, when he only sold a few bags and could only slam two or three times. On those bad days he debated whether to dip into his drug supply.

"If you're using and dealing," Chico explained, "some days you're using a little bit too much of your supply. Or maybe you don't have that much clientele that day. So you get in a hole as far as with the connection [supplier] in order to continue re-copping [resupplying]. . . . I didn't have reliable clientele and I wasn't a good dealer. I wasn't organized and structured. I was also using [heroin]. So, that messed everything up. I had to resort to committing crimes to make up for the lost money and lost time."

For instance, he sometimes did robberies, a high-risk crime with a lot of unknowns.[9] He mostly did burglaries, though. If no one was home, a murder was unlikely, a resistant victim was absent, and the crime happened out of view. Being seen during entry or exit was the greatest risk. But if a *tecato* felt the onset of sickness, carelessness ruled the day.

"Sometimes heroin withdrawal made guys brazen," Chico explained. "Individuals like myself, sometimes we just went brazen. We just had to do it quick and do we had to do. Sometimes I felt so impatient because I didn't want the withdrawal to set in that I just went by myself. I couldn't wait for my crime partner to show up. And there were other guys like me. We just go knock on doors to see if anybody was home. If no one answered, we just found a window to break in. There could've still been somebody inside, sleeping or something. But we didn't care. And I remember doing burglaries myself because I couldn't find someone to offer transportation. But I was sick, and the withdrawal was setting in. I had to whatever I had to do."

Heroin had Chico by the throat. It even made him rage against his second wife, a heroin user. He thought she had stopped earning money to enjoy the fruits of his labor. As a man, he felt that he could not let that happen. He controlled her body.

"There was this girl that I was with," Chico recalled. "She was my girlfriend, my using partner, and my crime partner. She was a white girl from Orange County. A Barbie doll. She was pretty, with blue eyes. But she was crazy, haha. That girl was something else. Later on she became my wife. One of the [drug] connections offered me a proposition. If I would give her to him [for sex], he would fix me up [with heroin]. I never took him up on the offer. One time I was tempted to. I brought it to her attention. She couldn't believe I was doing that.

"What happened, Randy," Chico continued, deeply embarrassed, "was that I was always a worker. I was always going and doing what I had to do to support both of our [heroin] habits. And I finally got tired of it, of her kicking back and looking pretty and getting loaded. We had talked about her cleaning up. I got tired of supporting both of us. So I finally told her, 'You want to keep using? Now it's your turn girl. I want you to get dressed up, put your nice perfume on, and paint your face real nice. I got some place to take you. It's your turn now to earn your keep.' She cried and cried and cried. She told me that I didn't love her, that I was a dog, on and on and on. We got into a big old fight behind that. It ended up not happening. But that's what brought me to that point."

Heroin, then, made Chico try to demonstrate the rawest form of what gender scholar R. W. Connell refers to as hegemonic masculinity.[10] The chaotic heroin subculture sometimes broke certain norms that men participants ascribed to, such as the sanctity of their girlfriend or wife. And the breaking of this norm was done in a gendered way. Chico and his wife did not sit down and equitably decide about her doing sex work for money. Chico certainly did not volunteer himself to engage in sex work. Rather, a gendered power dynamic was at play in which both Chico and his dealer relied on larger cultural norms that gave men greater value than women. Chico could thus sacrifice his wife's body to support their heroin addictions. Fortunately, she resisted.

By this point Chico was too far gone. He no longer consumed heroin to cure his heroin sickness. He devoured heroin, slamming as many times a day as he could. He always wanted to exist in that blissful world where the euphoria made sexual orgasms feel amateurish and cheap. "I mean there was a point where I was using up to two hundred dollars a day. I just went after opportunity after opportunity and before you know it, I got fifty spoons [doses of heroin]. Thirty, twenty spoons. And I'm the type of guy, I'm not gonna save [some of it]. Some guys call it having a 'get-up' or a 'wake-up.' They save something for the next morning 'cause they know that they gonna get up sick. Some guys were good at that. I was not good at that. I would use all day, even if I didn't need it. But I was the type of guy that was a pig. I had to nod out. I had to be loaded. I had to have that effect."

One day Chico and his wife invited some friends to their cheap motel room. Before the party, the hosts decided to do heroin. Once their friends arrived, Chico immediately fixed them with a spoon, or a dose of heroin. He took a spoon too, but his body could not take it. He overdosed.

"I don't even remember going out. I just remember nodding out. And they're slapping me, waking me up with cold water. I wake up and they're all scared. And I go, 'What's going on?' They look like they saw a ghost. They're like, 'Hey man, what's wrong with you?' My wife, she's scolding me, 'You stupid pig! What's wrong with you? You're going to OD on us! You're going to kill yourself!' They're all getting on my case. And my homeboy said, 'Hey man, you almost died on us. You didn't tell us that you just fixed [already].' I say, 'Okay, I'm good. Let's put the music back on.' I'm acting normal, right. And then ten minutes later, I'm like, 'Hey homey, you ready to fix again?' He's like, 'What's wrong with you? What do you mean you want to fix again? You just almost OD'ed on us? Chale! I'm good, homie.' I said, 'Okay, I'm going to fix with my wife now.' She goes, 'Hey stupid, wait a few hours!' I just wanted to stay loaded above and beyond. I couldn't just be cool."

Losing Family

Heroin created other problems. Chico had become a parent's greatest nightmare: criminal, violent, drug addicted, sometimes homeless, and disheveled, a billboard of stigma that brought sadness and shame to the family. His father wanted to help him stop using drugs, but ignored his own role in Chico's trajectory. Rather than productively nurture his son's drive and intelligence, he had led Chico into a life of drug use and crime.

"My father was more disappointed than anything," Chico explained. "I remember him saying one time, 'Man, I'm disgusted with my own son, a stinking dopefiend. A hype.' He called me a hype. We argued all the time though. He would tell me stuff . . . I don't know. Tell you the truth I never really argued with my father. I would just make comments and then walk away. I didn't want to get into heated arguments over stuff because it was the truth. So I didn't say much."

Chico's Pentecostal mother was distraught. Occasionally she saw Chico on the streets looking sick and unkempt, always in a hurry, with no time to chat. At least he stopped by sometimes to see how she was doing. But he had an ulterior motive. "I was living in my car, me and my wife. We were both hooked, up and running, doing all types of crazy stuff. And I remember sometimes going to visit my mom. She's cooking and doing the dishes and I would go and slam in her restroom, fix, and come out. That's pretty much what I would do. It was a safe place to slam, to get right. I'm sure it devastated her and bothered her. She never banged on the door and said, 'What are you doing in there?' A few times she knocked and said, 'Are you okay?'"

Once, after Chico returned from the bathroom, his mother asked when he would stop doing heroin.

"I told her, 'Mom, I hope to die high. I tried to get off and it's not happening for me.' I didn't want to tell my mom this 'cause it's not something you want to say to your mom. But that's how convinced I was that this was me. A zebra is a zebra. You can paint them, but that paint is gonna come off. Or dye its hair, paint them all black or all white. It's still gonna surface after a while. That's how convinced I was. I told my mom, 'I hope to die high, so you might as well accept it.'

"And it was almost as if I hit her with a baseball bat right between her eyes. She got real quiet. And she came back and said—like I said, my mom was a very religious woman—she goes, 'I refuse to receive that lie.' She said something else about the devil, I forget how she put it. She says, 'I'm gonna continue to pray for you so that you'll get delivered.' I said, 'Okay, do what you're going to do. This is what I believe.' And then I kissed her on the cheek and walked away."

Chico then described what happened on another visit to his mother. After slamming heroin in her bathroom, and sharing pleasantries, she walked him out into the Maravilla Projects parking lot.

"Son, I got something to tell you," she said uncomfortably.

"What's up, mom?" Chico asked, concerned. "Are you sick?"

"You're not welcome here anymore," she said, choking on her words. "I feel like I'm just assisting you with your lifestyle. And it's killing me."

"Is that what you were having a hard time telling me?" Chico asked, hiding the hurt. "Is that what you wanted to say? No problem, ma. I understand. No hard feelings."

"It's that I feel like I'm hurting you," she continued, sobbing. "I'm not helping you. I'm enabling and assisting you."

"Nah, don't worry, mom," Chico reassured her despite the pain he felt. "No hard feelings, ma."

Then, as he always did, Chico kissed her cheek and walked away. His mother suddenly broke down, heaved for air, and cried loudly in the middle of the parking lot. Chico turned around and saw his mother's anguish. But heroin prodded him back toward his car and soon erased the image from his head. Back to business.

Up and running again.

Spiraling Out of Control

Eventually their whirlwind lives of drugs, violence, and crime landed the young Maravillas in prison. Their drug addictions and endless drunkenness impaired their thinking. For instance, Emilio eventually got addicted to PCP and heroin, and despite being a PCP dealer, he always needed money to buy drugs. And he took on an unexpected crime partner: his father. The father-son team specialized in large-scale shoplifting: entering a store, grabbing lots of clothes, and walking out quickly. They received clothing orders from a fence, or a dealer in stolen goods.

"So we would go into the store bold and bad," Emilio explained, "and get to the [clothing] size we needed and arrange all the hangers so all the hooks are pointing in one way. That way when we grabbed the stack of things [clothes], the hangers would come off the rack with no problem. 'Cause if you had a hanger the opposite way, you'd be pulling and it won't come off. We would just go in there, go straight to the clothes, fix the hangers, grab our stuff, and walk out."

Emilio also burglarized alone. He once broke into a meat store and put pounds of meat and some money into a couple of trash bags. After leaving the premises, some do-gooders yelled at him and gave chase. Emilio dropped a bag, the one with the money. "But still," he recalled, "I went home with a bag full of meat. We ate steaks for about two weeks. Steak sandwiches, steak sandwiches, steak sandwiches. Even the meat was getting kind of discolored. 'Put it on the frying pan. It kills all of the bacteria and everything.'"

Even when not committing drug-related crimes, Emilio got in trouble. One night he and a friend walked home from a party in Monterey Park, just north of East LA. High on alcohol and drugs, they came upon a convenience store. His homie wanted to rob it. Emilio did not want to do it without a gun. Then his homie questioned his risk-taking masculinity. "My homie says, 'Come on, you're my homie. You're not going to back me up? Fuck it, I'll do it by myself then.' I was so loaded, so I'm like, 'He-e-re we go.' We walk in the store. I pretend I have a gun under my shirt. I start demanding money. Big ol' guy [cashier] don't want to give no money. And he's talking and I'm talking. Somebody comes in the store, and they call the cops."

As the police officers arrived, Emilio and his homie ran outside in different directions. He climbed into a dumpster to hide. He heard the officers debating about whether to continue the search. "Then I see the light go over the trash can," he remembered. "And I am praying like the Pope. 'God, please let me go.' I've never been in trouble really. I had been caught for small things, like trespassing at the school, so they really didn't send me away. And I'm praying. Then all of a sudden, I hear, 'He's in there!' And they tell me, 'Get out with your hands up!'"

Emilio was caught for a major crime and faced prison time. A few days later he was released on his own recognizance after he signed a promise to appear in court. Two weeks after his release, a PCP customer took Emilio to the home of a new client who wanted to buy drugs. Once there, they consumed alcohol and other drugs before settling down to play poker. According to Emilio, the host kept cheating, changing the rules of winning hands. Emilio felt disrespected. He said a few harsh words and went to the backyard to urinate. "I was loaded already," he remembered. "And he [the host] just opened the back door and had a gun. He then kneeled down and shot: Bam! I mean, the bullet went past me. I could hear it go past me."

The host then threatened him as he walked back inside, saying that if he tried anything he would kill him. Emilio sat down and played cards until he lost all his money. Calling it a night, he and his friend got up to leave. Then, according to Emilio, he politely asked the host if he could check out his gun. The host handed it to him but quickly tried to grab it back. A shot went off. The host dropped.

Emilio ran.

He hid in the front house of a property owned by his aunt. He stayed there with his aunt and grandmother as he watched police officers arrive and break into the back house, where he and his parents lived. His parents telephoned him, pleading for him to turn himself in.

Emilio ran.

As he hurried through the streets he saw an empty house. He broke in and found it littered with junk and trash. He saw a bottle of Courvoisier and drank some. He then used the home's telephone to call his girlfriend. After they poured their hearts out to each other and hung up, he got hungry and cooked chorizo and eggs. He finished the meal by drinking the entire bottle of cognac. He fell asleep.

He woke up gasping for air. The homeowner was choking him with a telephone cord. Emilio fought back, grabbing a piece of glass (the struggle had broken some household items) and stabbed the strangler below his ribcage. Still, Emilio weakened, faded, and passed out.

When he woke up again, paramedics were performing CPR on him. Handcuffed, he was then taken to the hospital at the LA County Jail, where he recovered from a lacerated neck. Then it dawned on him. In less than three weeks, he had amassed a pile of criminal charges. Attempted robbery. Murder (the gunshot victim had died). First-degree burglary, with an assault to commit bodily harm.

He was only eighteen years old.

Doing Time

Street life accounted for a only a small portion of the early Maravilla experience. The Maravillas' convictions resulted in periods of detainment and incarceration, which ranged from three years to as many as forty-two years. Sadly, during the late 1970s and early 1980s, the Maravilla participants were incarcerated during their emerging adulthood stage, or the foundational years that formed their adult identity.[11] They described horrific prison violence during this developmental period, much of it a result of the manhood-based inmate hierarchy. To survive they would learn how to control their fear, and to read fear in others. The jail and prison environment dictated what it meant to matter as men.

Emotions and Violent Masculinities

As a teenager, Emilio was released to his family after an arrest. But when he was arrested for murder as an adult, he was sent to LA County Jail to await trial. He feared for his safety but put up a masculine front. "Here I was, an eighteen-year-old man that never been to YA [California Youth Authority], never been to juvenile hall," Emilio recalled. "That's when I was afraid. But I couldn't let no one know. So, I get to the county jail, and right off the bat I met people from Maravilla and they bring you in as a family. 'You need some chanate [coffee]? Frajos [cigarettes]?' Boom, okay. Little by little I got used to it [the jail]."

Emilio relaxed as he reunited with homeboys and befriended Maravillas outside his neighborhood. The fear returned when he was sentenced to Soledad State Prison, which held some of the most violent prisoners. "They sent me to Soledad. Soledad back in the seventies, it was gladiator school. It was rockin' and rolling. Stickings [stabbings], riots. Here I am again feeling that fear. I get there, they RTQ you [restrict you to quarters]. They put you in your cell for two weeks. They confine you and escort you everywhere. Then you have all these guys asking, 'Órale, where you from?' I say, 'Soy de Maravilla.' 'Órale, homie!' And once you establish that you're Maravilla, you start getting help [from other Maravillas]. Cosmetics [toiletries], coffee, all that. They start taking care of you. Maravilla takes care of Maravilla."

Outside their warm community, the Maravillas witnessed deadly violence. It was no longer the long-range violence of a shooting. It was face-to-face knife attacks that aimed to kill. As a young man, Marcos, who was Chico's homie, saw how easy it was to extinguish a life in prison. He quickly adapted to the danger:

"Man, there's a lot of stuff in prison. You see death. You see a lot of stabbings. I remember the first time I seen a stabbing. I was out in the yard, and I seen this guy come up behind this other guy and just stick [stab] him. He just stuck him over and over. I saw a lot of blood come out from that guy. I saw a lot of other stabbings after that—I just got accustomed to it—I learned that I had to do the same thing too. I was like, 'Wow, that's what I gotta do now.' I already had a shank. It just gave me more power, man. I knew that I could fight back. That I could defend myself. I could stick somebody before they stuck me."

This type of violence sorted inmates on a masculinity hierarchy.[12] It was the prison's design—its harshness and poor resources—that influenced inmates to find meaning through a violent manhood.[13]

"One thing I learned is that prison is a lot tougher than the streets," Emilio explained. "You know why? Because you can't hide in prison. You've got to deal with your problem. You gotta deal with the situation when it happens. Someone says something bad about you, you gotta act on it, like that [snaps his fingers]. 'Cause if you don't act, you weak, man. You're a marked man and you got no place to run to. You live with everybody right there, man. You're confined like sardines in a can."

To accomplish violence, the Maravillas became experts at reading emotions. Sociologist Randall Collins argues that successful violence-doers learn how to master not only their own tension and fear, but also the emotions of their opponents.[14] Prison was the perfect testing ground. As Diego, who had been incarcerated with Emilio, stated, "You know what they call prison? They call it 'The University.' Because you learn how to read people like a book when you go to prison. You learn how to look into people's eyes. You could see the fear. You could see the hatred. You learn how to see all of that, brother."

Emilio passed the test with flying colors. His mastery of emotions turned him into the prison bogeyman that he once dreaded. He had internalized the prison's definition of manhood and now externalized it. For instance, Emilio often victimized two white inmates by using their weakness to boost his cruelty. It was also a masculine performance: he emasculated his victims in the presence of his homeboys. Others had to see that he was a violent man.

"It's that when people show fear," he explained, "then they become your bitch. You could see it in them. You could see it in their eyes. They ain't gonna do shit. I had this big ol' white boy in the county [jail], they called him Cherios. I had him washing my clothes by hand and ironing them. Cherios was a weak white boy. A fuckin' punk. One day he was going into a cell and the door just come closed. Wham! The CO's had this lever that shuts them [cell doors]. While he was out there talking shit, it took some of his fingertips off. I said [to him], 'Put a bag over it [the fingers]! Wash my clothes. Don't stop the show.'

"Another time I was hanging out with an older [Maravilla] homeboy and I tell him, 'Homie, you wanna get high?' He goes, 'Yeah!' I then went to this other white guy 'cause I knew he had weed. 'Hey, give me a joint.' I think it was ten dollars a joint. So he gave me the joint. He goes, 'Where my money at?' 'I'll get you [pay you] right now.' I leave, and me and my homeboy started smoking [makes inhaling sounds and gestures]. 'It's good, huh?' 'Yeah, it's good.' 'You want some more?' 'Órale, yeah.'

"So I go to the white boy again. 'I need some more.' He goes, 'Well, how much you need, you ain't paid me yet.' I said, 'I need it all.' He says, 'Aw, come on.' I go, 'Take it out of your asshole or I'ma take it out.' 'Cause he had it keistered [hidden in his rectum]. I had my homeboys out there. I took him to the restroom, and he had to shit his stuff out. Washed the bag out and gave it to me. Went back to my homeboy and he tells me, 'Est-a-a-as muy lo-o-co, Emilio. [You're too crazy, Emilio]. You're a fool, homes.'"

The Peseta: The Weak Man

Even when facing death, the Maravillas never sought help from prison authorities. Doing so would have them placed them into "PC," or protective custody, which was considered a haven for snitches and punks. Emilio preferred to be killed rather than seek such protection. "You could go PC up, or go into protective custody," Emilio explained, "but that's gonna follow you. Even when you come out, you won't have no more friends, no more homies. Because you're known as a peseta [quarter]. You're a PC. You're a punk. That's the last thing you want to do. Your own homeboys could take you out [kill you]."

Nando, who was Emilio's homie, criticized inmates who went into protective custody. "A peseta is a quarter [coin]," he explained. "Twenty-five cents is una peseta [a quarter]. Because peseta came from the word pesetiar [to lock up]. Tranquar [lock] yourselves. Lock yourselves under protective custody. A peseta is a vato that is no good. They PC because they got something on them. They a child molester, or they a fucking rata [rat]. The juras [police] get them to talk in different ways. They get weak persons who are barely getting into drugs and shit like that. And when they bust them, they say, 'If you wanna go, you gotta talk.' So the guys don't want to get busted and they talk. But then after a while, their [prison] papers come up, and shows that vato talked to the jura. Now when they hit the joint, they have to be a peseta. Se trancan [they lock themselves up] in protective custody 'cause they know that if they go in the mainline, they might get killed or something. They in a segregated unit, where everybody there are ratas [rats], child molesters, whatever."

So even if a Maravilla no longer wanted to project a violent masculinity, they had few options. They could not freeze the action, call a time-out, bring in a replacement, or quit or tap out. Even if quitting was the right choice to save one's life, it was the wrong choice to keep one's honor. It showed a willingness to be housed with child molesters, rapists, and informants, all considered disgusting and weak.[15] They could not let that happen. They had to keep their violent masculinity intact.

But an onslaught of violence waited for the Maravillas in the 1990s. It would test their courage. It would test their manhood. It would become the defining moment of their lives.

La Eme had made its move.

3 The Greenlight

La Eme. The prison gang is mentioned with caution. The gang name is mentioned with fear. When a Mexican gang member says its name, they always glance sideways in case someone can hear. Some gang members refer to it as "the organization" or use another veiled name. They know that La Eme can reach the streets from prison with a gun or blade. Between 1994 and 2006 this prison gang would target the Maravilla gangs, or put a "greenlight" on them. I cannot emphasize enough the salience of this historical moment in California's gang world. La Eme imposed a totalitarian regime that reorganized Mexican inmate society in its favor. The resistant Maravillas would then experience unprecedented violence and victimization. Their resistance bolstered their violent masculinities, since they never backed down. This also solidified their Maravilla identity, which they later believed represented being the ultimate gangsters, or the real men of the gang world.

The Rise of La Eme

In 1957 thirteen LA youths founded the Mexican Mafia while incarcerated at the Deuel Vocational Institution in Northern California.[1] The term *Mafia* referred to the period's Italian, Irish, and Jewish mobsters that inspired the youths. Their grand ambition concerned a pressing issue: Black and white inmates outnumbered Mexican inmates. For protection, the Mexican youths, who were from different gangs in LA, wanted to unite the facility's Southern California Mexican gangs. Like experienced statesmen, they succeeded. They also committed extraordinary violence, which made their peers comply with their demands.[2] Authorities transferred them to different adult prisons, hoping that older inmates could intimidate them.[3]

The plan backfired. Lore has it that when one of the founding members, Rodolfo "Cheyenne" Cadena, stepped into San Quentin's yard, a hulking Black inmate kissed his cheek and declared him his property. Cheyenne later stabbed the Black inmate to death—in front of more than a thousand onlookers. No one said a word.[4]

That was just the start. As the boys turned to men during the 1960s, they referred to themselves as La Eme (*eme* is the pronunciation of the letter *M* in Spanish), and they killed Black, white, and Mexican inmates who disrespected or disagreed with them.[5] During the 1970s they recruited hundreds of the best violence-doers from different Southern Californian Mexican gangs and controlled some of the underground prison economy.[6] They also stabbed and killed enemies openly, including in the presence of prison staff while on prison buses, and in courtroom waiting cells while under video surveillance.[7] The message was clear. They killed no matter what.

Capitalizing on Race Politics

The 1960s. Black civil rights activists led a historic movement that protested racial inequality.[8] Black masses marched the streets, marched on Washington, boycotted restaurants, boycotted department stores, picketed schools, picketed political rallies, faced police officers, faced police dogs, and stood their ground against fire hoses that tried to extinguish their spirit. The movement called for equal protection and participation under the law, with a larger aim to blur racial difference.

Yet Black militants, who were dissatisfied with the slow progress of Black church leaders, started a movement based on racial identity: Black Power.[9] It taught Black people how to defend themselves against police brutality, challenged negative portrayals of Blackness, and encouraged them to grow Afros in place of perms. *Black is beautiful!* The success of the Black Power movement stimulated the period's other ethnic movements, such as the Brown Power movement in California.[10] Its Chicano militants protested police brutality and supported worker unions and rights. They also inspired Mexican descendants to appreciate the history of indigenous peoples in the Americas.

These ideas struck a chord in the prison system.[11] Black inmates created the Black Guerrilla Family, which was modeled after the Black Panthers.[12] Mexican inmates identified as Chicanos and adopted leftist philosophies. White inmates solidified their racism through the Aryan Brotherhood. Race now overtook culture as the dividing line. For instance, La Eme emphasized an Aztec and Mayan heritage and promoted La Raza, or the Mexican race. Black and white inmates also focused on their own race-based concerns. Sociologist Robert Weide argues that race politics now prevented inmates from uniting as a class.[13]

Sociologist Rebecca Trammell and economist David Skarbek both argue that racial divisions in California prisons had also resulted from the mass incarceration of minorities during the 1970s.[14] The eventual overcrowding increased prison disorder and created large-scale divisions between Black, Latino, and white prisoners. Prison gangs then used racial identity to organize inmate life.[15] For Skarbek, these race-based prison gangs filled the governance void and instilled the order that prison authorities failed to provide.[16]

Drug profits, though, created a strange racial alliance. During the 1970s, the Aryan Brotherhood trafficked most of California prisons' heroin. La Eme, however, controlled the purchasing power of LA-based Mexican inmates. To tap into the Mexican market, the Aryan Brotherhood was forced to become La Eme's wholesale supplier.[17] Eventually the unlikely partners orchestrated a rhythm of drug market transactions that worked smoothly and allowed them to earn money. The dealers could now afford prison luxuries such as soap, soup, candy bars, and other simple conveniences.

The growing Black inmate population, though, started a war against the Aryan Brotherhood. At one point the Black Guerrilla Family began winning the race war, jeopardizing La Eme's drug income. It declared war against the Black Guerrilla Family. Fistfights, slashings, stabbings, and killings increased. But by the late 1980s, as sociologist Robert Weide documents, prison violence had tapered off.[18] The Black Guerrilla Family had lost. La Eme established prison dominance.[19] It now called the shots.

As sociologist Patrick Lopez-Aguado shows, race was not the only divider of California inmates. Geography divided them too.[20] It started in the 1960s, when LA Chicano inmates victimized Mexican inmates from Northern California.[21] The Northerners came from small farming communities, so LA Chicano inmates regarded them as hicks and called them "Busters," referring to people who busted sod for work. They also robbed them of their food and extorted money from them.[22]

One day, in either 1967 or 1968, and either in Soledad or San Quentin prison, a Northern inmate was gifted a pair of new shoes by his family. After a cell search by guards, he returned to find his shoes missing. Later he confronted a La Eme member who wore them and refused to return them. The next day, fed-up Northern Mexicans attacked La Eme. What became known as the Great Shoe War went on for days.[23]

In the end, La Eme won. The tiny group of Northerners lacked numbers and organization. Rather than submit, they formed Nuestra

Familia (Our Family) and later recruited hundreds of members.[24] The new group featured a hierarchy of military positions and a board of directors. And some of its founding members were from Southern California, defectors who perceived La Eme as a bully.[25] Later, Nuestra Familia killed Rodolfo "Cheyenne" Cadena, a founding member of La Eme who tried to broker peace between the rivals. From then on, La Eme and Nuestra Familia became mortal enemies.[26] No peace. No unification under La Raza. *Nunca.* Never.

The geographical division was set. All Mexican gangs below the city of Bakersfield, California: Southern. All Mexican gangs from Bakersfield and up: Northern. La Eme would later use this spatial identification to its advantage.

The Growth in Latino Inmates

During the 1980s two unforeseen developments helped La Eme: new crime mandates and a demographic shift in Los Angeles. Conservative officials had implemented harsh law-and-order policies that targeted minorities and immigrants.[27] And with the sudden growth of LA's Latino population, Latinos increased their presence in jails and prisons.[28] Soon La Eme had the support of the largest ethnic inmate population.[29] The Black inmates were terribly outnumbered. White inmates were fortunate to have La Eme on their side.

La Eme wasted no time in realizing its goal: the unification of all Southern California Mexican gangs as "Southsiders." In 1993, released La Eme members held meetings in public parks across Southern California.[30] Members from every barrio attended and learned that La Eme had formalized their jail and prison solidarity. New rules also regulated behavior both inside and outside the penal system.

When in jail or prison, for instance, they had to unite and let go of street rivalries. On the streets, barrios could no longer do drive-by shootings. They had to do their best to shoot rivals at a close distance. This rule left innocent bystanders unharmed, which reduced police attention and kept drug profits intact. They also had to show loyalty to La Eme by writing "13" after their gang's name since *M*—or Eme— was the thirteenth letter of the alphabet. Even the Mara Salvatrucha gang, which was started in LA by Central American youths, added the 13 to its name and became known globally as MS-13. The most important rule stunned park audiences. All barrios were now required to pay La Eme a tax on their drug sales. Drug dealers no longer had business autonomy.[31]

La Eme framed their demands as a security measure. The Southsider identity, rules, and taxes were needed for protection.[32] As Southsiders, inmates could no longer victimize each other willy-nilly. Instead, they had to present conflicts to proper Eme authorities who resolved problems. Jails and prisons became safer and more predictable, especially since rival prison gangs could not touch them.[33] Many barrio gangs felt relief.

La Eme, though, ruled with an iron fist. In fact, it acted like a totalitarian regime.[34] It repressed inmates and tried to replace traditional gang rankings and standings with a new prison structure that benefited its goals. It also reorganized inmate society, reoriented inmate identities, and redirected loyalties to its aims. And it contrasted Southsiders with an ethnic enemy (Blacks) and an impure geopolitical enemy (Northerners). This hurried Southsiders into war readiness through required military-style regimens of exercise. In all, it forced a common geo-ethnic identity or bond.

La Eme also punished anyone who defied the new social order. If an individual or gang resisted, La Eme put a "greenlight," or target, on them. All Southsiders (or all the Mexican gang members from Southern California) then assaulted the resistors on sight. Southsiders who failed to attack resistors were "greenlighted" too. The Southsider program resembled a well-oiled machine. It pumped barrios in and pumped a collective identity out. The stamp of "13" completed the process.

Some southern Mexican gangs, though, refused the stamp of "13." They would suffer, indeed.

The Greenlight

From the mid-1990s on, La Eme was California's most powerful gang. Its Southsider following meant lots of supporters—and lots of eyes and ears in prison and on the street. Gang members and non-members alike feared "the organization." People rarely mentioned its name. However, a few gangs took a stand. The Opal Street Locos in Boyle Heights and Lowell Street in Northeast Los Angeles refused to pay the drug tax.[35] But they paid a price. Surrounding Mexican gangs (who were now Southsiders) drove through their neighborhoods and shot at them. When they went to jail or prison, Southsiders stabbed and beat them. Their numbers then dwindled, making them unviable as gangs. They became chilling examples of what happens to barrios that refused to fall in line.

The Maravilla gangs in East LA remained defiant. They represented close to twenty neighborhoods, and as far back as old-timers remember, the Maravilla gangs always united in jail and prison. Many members had brothers, fathers, uncles, cousins, and childhood friends in various Maravilla neighborhoods. This had allowed them to collectively grumble about La Eme's intrusions as early as the 1960s.[36] When La Eme demanded Southsider unity and a drug tax in the 1990s, the Maravillas felt disrespected.

In 1994, the Maravillas held a meeting at Belvedere Park in East LA. Old-timers claimed that between three hundred and seven hundred Maravilla gang members attended. Newspaper stories of the time corroborated this historical gang event.[37] Respected Maravillas took the lead. Luis, a Maravilla in his late fifties, remembered:

"We got together in Belvedere Park. I mean, there was about six hundred guys. I didn't even know half of them! I was like, 'Fuck, where all these guys come from?' They had fuckin' narcs [police officers] in every side of the street. They had fuckin' patrols of sheriffs all around. They had a helicopter flying around and shit—that's how many guys were there. . . . And that's when we learned that we were not gonna pay taxes to the Mexican Mafia. The guys that were talking were older dudes from Marianna [neighborhood] and one from Arizona [neighborhood], and they said that everybody has to watch out. That whatever money we made was our money. That Maravilla always stood for honor and we weren't going to bend over for them. But now we gotta take care of each other 'cause they gonna try to come after us."

The Maravilla participants, who were in their thirties at this point, also believed in East LA's importance for the Mexican gang world. They claimed that it was where the pachuco fashion and the slick talk—the "órale," the "simón que sí"—first became cool. It was also where masculine codes of honor, respect, and resistance arose. No outsider had the right to tell Maravilla what to do.

"We never listen to nobody," Nando explained. "I'm talking to you about politics. Prison politics. Street politics. The Mexican Mafia [La Eme] took over a lot of territory. And we never considered ourselves with them. We're just Maravilla. We don't claim '13.' In LA, they [other neighborhoods] pay rent. We don't pay rent. You know why? Because this is the first barrio, the first neighborhood in LA. How the fuck we gonna pay rent to another man? We fuck up other motherfuckers. So how is another man gonna tell me that I have to pay a tax? What the fuck? Como le voy a pagar? [How am I am going to pay them?] No way, homie. Si yo no le doy a mi jefita feria [If I don't give my mother money], you think I'm gonna give feria to another puto [fucker]? That's why the pedo [conflict] started in the joint with us. Because they tried to charge us renta [rent]. And we say, 'Chale! We're not gonna pay no rent.' We're gonna go in guerra [war]."

Maravilla's unification was an amazing achievement. Every Maravilla that I spoke to had homeboys who had been beat up, stabbed, shot, or murdered by rival Maravilla gangs. But La Eme's demands threatened their independence.

"Everybody was against each other," Nando confirmed. "My barrio was fighting against Marianna, against El Hoyo, whatever. Back in the day, there was guerra [war] between us. But when that shit happened that they [La Eme] wanted to charge us taxes and shit like that, it made the neighborhoods make the meeting in Belvedere Park. We came together and we said, 'Sabes que? [You know what?] Now la guerra between us is over. That shit is over.' We came fuckin' together."

Several Maravillas claimed that they had no intention of overthrowing La Eme. They were resisting from a defensive stance. "We weren't trying to start a war," Chico explained. "We ain't that stupid. We're not that naïve to try to start a war with these vatos. We were defending our rights. We were defending our space. From being overruled. From being dictated at."

The Southsiders, though, outnumbered the Maravillas. When ordered, the Southsiders relentlessly attacked the Maravillas in holding pens, dormitories, and yards. Maravillas had to be on constant guard, always wondering not *if* but *when* they would be attacked. For instance, Pelon, who is forty-eight years old, was targeted by La Eme several times while in prison. Most of the time he got away with only bumps and bruises. On one occasion they injured him badly.

"I'm in the yard, and these vatos come up to me and tell me to put on my shirt. They say that I'm disrespecting them 'cause they could see my placa [tattoo] that says Maravilla. I told them, 'Fuck, aye, soy de Maravilla [I'm from Maravilla]. I don't follow no orders from nobody.' Then like five or six of them start swinging and I'm fighting back. Then I fall down—I trip or something—and that's when one of them fuckers got me. That fucker stabbed me everywhere. He got me in my back, my stomach, legs. . . . I [still] walked the mainline later. I didn't give a fuck. I told any fucker who asked where I'm from, 'Soy Maravilla!'"

Some Maravillas fell prey to Southsider trickery. The Southsiders often pretended to be Maravillas to catch them off guard. Smokey, an almost toothless Maravilla in his late fifties, recalled being fooled.

"Everything was fucked up in jail. Those Southsiders were hitting us from all over. They put me in a module and some of the vatos where like, 'Órale, homes! Where you from?' I go, 'Soy de Maravilla.' They go, 'Órale, homes! We're kicking it here because they [South-siders] are moving on us, homes. So, when you get in here, come out to the back. We gonna be in the back.' So I felt that I had some Mara-villas to back me up now. I go back there and they surprised me. Those guys weren't Maravilla. They were fuckin' Southsiders. They got me real good. They knocked all my teeth out, that's how good they got me."

When I came across Southsider old-timers in my everyday life, I asked them about the Maravillas. Most of them confirmed that dur-ing the greenlight years they were required to assault Maravillas in jail or prison. They often waited for orders from "the organization," which sometimes paused attacks on Maravillas to get their support in race riots. Other times the greenlight was paused for business or per-sonal reasons that were unclear. Still, the greenlight card was in the organization's back pocket. When it slammed the card on the table, the Southsiders attacked.

"When I was in prison in the nineties," a former Southsider said, "they [Maravillas] were really getting attacked. One time I was in a prison, and something happened where they [La Eme] said, 'Get all of the dudes from Maravilla off the prison yard.' They started beating them all up, wherever they were at. It was coming down from the top. They were getting jumped on, beat on, taken advantage of because of the greenlight. It was like if you go out hunting and you say, 'Okay, we gonna take out all of the fuckin' elk, or whatever.' That's how it went. And in a yard, there were only five to eight Maravillas and then the rest of the yard was Southsider. There was a gang of us! Sometimes it was ten to one against Maravilla."

Maravilla Strikes Back

Chico, Emilio, Diego, Juano, Nando, and others admitted that La Eme deserved respect for their violence. "Some people don't understand their brilliance," Chico explained. "It's a combination of the politics, the power, the brilliance. These guys are sharp, sharp, sharp, sharp. They'll be able to notice a single pelito [strand of hair] on somebody's head that stood up. They know how to read people like a book. That's just the nature of the lifestyle in prison. Some of these guys are extremely bright."

Once the shock of Southsider attacks wore off, Maravillas mounted a defense through offense. For instance, they checked the wristbands of fellow inmates for clues that indicated a committed Southsider—someone they wanted to stab. And after their release from LA County Jail, other Maravillas waited outside the facility to surprise exiting Southsiders.

"We waited for them outside of the county [jail]," Juano recalled. "We would ask them, 'Aye, how you doing man? Where the fuckers from so and so [neighborhood]?' They would be like, 'I don't know.' Then we're like, 'We're from Maravilla.' They would look at us and be like, 'Is that right?' Then: Paah! Give it to them motherfuckers. They started [saying], 'Aye, man, fuckers from Maravilla are outside, aye.' We waited for anybody to fuckin' walk out and fucked them up. 'Aye, homie, remember what you said in there?' Paah! We got ours back. We didn't back down to those fuckers."

An inactive Southsider confirmed the accounts of Maravilla's offensive. He added the following: when Southsiders were released from the county jail, they often used an outdoor pay phone at a nearby Denny's (a chain diner) to call friends or family members for rides home. Maravillas, however, hid like snipers in the area and shot at them as they made calls. Some of his jail homies got shot, including two members of his neighborhood. Southsiders now feared using the pay phone. When they did, they put hoods over their heads to disguise their bald heads, which signaled Southsider membership.

In all, the battle was no longer one-sided. Injuries and deaths hit both groups hard. Of course, the Maravillas were outnumbered and racked up more losses. Yet they refused to go into protective custody. They preferred to die rather than be called cowards or "rats." They also refused to be housed with the lowest of the low—the pedophiles, child murderers, child abusers, elder abusers, and so on. Chale! They had to show they were real men.

Blood continued to be spilled.

The bloodying then slowed a bit. A few participants claimed that some mothers of Maravillas complained to local politicians about their victimized sons. The politicians then pressured jail authorities to reduce the greenlight violence. A Maravilla gang module was created, which many Maravillas hated. The Southsiders now ridiculed them for "locking it up" even though it was the jail authorities that forced them out of the general population. But even under segregation the Maravillas were treated as dangerous, which reinforced their violent masculinities.

"Being who we are," Papo, who was in his mid-fifties, proudly explained, "we always had to be handcuffed. If we had a medical reason or something like that, they'll handcuff us to take us down there so that we don't go after anybody. . . . Even when I was going upstate [to prison], I was handcuffed on the way. I was put way in the front [of the bus] because of where I was from. I was like in a special unit. I was like a special person."

Despite the Maravillas' resistance, La Eme continued unleashing Southsiders, who were in never-ending supply. Outnumbered, the Maravillas bravely fought on. They had good reason. Within their ranks, a special unit of fighters existed. They committed violence regardless of the consequences. They were the baddest vatos in Maravilla. They called themselves the *Maravillosos*.

The Marvelous Ones.

The Maravillosos

In California, the most violent inmates created La Eme, the Aryan Brotherhood, Nuestra Familia, the Black Guerrilla Family, and other prison gangs. Sociologist Randall Collins refers to such individuals as violent elites, or the small percentage of people competent at violence.[38] Like theoretical physicists who analyze and predict phenomena in the physical world, violent elites analyze the emotions of potential victims to predict their behavior in the human world. As a result, they understand how to overcome fear and emotionally deflate opponents to do violence.

In jail and prison, however, violent inmates live alongside other violence experts, such as fighters, shooters, murderers, and robbers. So the playing field becomes level, and a new violent elite emerges. They are brilliant, brave, and relentless: they kill during courtroom travel; they kill despite being outnumbered or in the presence of correctional officers; and they pursue targets endlessly. In the jail and prison context, the following four attributes distinguish them from other inmates:

1. The desire to organize inmate life through physical dominance
2. The doing of violence that risks more prison time and their lives
3. The embrace of being a target
4. The willingness to kill

During Maravilla's greenlight, one violent elite, La Eme, clashed with another violent elite, the Maravillosos. The Maravillosos were a self-selected group of individuals that came from different Maravilla gangs. In other words, no one recruited them; they chose to protect Maravilla on their own. Clearly, other Maravillas were not cowards. They just had no desire for a glorious prison death. They preferred to do their time and return home. The Maravillosos, though, had a *qué se joda*, or fuck it, mentality. They hunted La Eme to prove that they were ultraviolent. The Maravillosos had the following four characteristics:

1. They volunteered to protect Maravilla
2. They targeted La Eme and its associates
3. They regularly engaged in risky and deadly violence
4. They embraced being targets by displaying a Maravilloso tattoo

I heard many inconsistent accounts of how the Maravillosos formed. I did meet three old-timer Maravillosos, though, all of them sporting bold tattoos with the group's name. One of them was a homeless dopefiend who pushed a shopping cart that carried his belongings. Chico considered him so deranged that he refused to broker our relationship. At a neighborhood barbecue, I met another Maravilloso, who later told me stories about his prison violence. However, he belonged to the neighborhood that I cut ties with (though whenever I saw him, he eagerly asked about the book's progress).

The third Maravilloso, Giant, I came to know well. Though he was a homeless heroin addict, he was charismatic and wise. He also radiated confidence, walking as though he were six feet tall despite being under five foot five. And Giant's homeboys, who had seen his violence, assured me that whatever he said was true, that he had no need to lie. Through him I learned that not just anyone became a Maravilloso. Only those who wanted to dominate the most violent men volunteered for the elite group. I also learned that his violence and sense of self (which some readers may mistakenly categorize as purely sociopathic and narcissistic) had origins in his family environment, gang-related notions of masculinity, and the emotional highs he got when peers praised his violence.

Mattering as a Maravilloso

During the 1960s, Giant grew up surrounded by gang members. His father, uncles, and cousins were Maravillas, and his mother and aunts were supportive of gangs. Giant's grandfather was also a legendary gangster, which made him feel like he had to live up to his family's name. When Giant first went to prison in the 1970s, he got his chance. Surprisingly, it was his guitar skills that first got him noticed. His grandfather, an avid guitar player, had taught him to play Maravilla songs.

"I know how to play the guitar and shit like that," Giant explained. "That's how it all started. I seen the guys [inmates] there and I see this guy struggling [with a song], and I go, 'Hey, man, con todo respeto [with all due respect], you know what, there's a different pisada [chord] on the guitar that's made for that song.' He goes, 'You know it?' I say, 'Yeah.' Then he gave me the guitar and I put it down on him, you know what I'm saying? 'Cause I'm one of them eses that can turn the channel to English to put it in Spanish, you know what I mean? So, I'm getting down on it, and he goes, 'That's the motherfuckin' chord that I've been looking for! For ten years! How in the fuck did you learn this chord?' I says, 'I learned that shit in some alley down there in Maravilla from some winitos [winos].' He goes, 'A wino taught you that? I gotta get with you, man. I'm serio [serious], man, we gotta get together.' That's how I got that trust."

Soon Giant played guitar in the prison chapel, the only place inmates could play for an extended time. One day he played an old Maravilla song, which he thought the old-school vatos would appreciate. The song, "Así Vas Pa Maravilla," was about using heroin, its lyrics foreshadowing the heroin addiction that many Maravillas would experience in the coming decades. Giant sang it for me in a strained voice:

Así vas pa Maravilla,	You go to Maravilla
Te compro un boltero,	I buy you a steel bull
una vaca de acero,	A cow of steel
Y carga pa loque-a-ar	And heroin to get crazy
A nadien les hace ca-s-o-o-o,	You pay attention to no one
Y solito te amarras bien el braso,	And you tie your arm well alone
Te das tu filoriaso	You inject yourself
Y verás que va sin dolo-o-o-r . . .	And you'll experience no pain

"That's the way that song goes," Giant said after singing it. "From there, it was like saying, 'Open sesame,' you know what I'm saying? That's when all the vatos wanted to rewrite that fuckin' song. I go, 'Chale, I can't do that. That's my neighborhood song. That's a Maravilla song.'"

The guitar playing, his grandfather, and his Maravilla origins all endeared him to his prison mates. But, as always, a moment of truth arose in prison that answered questions about one's manhood. The moment found Giant. He knew what to do.

"Shit fell down in the fuckin' yard against the Blacks. I don't know who got disrespected or anything like that. What I do know was that it was all hands on deck. So among the young guys and among the old guys, it was 'Who's gonna fuckin' deliver the shanks to the yard?' So we're all kickin' back and there was about three vatos that vouched for me. They says, 'Hey man, sabes qué [you know what]? Get Giant. Have him take the fuckin' fieros [shanks] out. He just got here. We been here and we're burned out [caught a lot]. They gonna search us down.'"

A homie asked Giant if he could transport the knives to the yard. No problem, he answered. Giant then used hair grease to keister, or hide in his rectum, seven shanks wrapped in plastic. He walked past officers to a secluded area, where he emitted the weapons. He handed them to a homeboy, who cleaned each knife with a towel before giving them out.

"Then we just got busy, started fighting. Pull out the fuckin' fiero. Boom! I hit this dude and the dudes ran around the tables. Truchas [clever], you know what I mean? They had fieros and all this shit like that, man. And a motherfuckin' prison guard comes in trying to stop everybody. And the commotion, the combat, it's right by the weights. So I got the fuckin' weight bar and bam! I hit the fuckin' prison guard with it. That really boosted up my name afterwards. 'Hey homes, you seen homie? He hit the fuckin' jura [guard] with the fuckin' weight bar.' Well, that there got me sent to level four. And I was up in the motherfuckin' hole [isolation unit]. I'm up there and they take you back to court, you take a deal, and they add two years to your sentence 'cause you gonna do it in lock up, in the hole. So I did two years there."

While in isolation, Giant learned that other Mexican inmates had heard about his attack on the guard. His name began to be spoken with respect. He was off to a great start.

Later Giant was released on parole. However, he had had a heroin habit since the age of sixteen. It started on a day when he was heading to his PCP dealer. On the way, he came across a dopefiend homeboy who was short on cash. The friend offered him heroin if he chipped in. Giant agreed. He thought he would be immune to heroin withdrawal, but he got hooked after the first shot. It led to repeated incarceration for the rest of his life.

When he returned to prison, Giant picked up the violence where he had left off. In the late 1970s (before the greenlight), some Eme members noticed his violent potential and made him a bodyguard. He recalled, "A guy from the Eme had me standing there [in the cell] all fuckin' night, by the bars while he was asleep, making sure that when the thing [cell door] opened, nobody ran up on him. I was about twenty-four years old. I had to look out for him. I had to have a shank because we were up north. There was a lot of Norteños [Northerners] up there. So, if he had to go down, I had to go down with him. But I had to go down first. If the cops came in and made a cell instruction [search], I would have to push the jura [guard] out of the fuckin' way until this guy got up. Ain't that crazy?"

When he was transferred to another prison, his career of violence took off. He landed in a yard controlled by about forty Maravillas. They dealt drugs and gifted heroin to addicted homeboys. But, according to Giant, a few Eme members tried to strong-arm them. "They wanted some of the homeboys' dope. Homeboys were so strung out, they said, 'Fuck no! I ain't gonna give 'em no fuckin' dope. Who the fuck is he?' You talking about older vatos that's been around with these guys [Eme members] from the beginning, when they sprung up and created the Mexican Mafia. So they know each other and they know each other's characters. He goes, 'Hey homie, what's this shit that you want my dope? Vete a la verga! [Fuck off!] I used to slap you around in juvenile hall, motherfucker.' And he [an Eme member] said, 'Well, this is what's happening.' My homie goes, 'Naw, that ain't happening.'"

A day later the resistant Maravilla was killed.

Giant recalled tensions rising between the Maravillas and La Eme. They had words with each other: *Chale, why you gotta do him like that? Who the fuck do you think you are talking to us like that?* Then a slap occurred. Someone fell to the ground. Later, a fight happened. Much later, the loser knifed the winner. *Guerra, homie!* The war was on.

According to Giant, the Maravillas attacked La Eme members in the chow hall and yard. And one day, a lifer high on emotional energy yelled out, *Qué rifan los Maravillosos de Maravilla!* (The Marvelous Ones of Maravilla rule!) Then days later other Maravillas, who led the resistance, shouted, *Somos los Maravillosos de Maravilla!* (We are the Marvelous Ones from Maravilla!) Then they organized. Word hit the streets about the group that took on La Eme.

The new fame made Giant feel like a barrio star. His job was to protect Maravillas in prison. It was dangerous work. First, he could get more prison time. After a stabbing or a killing, an initial two-year sentence could turn into three or four or five, or an added lifetime of years. *Híjole!* Second, he could get killed. Most Maravillas refused such a risk. This was why Giant earned so much respect. He cared more about their welfare than his own.

Like other Maravillosos, Giant got a huge tattoo that boldly stated MARAVILLOSO. It was now clear that he hunted La Eme and did not care that the tattoo put a target on his back. It was a status symbol, just like the tan and green berets that indicate membership in the US military's Special Forces. He went on "search and destroy" missions as a violent elite.

"I took it upon myself to put on the tattoo. Because I stopped talkin' about it and being about it. In other words, I said, 'I'm involved and I ain't gonna just be a soldier. I'm gonna be somebody.' And they [homies] saw your authority and they said, 'Aye, watch that tattoo on the vato. He's with the business [violent prison politics].' . . . If you're putting on the tattoo and you don't do nothin', people from your own order are gonna fuck you around. Because then they gonna say, 'Aye, homie, you know what? You ain't never done nothing, homie. You talk a good game, but you don't follow through. Now if you want to get advanced like me, you better sit your motherfuckin' ass down and learn something. Step it up homie or step down.' Now if the guy becomes argumentative, my mentality is, 'Okay, I gotta take this motherfucker out [kill him].'"

Being a violent elite attracted attention from prison authorities, adding another notch to his belt. The prison staff treated Maravillosos as dangerous men who needed strict monitoring. "So even the fuckin' COs, the staff in the prison, they were aware of us," explained Giant. "They were like, 'Aye, man, let me see that tattoo. Okay, you're a Maravilloso. We gonna have to lock you down for the safety of this penitentiary, for your safety, for the safety of others.' They knew what we was about, you know what I'm saying? We're with the business [violent prison politics]."

For violent elites, being "with the business" meant killing enemies. It also meant that enemies tried to kill them. Again, La Eme and its associates were brilliant at violence, or figuring out how to victimize enemies despite being under heavy surveillance. The Maravillosos, though, believed that they were just as good at this deadly game. And success meant becoming known in prison despite its dangers.

"You have to have what I could say is a 'solidness,'" Giant explained. "You show that you don't back down and that you take care of business. But if you don't want trouble, [then] you don't want to be around too much solidness. Because solidness is what creates your fame. It gets you too recognized as a rebellious person, man. [Saying as an example'] 'Aye, man, there's goes that vato, Randy. Ese pinche vato está loco [That fucking guy is crazy]. He don't listen to nobody. He does what the fuck he wants to do. I seen that vato cacquiar carneles, beat up vatos from La Eme. He whacks somebody, they put him in the hole. Every time he comes out, he whacks somebody. He don't give a fuck.' So everybody starts getting to know Randy. You know what I'm saying? So, within all this sum of people that heard about you, maybe 80 percent are scared to death of you. But there's always one that wants to make [earn] his points that says, 'Fuck it, man. I'm gonna try to take down homeboy.' There's always that person, you know. You gotta always watch for them."

There was a superb reward for that never-ending tension: the emotional high that came from doing violence.[39] Like the tension felt by competitors in a low scoring game, the act of hitting a home run, or scoring a touchdown or three-point shot, released an emotional high that often resulted in chest bumps, mighty leaps, and high fives. The emotional payout was even higher when the game involved death.

"So, if you're exposed," explained Giant, "and you're getting a lot of fuckin' bad vibes because the main motherfuckers [La Eme] is there, you gotta attack them. You gotta whack [kill] him before they rejuvenate [*sic*] some kind of fuckin' plan to whack you. And I was blasting my [Maravilloso] tattoos, homie. I'm walking dead, homeboy. People wanted to take me out."

The emotional payoff that came from a stabbing or killing made such risk seem worth it. After one of his attacks, Giant felt sky-high. "You know, when I stuck somebody, you know what you feel?" he asked rhetorically. "You feel le-ecstatic [*sic*]. You feel the ability to do anything you want. Put it like this: you got the potential, you know what I'm saying? You're built to go that fuckin' extra mile, where nobody else does it. You standing apart, you know what I mean? It's like that fuckin' *Speed Racer*, that cartoon. You know how *Speed Racer* gots a car that could go in the water and everything, and some people don't got a car and they can't go underwater? That's how you're built. That's the way you are. You feel like you can do anything. Nothing can stop you, you know what I'm saying?"

"So how did you feel emotionally before you had to go stick somebody?" I asked.

"Emotionally, I felt *hi-i-i-i-gh*," answered Giant. "I felt high and I felt like a kite. I felt the adrenaline, you know what I'm saying? It's a rush that makes you feel so *hi-i-i-i-gh*. You about to do something that nobody else can do. Like I told you already, you know you're built different. You do it and you get a rush. It feels like a new star is born [in the galaxy]. You know what I mean?"

Giant also equated being a Maravilloso with a religious calling. This showed how his violence was not the behavior of a sociopath, or a cruel human being unable to form genuine human relationships or emotional attachments. His violence was supported by a social network—by the Maravilla community he loved. The emotional energy of the Maravillas—the praise, the respect, the unity; the chants, *Somos los Maravillosos de Maravilla! Qué rifan Los Maravillosos de Maravilla!*; the belief that Maravilla was the sacred birthplace of the original LA Mexican gangsters, and that they descended from the Abrahams of the Mexican gang world—all of these carried Giant on a powerful emotional wave that was almost religious in its intensity.[40] Thus, when he botched his duties, he felt the guilt of a sinner: *Forgive me, Maravilla, for I have sinned . . .*

"You have to take care of the brothers that are busted," Giant explained. "That's number one. I always take care of my brothers. You can't let them suffer in there. Then I get home and everybody says, 'I saw you get down [do violence] in there. Órale, you hold it down for Maravilla.' It makes me feel good, you know what I me-e-e-an? 'Cause we're from Maravilla. We're the first and not the last [gangsters], you know what I me-e-e-an? We're proud of who we are. We try to really stand on our bond, on our word, like the Christian stands on faith, you know what I me-e-e-an? So that when you fail, you actually feel bad. You actually feel that you owe it and you gotta make it up."

These religious feelings, though, eventually gave in to rationality. It was an uneven match between the two violent elites. La Eme had Southsiders from hundreds of Southern Californian gangs wanting to join their elite group. They did violence for La Eme to prove their worth. The Maravillosos could only rely on the twenty or so Maravilla neighborhoods for members. Thus, they played a death match without enough replacements for those that got hospitalized, put in solitary confinement, or released home.

Fortunately, the Maravillosos got more help from other Maravillas after the greenlight. As mentioned earlier, many Maravillas defended themselves through offense, attacking Southsiders on sight. Giant and other Maravillosos, though, were the ones who dared go after La Eme—the violent elite.

The End of the War: Southern Unity

2006. The greenlight was off.

Many of the Maravilla participants, who were now in their mid-forties, were confused. As they aged, they spent less time in jail and prison since they committed less violent offenses. Many of them had also moved out of East LA to live in cities with cheaper housing costs. Others had entered drug rehabilitation and were trying to live conventional lives. They had no clue why La Eme canceled the greenlight. A few argued the following with bravado: *La Eme had grown so frustrated at its failure to defeat Maravilla that it bargained a truce.* Others offered the following with a snicker: *The Eme member responsible for putting the greenlight on Maravilla had dropped out of La Eme and become an informant, a snitch or rat. Once he left, the greenlight was turned off.*

But most old-timers claimed that the new generation of Maravillas had negotiated peace with La Eme for drug profits. Some even claimed that a few Maravilla neighborhoods paid a hefty fee to get into La Eme's drug network. Others claimed that some Maravillas joined La Eme to cancel the greenlight only to put a drug tax on their own Maravilla neighborhoods. Some of these reasons seemed plausible. Maintaining a separate identity as a Maravilla promised no riches for the younger generation. The latter came of age during the late 1980s, a period of extraordinary prosperity for the rich, when the "greed is good" message took off, and when images of financial and material excess bombarded them.[41] It made little sense to risk one's life under a greenlight if one remained broke. None of the older Maravillas, though, gave evidence to back their claims. It was all speculation.

Regardless, the Maravillas were now integrated with Southsiders. In fact, they followed La Eme's *reglas*, or rules. When these old-timers went to jail or prison, heroin-related health issues weakened their influence. The prominent Maravillas now comprised vibrant youngsters, the Pepsi generation (as the old-timers called them). This generation preferred bald heads to long, comb-backed hair; preferred pricey Air Jordan sneakers to dressy Stacy Adams shoes; preferred oversized football jerseys and baseball caps to buttoned-up Pendleton shirts and hairnets; and came of age during the crack era and saw drug market riches—and wanted to become rich too. And they were sharp and violent men. The old-timers had to fall in line. Their time had come and gone.

Even Giant, who once proudly took off his shirt—showing his MARAVILLOSO tattoo—to announce that he was with "the business," fell in line. The younger Maravillas did not want him to disturb the peace. In the mid-2010s, for example, Giant, who was then in his fifties, did a few months in the county jail for drug possession. After his release he recounted how he had to follow the Southsider lead while detained.

"When you get to the county [jail], at night you hear the announcement, 'For all the homies that just arrived, it'll be suitable for you to announce your barrio, the cell you're in.' So you'll hear like thirty vatos in one chingaso [shot]. You'll be hearing, 'Soy Giant de Maravilla gangs, cell 6, announcing my arrival! Gracias, Raza! [Thank you, my race!]' Then everybody'll respond, 'A ti! [To you!].' And everybody'll flush their toilet, and then the next vato will say it. That's the regulation, and it comes from the high power [La Eme]. And the next thing that comes down is they ask you, 'Did you bring any clavo [drugs]?' Because if you did, you give a third to them and they take it back to them vatos [La Eme]."

Giant also had to stop his Maravilloso activities. Reviving the war would harm the younger Maravillas who benefited from the current relations. "Like now, the Maravilloso car [group] is like, hush, you know what I mean?" Giant explained. "Everybody's like dormant. Nobody says nothing because they don't want the youngsters to get all fucked around by La Eme and all that shit. So, we're just like dying out. It's better for us like this because La Eme is strong, bro. Believe that! In prison, they're strong. They're all over the fuckin' place."

Though he no longer targeted La Eme, Giant still had his huge Maravilloso tattoo. He managed his safety by projecting a violent masculinity. "There was a guy where I had to project my solidness right there and then. It was a vato from [a Southsider neighborhood]. He goes, 'Aye man, where you from?' I go, 'Soy Giant from Maravilla.' And the vato goes, 'Oh, I heard about you. You one of the crazy ones.' I tell him, 'That's right, baby boy. I never sleep. I sleep standing up.' I tell him just like that. So he caught wind right there, you know. We just put it on hush. Because if any weirdness would've jumped off, I would've hit [stabbed] him first because he's the one that exploited it [brought it up]."

Giant's other safety strategy was to outdo Southsiders at their own game. Despite his age, Giant was competitive, with a masculine preoccupation of not being physically outdone. While in jail, he could not show weakness.

"With my discipline, with how I project myself, once I get all that veneno [poison], all that brujería [witchcraft] off of me (I'm talking about the drugs, the heroin), I put it down. I burn out youngsters on routina [Southsider military-style group exercises]. I do burpees, jumping jacks all day long, two times a day, burnout. And then I'll take a birdbath [light wash] in a cell. And then with that I feel like relaxed and go to sleep good. . . . One time there was a llavero [shot caller] that came down. He stops at one of the cells and looks at one of the [young] guys and goes, 'Ay, what's wrong with you?' The guy goes, 'What you mean what's wrong with me?' He goes, 'Yeah, what's wrong with you? Why you always sleeping when I pass by? Look at this old man. He's old enough to be your father, ese. I always come and he's up early in the morning working out and he's working out right now, and your ass is on the mat asleep. I'm gonna talk to you later.' And he splits. The guy goes, 'Ah, you see OG [original gangster], you got me in trouble.' I go, 'I didn't get you in trouble. You got yourself in trouble. Here nobody covers up for nobody, man. If you walk straight, your ass will follow. Straight up.'"

Mattering in the Gang World

In all, the greenlight years had a lasting impact on the Maravillas. According to participants, they were already LA's original gangsters. Now, after their greenlight status, they felt that they were LA's gangsters who showed the most heart. Their encounters with non-Maravillas cemented those feelings. "Imagine," Juano explained, "we were walking the yard [in prison] and the Busters [Norteños] see us and they say 'Dale Maravilla!' [That's right, Maravilla!] You know how fuckin' proud it makes you feel walking the yard and the fucker that's from up north tells you, 'Aye, simón, ese.' Shit like that makes you feel like you're the big dog."

Chico also recounted similar moments when he left East LA to visit family in other areas. He claimed that old-timer Southsiders often admired Maravilla for taking a stand. "I remember that I was all the way out in Riverside County and these two guys about my age [in their fifties] see my tattoos. They ask me where I'm from. I say, 'Soy de Maravilla.' And they're like, 'Maravilla? Aye, mucho respeto. I got much respect for you guys.' And we shook hands and you know, talked for a little bit. Randy, when he said, 'I got much respect for you,' that made me feel like I was on top of the world. That wherever

I go, people know what Maravilla stands for. It stands for pride, respect, and honor."

However, not all older Southsiders admired them. When I told one Southsider that I was researching the Maravillas, his response was the following: *Fuck Maravilla! They're fuckin' weak! You should study a real neighborhood, like my neighborhood.* He then told me of his prison encounter with a Maravilloso—how, shank in hand, he grabbed the Maravilloso from behind and stabbed him several times. However, he could not slash his throat since the victim squirmed too much. Later, he felt like crying for failing to kill the Maravilloso. He hated Maravilla that much. Yet his wrath showed that Maravilla's resistance impacted him. Maravillas had become known in the gang world.

This all meant a lot to the Maravillas. Chico: for most of his life he was a heroin addict. Emilio: for most his life he was a heroin addict. Giant, the mighty Giant: for most of his life he was a heroin addict. Each of them held a marginal position in the US, a nation that historically has stigmatized and placed limits on places like East LA. Given their social circumstances, these Maravillas struggled to succeed in conventional ways. They then created violent masculinities on the streets, in jail, and in prison. And they had the greenlight to show that they mattered in the gang world.

Somos Maravilla!

The greenlight, though, was only one part of their story. Some of them stopped their violence and self-destruction to find fulfillment elsewhere. Others suffered dearly as they struggled with homelessness and drug addiction. They would turn to religion for hope, then back to heroin and alcohol in despair. Then they went back to religion, in the name of Jesus, then back to the streets when their souls seemed beyond repair. We now move on to the next part of their lives: redemption, guilt, and pain.

II *Mattering in the World*

4 *In the Name of Jesus*

Chico sat in church. Fidgety. His eyes wandered everywhere. He picked up a water bottle. Put it back down. Grabbed a pamphlet. Opened it, closed it, put it on his lap, and then put it back in the rack. Picked a piece of paper off the floor. Put it in the rack. Took off his hat. Put it on his lap. Put it back on. Put it on his lap. Eyed the neighbor to his left. Eyed the neighbor to his right. Something made him tense, uneasy. Nervous. It was as if he prepared for a major event—a fight, a job interview, or a speech—for the first time. Or preparing to let the Holy Spirit enter his body, let the emotion lift him to a higher plane.

The sermon started. Chico sat back. It was time.

Chico was one of many Maravillas who transformed their lives through Christian Pentecostalism. To clarify, Pentecostals are a subcategory of Evangelicals, and Evangelicals are a subcategory of Protestants. So Pentecostals and Evangelicals share their main religious beliefs with Protestants.[1] The religious Maravillas joined the historical wave of Latinos from the United States and Latin America that had recently turned to Pentecostalism because of its high energy and emotionalism.[2] The church's emotional intensity—its congregants sometimes spoke in tongues—made them believe that the Holy Spirit entered their bodies. This belief personalized their relationship with

God in a way that they had never experienced in the more rigid Catholic or typical Protestant church.[3] Spirituality, then, became a way for them to interpret the world—the drug world, the gang world, and the divine recovery that now defined them.

Battling Heroin: The Lord's Way

Throughout the 1980s and 1990s Chico often spent time incarcerated. It happened so much that it no longer felt like a disruption. It did not unsettle his family life, work life, or social life. It interrupted only one thing: his heroin use. Heroin was Chico's priority, what drove him to be devious and brave. He pursued it endlessly since it crumbled the insides of followers who did not get their daily fix. A dose of heroin—and look: the bone chills, stomach cramps, and anxiety were cured! It was a life measured not in prayers, but in heroin spoons. But after close to twenty years of kneeling before the drug, of performing the ritual prayer—measuring and heating the drug, drawing it into a syringe, searching for a usable vein, and then injecting the drug for the divine euphoria—Chico pleaded, "No more!' Yet it was easier said than done. He believed that one of heroin's main ingredients was literal evil.

"When that stuff [heroin] is produced, manufactured, processed, there's actually black magic involved in it," Chico told me one day as we sat on a park bench. "There's brujería [witchcraft] mixed with it. That's part of the finishing touch. They go through a ritual in most cases, ones that want to have it blessed so that people could get hooked and they'll need it, and they'll crave it, and they'll desire it, and they'll have to have it."

"I know someone that was actually there [during the heroin production process] that told me about it. I could say his name because he's dead now, but I won't go that far just to respect his family, his kids, in case this information gets to them [he pointed at my digital recorder]. This guy was big time, him and his brother. He was a transporter. He would go to Mexico and bring it [heroin] back. Kilos of pure stuff. He said that it took two guys or more to make [process] it. It was a twenty-four-hour process."

"One time, one of the guys that does the process wasn't there, and he couldn't wait. So, the [processing] guy asks him if he wants to help him. He agreed. So it was like this: One guy was doing the mixing at a certain temperature while the other one rested and went to sleep. When it was his turn, he did the mixing while the other guy took a nap or slept. And—I don't know how I should say this—he saw something in the pot that was supernatural. He saw faces come out of the pot. He heard voices and everything coming out of the pot. And he drew a gun on the [processing] guy and told him, 'What did you get me into?' He felt like he was framed or set up."

"Do you think that he saw the spirits and faces because he was inhaling the fumes?" I asked. "Because you know that people who produce drugs have to wear [protective] masks."

"That's a probability," Chico answered. "But the guy told him, 'Es parte química, parte brujería [It is part chemical, part witchcraft].' And that explains it. When I think about all the stuff that I've been through and all of the things that addicts go through when they're hooked, that doesn't surprise me a bit. Because I'm a monster, Randy, when I'm using. I'm not the same guy. Believe me, I've done some pretty heinous things. Heinous is like cutting heads off. That's my definition. Go to the extreme. You do some pretty extraordinary harmful things to people. Some of the acts I did, the burglaries and the robberies, I went that extra step. That's out of my character. That's what the brujería [witchcraft] brings out in you."

I understood why Chico believed that witchcraft produced heroin addiction. He had grown up observing his Pentecostal mother, a *religiosa* who attended church often, told Bible stories, evangelized to friends, and could recite Bible verses by heart. And she prayed and prayed and prayed, in the living room, in the kitchen, in the bedroom.

She prayed for neighbors experiencing hardship; for her husband, who sold weed; for her long-haired hippie children who experimented with drugs. And she prayed for Chico—*Oh Lord, Jesus Christ*—the gangster Chico, who did everything she rebuked. *El diablo* had taken her son. She wanted him back. She prayed.

"I would see my mom praying and crying," Chico recalled. "And actually, I would get really emotional. It would kind of touch me, man. 'I gotta get away from this. This is too deep, man.' One, I was trying to be a tough guy. I was trying to be in control in all that. 'Cause I was already exposed to that when I was a kid. I would come home after partying. I'm talking about twelve, thirteen years old. I'm just a kid, just became a teenager, and I'll be in the street sniffing glue, getting high, doing whatever, and I'll come home at ten, eleven o'clock [at night]. I walk in and I hear my mom in the room praying. Sometimes, it was for me 'cause I was in jeopardy. And I would see her. I would open the door to tell her that I was home. I would see her praying, crying, praying for this, praying for that, deep prayer. I would close the door. I don't want to interrupt that, man. So, I was exposed to that."

This spirituality influenced Chico's path of drug recovery. He first attended secular programs where people talked about their problems. Nothing dynamic, nothing spectacular, nothing that made him feel like he had struck gold. According to him, people just told horror stories and looked for sex. Chico was disgusted. It was surprising to hear him reject carnal pleasures. He was a charmer who lit up around women, looking for signs of their discomfort: he offered his jacket if it was chilly; a bottle of water if it was hot; guide services if they needed to get somewhere; and he quickly picked up items that they had dropped. He was a smooth dresser, a smooth talker, and he deepened his already rich East LA accent when telling stories to make the ladies smile. Chico loved women. He interacted with them as though he always had a chance.

But pious Chico now spiritualized his drug recovery. He framed drug rehabilitation as sacred, a process in which personal transformation came before sexual desire. He argued that in a rehab center such desire abounded, and that women wanted to hunt him, devour him, lustfully tear his flesh apart. He felt objectified, like a piece of meat. This was too much. *Adios.*

"I tried Narcotics Anonymous and tried AA [Alcoholics Anonymous]," Chico explained. "I went to those places for a while. But to me it was like a big meat factory. I was sincere. I really wanted to find methods other than Christianity to clean up. So I would go to these meetings and try to mingle with guys that were dopefiends. A bunch of friends from Maravilla, they were part of Narcotics Anonymous. And I started realizing that it became like a meat factory. Everyone was trying to hook up. In fact, I was approached by a couple of females that were interested in starting a relationship with me. To be honest with you, Randy, that turned me off. They just wanted to hook up with me. I said, 'This is not what I'm looking for.' And I walked away and I continued using. I fell back to using."

He fared no better under methadone and detoxification therapies. They were nothing great, nothing exciting, nothing transformative, nothing spectacular, nothing out of this world. They just replaced one drug for other ones. "I did the methadone thing a few times," Chico recalled. "I did it even though I knew it wasn't the solution. I was too much of a pig. Because I was using methadone and heroin and smoking weed all at the same time. It wasn't fulfilling my needs. I also went into treatment, into detox. It was a medical facility where they give you medication to detox you, to help you go through the withdrawals. I kicked pretty bad. The medication that they were giving me wasn't even helping me. It was almost like giving me nothing. I was feeling the kick coming and going. If you see that movie *Ray* [about Ray Charles], when he's in the hospital detoxing, seeing nightmares and falling off his bed and hallucinating, going through severe withdrawals, well, I was that guy in the movies. I was Ray Charles in the movie, but without the fancy pajamas, haha."

Chico persisted. He gathered his might and used his last stint in medical detox as a springboard. It was only a nine-day detox, and when he was released his knees felt wobbly and the angst remained. It was still a start, which put him on the road to recovery. Finally, oh finally, as he recalled, he opened his heart to Christianity to reject, to repel, to repudiate heroin use. His ears opened: he finally heard the meaning of the Word spread by his mother and friends. His eyes opened: he finally saw how the Word transformed devious dope-fiends into kind human beings. Slowly, he opened: he let the Word warm him, shine on him, pour on him to start the new season of his life.

"That's when the miracle happened," Chico explained. "It didn't happen overnight. I didn't get hit by a bolt of lightning from heaven. But something started happening gradually in my heart, in my mind. Started to sense that this was something that I needed all along. And the more I opened up, the greater the miracle that began to happen."

But the evil residing in heroin, as Chico saw it, tempted him away from Christ. It intruded on his gentle thoughts, reminding him of the drug's bliss. All he had to do was stray from the Lord and—*órale*—he would be nodding out in pleasure again. Chico stood his ground. *In the name of Jesus Christ!* His mind and body, though, revolted.

"It wasn't that I could just walk away from it," Chico explained. "I still went through severe post-acute withdrawal syndrome. And I would get it now and then even after six months. And I was like, 'Man, what the heck's going on?' One of the scariest ones, one of the ugliest ones, is restless legs syndrome. It's a sense of anxiety that your body feels like you have a thousand ants running through your nervous system. Not only is it uncomfortable, it can even be painful. It certainly is psychologically traumatizing. You can't think up or down. It's kind of hard for you to make a move to do something. You don't know whether to cry or laugh, or shit on yourself or throw up. You feel a sense of anger, anxiety. And the worse part about this is that it happens about ninety percent of the time after midnight, when the lights are off, things are quiet, stores are closed, and you have to deal with it alone. Any dope-fiend will tell you that that's probably the worst part of withdrawing."

Chico doubled down on prayers. *Be gone, devil!* But the temptation lingered. For him, it was like being enticed daily by a dish of fried ice cream and promising oneself that one bite would do no harm. "We start romancing with the devil," explained Chico, "and before you know it, one fix leads to another one, and another one leads to another one. Before you know it, you're hooked. We think that we could play with the dragon's tail without getting flamed on or burned."

It took several years, but eventually Chico overcame his heroin cravings. He began seeing drugs as impure, disgusting, and the Word of God as sacred, pure. He felt a state of grace when he attended church or Bible study, or when he sang or spoke about the promise of everlasting life in heaven. He had come a long way. He certainly felt more secure. Of course, there would be slipups here and there as he as walked toward God.

Interpreting God and Jesus in Gangs

Back in 1993, Marcos was at home, paralyzed from the neck down. About six homeboys stopped by to tell him about La Eme's new rules. They wanted to take him to the Maravilla meeting at Belvedere Park. His wife refused—*no, no, no, he ain't going*—so they promised to return with information. Weeks later he saw how Maravilla's alliance against La Eme relaxed territorial boundaries. Maravillas from different neighborhoods now partied together and walked through each other's turf with little *pedo*, or conflict. It would be a long time, though, before Marcos experienced the freedom of moving his body.

Months earlier Marcos had broken up with his wife and moved in with his parents, who still lived near the neighborhood. One night he and a few younger homies did drugs and got hungry. It was a wet, drizzly January night (equal to a blizzard for Southern Californians), but they braved the bad weather to walk to a pizza shop. They ordered a large pizza and, as they waited, a younger homeboy alerted the twenty-five-year-old Marcos to a slow-moving car. He dismissed it. They were not on enemy turf. He stepped outside to smoke a cigarette.

"Then I see a guy pointing a gun at me," Marcos recalled. "I looked at him. My first instinct—'cause I was high, buzzed out—[was to] bob and weave, you know? Dodge. Dodge ball. Pah, pah, pah, pah. While the guy's shooting, he's asking me, 'Where you from?' I'm trying to dodge him; he's shooting at me. Aw, man. I'm buzzed out, bro. I see somebody else, different, on the other side of where I was at. And I see him pulling the trigger too. One of them took me down. The guy that I was running from was behind me and when I ran away from him, the other guy was on the side. Pah, pah, pah. I went down."

Unconscious. Conscious. Unconscious. Awake. He heard cars. *Vroooom!* He heard people. *He's not over here! He's over here!*

"I don't know how I landed across the street behind a two-foot wall. The cop came, stopped, got off [out of the car]. 'You alright?' 'I can't move, man.' 'Ambulance is on its way.' They came and took me to General Hospital. They diagnosed it as a paralysis. I was shot through the neck. Completely paralyzed. That was it. That was my last tragic thing that happened."

Marcos was angry. Before the shooting he had become interested in Christianity. He was tired of the paranoia and violence of gang life, tired of the heroin addiction that had him up and running to nowhere fast. He had attended church a few times and admired the stable born-again homeboys. Though he was still a long way from a total Christian transformation, he had taken the first step. Now he was bedridden, unable to lift a finger or wiggle a toe. Jesus was far from his mind. Payback. That was the way to go.

"Then I found out that the whole thing was a case of mistaken identity," Marcos explained. "They thought I was somebody else intruding on their territory. The shooter's friends came to the hospital, and they spoke to me. These guys came to visit me, giving me their love, man, affection. They came and apologized. It was hard for me, man. It was hard. The only reason I decided not to do anything is because a lot of my homies were like, 'You know what, you gotta let it go man.' My friend's like, 'Easy, man.' He's an older homeboy, an older cat. So friends like that helped me stop. It was the Lord that really helped me. He put forgiveness in my heart. He put goodness in my heart. I stopped everything. Smoking, drugs, everything. I stopped drinking too. I quit drinking for about eighteen years, man."

This was a transformative moment. Any shootings, knifings, or harm done by outsiders required retaliation. An eye for eye, a bone for a bone, a bullet for a bullet—a paralysis, oh man, oh man: *Get the cuete, homes!* But the shooters' remorse, their apology, and the homeboys telling Marcos to let it go—all of that meant something. He felt something greater than him, something beyond him, something above him; he believed that God and Jesus, the Almighties, had teamed up to instill mercy and kindness in his heart.

And look: Marcos walked again! He had worked hard through physical therapy, one assisted step at a time. He also gained some use of his arms and hands, which allowed him to drive again. "I got shot in my neck, upper neck. My C6, C7 vertebrae. [The bullet] lodged in my spinal cord. I was told that I was never to walk again. Here I am walking today. That was my diagnosis: completely paralyzed, the neck down. Here I am walking, man. I get around just like everybody else gets around. I walk, I drive, I do everything. That's the Lord helping me, showing his love for me. That guy up there [motioning to the sky], he's real. He made this miracle happen."

Marcos, who now walked with a pronounced limp, committed himself to Christianity. The problem? Christianity did not instantly eliminate his gang reflexes. When Marcos felt threatened, his street instincts kicked in. Eight years after being paralyzed from the neck down and becoming a born-again Christian, he put a gun in his hand.

"There was this guy that used to mess around with the girl I was messing around with. He was kind of disrespecting. So my mentality came back out. I made a phone call and he [a friend] delivered what I needed, what I wanted. A nine-millimeter [handgun]. I was going to hold on to it until I seen this guy. But I never seen him. I guess he caught wind of what was going on or heard something, so he stopped coming around. And I was like, 'No, I'm gonna hold it [the gun] until this guy comes back around.' My mentality was protection, you know, protect myself."

One night some family members invited him to play pool. They called a taxi, and as they waited he told him that he forgot to put on cologne. He went back in the house, got the gun, and put a clip of bullets in it. "So we got to the bar. I started contemplating, 'Man, if I get caught, oh Lord!' The girl I was seeing, she had a backpack. I said, 'Come here.' She says, 'What? What are you gonna do?' I said, 'Come here. Just stand right there.' Opened up the bag, put the clip in there. She says, 'What the hell is wrong with you?' I put the nine [millimeter] in there, closed it up. She says, 'There's no reason to bring that!' I say, 'I don't want to talk about it.' She took off the bag and put it under the table. Somebody seen me put the gun in the bag. They called the Montebello police. They were there in no time. Ten minutes later I'm in a cop car being transported to the Montebello police station."

Then, a miracle! For possession of a firearm, Marcos was required to do only three years on probation. "That's another blessing! Psshh. That man [Jesus] is real. He is real. I did three days. Within three days, I went to my arraignment. They rescheduled it for my preliminary [hearing] in two weeks after my arraignment. Then they offered me three years [of] probation, time served. I'm a two-striker. If I got another conviction, I would never come out again, man. Throw out the key and lock me up for good." According to Marcos, the judge took a lot into his consideration: his community work with gang youth; glowing reference letters; and his argument that he carried the gun for self-defense. He felt the Lord on his side.

A year later, Marcos was in the probation office for his scheduled appointment. He had brought his daughter along, with plans of getting something to eat with her afterward. A probation officer walked up and told him that his probation was terminated.

Marcos was free!

"I broke down and cried right there. My daughter, she never seen me cry. At that time, she was about twenty and she never seen me cry. That was an experience for her too. Like they say, God works in mysterious ways. She experienced that. She was there at the time, witnessing it. It blew her away too. It was alright. I'm not the type of guy to cry. Life can do that to you. I don't know what it is, but somebody up there, or something, is watching out for me. That was a good feeling."

Jesus in Gang and Prison Politics

The Christian Chico was still a Maravilla. In fact, those two identities—religious and secular—intersected, both joining hands to define Chico. Chico still hung out with homeboys, which reinforced his neighborhood status. Most of his friends, though, were nonreligious and offered him not grape juice or bread but weed, liquor, and beer. Chico respectfully declined.

"I go back to the neighborhood," he explained, "and they all be drinking beer. I'll see beer drinkers and a couple of heroin users in the mix. And this one time, one guy kept offering me a beer just to be cordial and friendly because he saw that I was just drinking water from a bottled water. And I would say, 'I'm good, thank you.' But after a few more times, I said, 'Hey, I'm a born-again Christian. I don't drink.' He was really bothered by it, like he was the devil trying to entice me. I told him not to trip, not to worry about it. I knew that out of respect he was just trying to be cordial. He kept coming up to me saying, 'Man, I feel bad now about this.' I said, 'Don't worry about it, homie. Just enjoy yourself.'"

Marcos also experienced drug and alcohol temptations at neighborhood get-togethers. However, he claimed that Jesus pulled on his heart, allowing him to win the tug of war between Christianity and vice. He wanted to experience everlasting life in heaven. "I got nothing to worry about," Marcos explained. "I'm comfortable being myself. There's a better place where I want to go [heaven]." Looking up and laughing, he said, "Take me now!" Yet he admitted that he still thought about doing heroin and violence. "Of course, I get those thoughts. I grew up doing those things. That's part of what created me."

But he was determined to overcome his life experiences—to overcome his upbringing in a marginal East LA neighborhood with parents who tried to escape their marginality not by rejecting racism, sexism, and classism through collective action but by joining the neighborhood gang. They raised children who later joined the neighborhood—who later shot rivals and got shot. Gangsterism was an embodied experience. It took a lifetime to build; it also took a tremendous effort to tear down. Marcos felt that only God could hasten his personal transformation.

"I gotta overcome that," he reflected. "That's what the Lord says. When your homeboys bring things up, you gotta change the subject. You talk about living. You talk about your health. Stuff like that. Ask them, 'Whatta you do at home? How's your car?' Things like that. . . . They might be talking about, 'Well, this guy's no good' or 'He snitched on him, so and so.' You could [give] input about what he should do about it. 'What do you want to do about it?' But from my view, what comes around, goes around. So all I do is change the subject. They talk about issues like a conflict or who has the best drugs, I change the subject."

"They talk about those things in front of you?" I asked.

"Sure! They talk about who has good stuff [drugs], 'Do you want a beer?' or 'I got some good stuff.'"

"Do they still offer you?"

"Nah, they don't offer me anymore," he answered. "And if they would, I'll comment on it, make a joke about it, and next time they know not to talk about it or bring it up. One time an old friend of mine came up to me and pulls out what looked like a kilo [of heroin] out of his pocket and said, 'This is yours. I know you don't mess around anymore, but this is yours. If you want it, here.' I hesitated. I looked at him. I said, 'You ever show me something like that again, I'll kill you.' I told him right there. He says, 'Oh, okay, sorry.' He thought he was doing something good. What's that saying? 'Right motives, wrong intentions.' He wanted to give out of respect, but he brought it about the wrong way. He should've offered me a thousand dollars! [Laughter] Then, okay, I'll take it! He has a good heart. But he showed it the wrong way. Sometimes people say, 'Oh, here's a gun' or 'I know somebody who you could score on.' They want to help you. But like I said right now, 'Wrong intentions, right motives.'"

Sadly, Marcos had few places to go where friends did not discuss gang life, drugs, and violence. At least the Maravillas still loved their born-again Christian homeboys. Their parents perhaps had influenced them to be whisper quiet on the topic of God, so they accepted peers who now claimed to walk a holy path. *Órale, con suerte, homie.* The reborn homeboy was now considered inactive, with no more duties or obligations. If they fell back into heroin use, life went on as though the rebirth had never occurred. Christian or non-Christian, there was only *puro amor*, or pure love, between the homeboys.

At least most of them showed love. A few homeboys were skeptics, seeing religion as a scam. They argued that religion's trickery shifted one's loyalty from the neighborhood to an imagined figure in the sky. They told their homies to remain barrio warriors and only believe in what they could actually see and touch.

"I have a friend, his name was Memo," Chico explained. "He was from the barrio and probably about seven or eight years younger than me. I was a lot more active than he was. He eventually came up in rank and I had just become a born-again Christian. And he heard about it. He approached me and said, 'Órale, Chico, why don't you snap out of it, homie? Christian? Are you serious? You're really becoming a Christian?' He was kind of mocking me. And I said, 'Hey Memo, this is me. This is really what's happening. I'm not leaving the barrio. I'm still from the neighborhood. I'm just not active. You're only going to find me in church.' And then he was mocking me. He was trying to convince me that it was all a sham. That it was just a little phase that I was going through. And I told him that he was wasting his time. Now, about two weeks later, he was gunned down. They caught him in the neighborhood and ambushed him. He died a pretty violent death. I was thinking, 'Man, this is what happens to people when they mock me?'"

In true religious form, Chico now believed that God sometimes worked on his behalf to smite those who scorned Christianity. Forget about how his homeboy was a violent gangster with a target on his back. Forget about how the violent death probably would have happened whether he encountered Chico or not. But he interpreted signs everywhere. God was on his side.

Even in jail.

Despite the fact that Chico was a born-again Christian, heroin held on tight, using the body's physiology to make him use again. And he did. He was soon arrested for drug possession and sent to LA County Jail. He reasoned that God punished him for straying from righteousness. He prayed again—*Lord Jesus Christ, forgive me for my sins*—and asked the Lord for help, to guide and protect him through the greenlight drama. Since he was a Maravilla, the Southsiders could pounce on him, and he would have to use violence to protect himself—*Please Lord, I do not want blood to be shed.* Chico, though, was also prideful, a deadly sin. He took pride in being a Maravilla who refused to back down. He did not want to be seen as someone who used a Christian identity to punk out.

"When people use religion as an escape, they call that 'hiding behind the Bible,'" he explained. "You see that happening in the system [jail and prison]. You see some guys that don't want to get involved with gang politics or add more time behind an assault. They start going to church or they start carrying their Bible to get away from the gang politics in the system. They call it 'hiding behind the Bible.' Now, I happen to have a situation myself where I was already a Christian. I was already a born-again believer. I was already serving the Lord when I caught a [criminal] case and went to jail. So I was worried that they [his peers] were going to think that I was one of these guys hiding behind the Bible to stay out of the gang life in there."

He prayed: *God, can we postpone this* [the violence]? It was a long shot, but at least he tried. Still, he interpreted what happened next as a divine intervention. "One time it was shower time in my cellblock. There was anywhere from seventy-five to one hundred inmates in that cellblock. And I was the only guy from Maravilla in there. And during this time, the guys from Maravilla, we're being assaulted. And I'm branded Maravilla. I have it all over my body. I have it on my arms, my back, pretty large-size tattoos. So what happens is that when you leave to shower all you got is a towel around you. A towel around your waist and bar of soap and if you're lucky some slippers. And I said, 'This is it. This is when they're going to stick [stab] me. This is when I'm going to face the music.'"

Alert, tense, he went into the shower, washed himself, and left. Nothing happened. He was like an invisible man. Later he spoke to the shot caller, or the La Eme associate who controlled the cellblock. "I explained to him that I was already a Christian before I got there. And I actually told him that I'm Maravilla, 100 percent, born and raised, but that I'm a born-again Christian, that I'm waving the *bandera* [flag] of the bloodstained banner of Jesus Christ. The guy tripped out on me. He thought I was nuts. But he pretty much detected that I was genuine with my faith, with my commitment. So they pretty much gave me a pass. It was a divine intervention."

Later Chico was housed in another part of the jail, a section called Wayside, which he claimed contained about three thousand inmates. He was in the same dorm as another shot caller, who he also pulled aside. "I was able to sit down and talk to him face-to-face. We sat and talked, and I shared a little bit about my faith. And we had a cordial conversation, and it was a real short conversation. We had to part ways because he was a busy guy, and he had a pretty strong reputation. But he gave me a pass."

Chico encountered no more problems. He even played handball with his shirt off, showing his Maravilla tattoos. The Southsiders, though, respected his religious stand. Another divine intervention, Chico thought. But a moment of truth arose. The Southsiders planned to riot with Black inmates again. A message passed through the dorms and cellblocks: *All Latinos must unite regardless of greenlight status or conflicts.* And the Maravillas would participate because their hatred for Blacks exceeded their dislike of Southsiders. Chico had to choose a side: Jesus or the Southsiders.

He chose Jesus. He could not risk his standing with God by striking another human being who had done him no wrong. He was trying, trying, Oh Lord, trying to stay on the right path. And this was a monumental moment, the moment when he turned away from everything that he had once honored: the decades of prison politics that existed before him and would remain after him; the politics that guided his life in and out of prison; the culture and ideology telling

him where to go and what to do; the need to display toughness, man-
liness, and violence; the street creed never to back down. *Oh Lord!*
What a monumental moment it was for Chico when he chose to stay
out of it.

"Because a few race riots jumped off and I didn't participate as a
born-again Christian," Chico explained, "because as a born-again
Christian you don't get involved with any gang politics. So there were
a few riots that jumped off and the shot caller looked at me knowing
that I wasn't going to participate. I just stood on my bunk and watched
all the melee that went on. The stabbings and all that. It was between
the Blacks and the Sureños. At one time I would have participated,
Randy. You didn't even have to ask me. But because of my faith, because of my commitment, because of my stance as a believer, I had
to make a choice right then and there. And I made my choice. Actually, I made my choice before I went in there [to jail] that I was going
to do my thing as a born-again believer. And my faith was put to the
test. My reputation was put to the test. Everything was put to the test.
And I walked out with flying colors. I was able to do my time, get out
of there, walk unscathed."

Chico made it. He felt that God walked by his side.

Religious Emotions as Thrills

Bible stories are fantastic: an invisible force parts seas, smashes
fortress walls, and hails fire on cities; people turn into salt, walk on
water, and rise from the dead; and the world's end features a seven-
headed dragon. But, apart from his mother's influence, why would
the hardened, street-savvy Chico accept Christianity or practice Pentecostalism?

The answer: emotional energy.

In the early twentieth century, sociologist Émile Durkheim argued that religion arose not because of a real God or deities. It arose

because of the social: a moral community that celebrated sacred acts, ideas, and objects, whether they were rocks, trees, animals, the moon, the stars, or an invisible force.[4] Its ritual-based ceremonies produced powerful emotions among the gathered, a unified emotion that Durkheim called *collective effervescence*. Together, like-minded people felt energized and behaved in ways they never did in ordinary life. The experience confused them so much that they could only explain it as the work of the supernatural. Durkheim states:

> The very fact of assembling is an exceptionally powerful stimulant. Once the individuals are assembled, their proximity generates a kind of electricity that quickly transports them to an extraordinary degree of exaltation. Every emotion expressed is retained without resistance in all those minds so open to external impressions, each one echoing the others. The initial impulse thus becomes amplified as it reverberates, like an avalanche gathering force as it goes. And as passions so strong and uncontrolled are bound to seek outward expression, there are violent gestures, shouts, even howls, deafening noises of all sorts from all sides that intensify even more the state they express.[5]

About a century later, the sociologist Randall Collins argued that religious ceremonies, sports games, lectures, meetings, concerts, and other events can intensify emotions.[6] The events needed not only a gathering, but also focused rituals, such as praying, chanting, singing, sitting quietly, or booing loudly. When rituals succeeded, people felt exhilarated. When rituals failed (as in a dull meeting), people felt unmotivated. As a result, individuals searched for a series of energizing rituals, or a chain of interactions that raised their emotional energy and gave them meaning.[7]

Sociologist Robert Brenneman later used Collins's theory to understand gangs in Central America.[8] Brenneman focused on youths who tried to escape the shame of their disadvantaged circumstances. Some of them looked for empowerment in gangs, whose members showed loyalty, valued gang symbols, and performed risky acts. Belonging to a gang raised their emotional energy, which made them feel confident and proud. Such a life, Brenneman found, eventually drained gang members. The initial excitement wore off as retaliation by rivals and arrests by police increased. Soon they experienced constant fear and paranoia, and wanted out after the emotional payoff was gone. But they needed a substitute that would accept their gangster past. They considered the Pentecostal church, which preached salvation through personal transformation—and called anyone walking through its doors an *hermano* or *hermana* (brother or sister)—their best bet.

Of course, joining the church came with a price. It demanded that one accept Jesus Christ as one's Lord and Savior and focus on one's own faults. But it was not the actual Word of God that won them over. Brenneman found that it was the tremendous emotional experience of admitting their shame while being surrounded by congregants who prayed for them. The intense act made them cry, weep, and beg for acceptance and forgiveness. The emotional energy made them believe that a higher power must be present.

This was one reason Chico believed. He felt the collective effervescence of the congregation (Durkheim); he experienced an emotional high that he wanted to repeat (Collins); and he felt that only Pentecostals accepted him and allowed him to express shame and tears without consequence (Brenneman). His emotional energy soared. For Chico, there was only one explanation: the holy spirit had entered his body and mind.

"You know, Randy, I feel some stuff that is not taught," Chico told me one day. "I experience God in a personal way, a divine way, that has no real scientific or logical explanation except for something divine. And that's been going on seventeen, eighteen years now. I'm still amazed at it to this day. The things I've experienced, and the things I'm still experiencing."

I observed Chico's divine experience whenever I went to church with him. He attended a large Pentecostal church in a gentrified community, which was surprisingly ethnically diverse. White, Asian, and Black congregants were preached to by a white pastor who sometimes referred to stock portfolios, IKEA furniture, and recreational travel to make his points. The visit always started in a parking lot next to the church, where Mr. Serna, a former parole officer in his late eighties, set up a table with free tamales, chicken, and bottled water. The smiling born-again homies would call out to passing congregants, "How are you today? Would you care for some tamales? How about a bottled water? God bless you." Their Christian brothers and sisters smiled back and often took them up on their offers.

The mood was festive, with Mr. Serna playing salsa music on a small radio. I could never tell if it was Christian salsa because I always got caught up in the beat and just wanted to dance (though I never did, because it might be considered sinful). But it was an emotional preparation, like a warm-up before a workout, that made most of us share pleasantries and feel giddy and light. Then, about fifteen minutes before the sermon's start, some of the guys helped pack up everything and put it Mr. Serna's car. We then entered the church in good humor. After finding seats, though, we mostly stayed quiet. Chico acted nervous. Marcos and Emilio seemed meditative. All of them prepared for the seismic emotional wave that would soon sweep them into another dimension.

It began. A small band on stage played guitars, drums, and violins. The melody was modern and the drumbeat fast: *tatta-doom, tatta-doom, tatta-doom, bah-boom-bah-boom—chaaa!* It felt like a concert, not a church service; like a secular performance, not the sound required to praise God. That was how I felt as a nonbeliever who had not seriously attended church since I was about ten or eleven years old. I held onto the stereotype that church music was old and traditional, so I was surprised when I wanted to tap my feet and nod my head to the rhythm and beat. I was surprised when I felt enjoyment. But the believers, like Chico, Marcos, and Emilio, were focused, entranced. The lively music opened their emotional pathways so that they could take in the pastor's sermon under amplified emotional conditions.

The music stopped. The pastor entered.

Thank you, God. Thank you for the season, Lord. While there are many sorrows, this is a time of a great joy. For you came to us, came to us to redeem us. . . .

Amen.

You can be seated.

The congregants listened intently as the pastor preached, with some of them nodding their heads and a few of them smiling when hearing something that resonated with them. Then, after about fifteen minutes, the pastor stopped and the band played again. The band seemed even louder and more energetic this time. A soloist then sang a religious song, the congregants singing with her. She had a marvelous high voice, which made me fall in love with her gift. The music often crescendoed, the mood swelling with it too. *Oh Lord!* People raised their arms, palms facing up, as though they were lifting an easy weight, as though their heavy burdens had miraculously become light. *Oh my Savior!* I became entranced as well. I became one with the congregation. I did not know the song lyrics, but it did not matter. I understood the moment, the mood. I could feel the music pulsate through me as it pulsated through everyone else; I could feel joy as everyone else felt joy; the music had lifted me, had made me forget about the outside world. It was so strong, yet so beautiful and peaceful. Chico was crying. Emilio was crying. Marcos had tears in his eyes. They raised their arms and swayed from side to side. In that moment, I loved them. How could I not? Under the emotional circumstances, did they not love me too? The band transitioned from one song to the next, and the woman with the soprano voice that could melt the iciest heart kept up. The violinist played forcefully, and I fell in love with her gift too. The people sang as one and knew the meaning behind the words, which raised their emotions higher than mine. And the drummer—*Almighty Jesus Christ!* He played louder and louder. The spirit. I finally understood what they meant by the spirit.

Finally the music slowed and decreased in volume, the singers harmonizing softly. When the music ended, the congregants clapped loudly. Later, when I checked my recording, I discovered that the music had played for about twenty minutes, a hefty chunk of the service. Later, when I attended other church services, I found that roughly the same amount of time was allotted for music. Though I never spoke to church organizers, it seemed as though they used music to keep the emotional energy high.[9] Like Durkheim and Collins, they understood the power of unified emotions, how inspiring music and united singing put congregants in the proper mood to accept their message. The emotional high also increased the chances that congregants would return weekly to create a chain of emotionally charged events. Emotional energy feels great, especially when experienced with others, so most of the service focused on mood enhancement or emotional manipulation to ensure that congregants felt the spirit, or higher power.

For the remainder of the service (about forty minutes), the pastor preached about the dangers of thinking that one was wiser than God. He claimed that many congregants understood God's guidelines, but "nevertheless" ignored them and took a different path. The result was intense suffering until they acknowledged that God had the greatest wisdom of all. *Do you have a "nevertheless" in your life?*, asked the pastor. *Something that you know that God has instructed for your good, but you think you know better?* Tears ran down Emilio's face. The words seemed to evoke the shame of his past and present, and he felt comfortable expressing that shame through crying—a taboo in the gang world. This church, though, accepted anguished emotional displays because it was a sign that one looked inward, not outward, to account for their life's suffering. The more Emilio cried, the more the church did its job.

At the end of the service a guitar player played a soft melody while another pastor, a woman, stood at the lectern to summarize the day's sermon. She then called for congregants to accept Jesus as their Savior: *So tonight, I just want to invite you, take a minute and say yes to him [Jesus], the one who came for you. He didn't just come so that you would say, "Okay, I accept Jesus, forgive my sins and now I'm a Christian." He came so whatever it is you're battling tonight, he sent his Holy Spirit so that we wouldn't have to do it alone.* Chico cried again. Those words within the context of a ceremonial Christian gathering, the ritual of music and singing, of jointly praising the Lord, of a united focus on the pastor and his words, and now on this pastor and her words, made tears drop from Chico's eyes. Despite his ugly past, he felt that Jesus was with him. His Christian brothers and sisters were with him too. He was not alone on the journey to renew his life.

We surrender ourselves again, and we do so in Christ's name.

Amen, the congregation answered.

After several church visits I spoke to Chico about his religious experiences. I told him that although he was a Christian and kind to others, he still had a toughness about him, in his talk and his body. I was surprised to see him cry so freely around others.

"I'm not surprised that you were surprised," he answered. "It's like I think I told you once, being in church is almost like being welcomed into a beautiful mansion with the best food, the best furniture, the best everything, and being treated with respect and love. You're being welcomed into this place, and you're being treated by servants, and they're treating you with dignity and respect. You get a sense of gratitude, of awe, of appreciation for even being invited to this place. That's why I get emotional. Part of it it's just about being happy of where I'm at. There's been times when I'm just bawling, like a little baby on my knees. And people at the church come up to me and say, 'Are you okay? Don't worry about it. It's going to be okay.' They think that I'm going through something traumatic. I'm actually [feeling] grateful. I'm actually in a good place of gratitude and happiness—that I am where I am, and that God has done what he has done in my life."

Chico felt thankful. The Pentecostal church embraced him despite his gravelly voice and despite his throwback self-presentation, which represented the neat and polished gangster look of the 1970s: hard-pressed slacks or jeans; a leather blazer over a button-down dress shirt; pointy, shiny Stacy Adams shoes; a thick, bushy mustache; and visible tattoos. This reminded me of what sociologist Edward Flores referred to as a "reformed barrio masculinity" among gang members who became born-again Christians.[10] While they kept certain cultural practices of the barrio—the gang lingo, tattoos, and fashion—the church encouraged a masculinity that featured kindness, legal work, and nonviolence. For Chico, the church provided the chance for him to transform from a violent drug addict into a gentle human being.

"It's almost as if you've been sentenced to life, you've been sentenced to execution, and you got a date to be executed, and the mayor, the president, or the vice president, or someone powerful walks in and says, 'We're not only going to pardon this guy and take him off of death row, but we're actually going to give him a break and allow him to get out and get back on the streets. We're going to give him a second chance after being guilty, a convicted murderer, on death row.' So, you're grateful, happy, especially if you have a family and children. It's unbelievable. You know that God has forgiven you. That's where emotions come in, Randy."

Chico then spoke about the emotional energy he felt around like-minded others, and how it motivated him to continue following the Lord's lead and worshipping God Almighty, who in his eternal wisdom created the rules to live a peaceful and happy life. And the music and songs of the religious ceremonies created an emotional charge that made him keep attending church. It made him feel *high*—a high he could only explain by invoking the Holy Spirit.

"It's like walking into a gym," he explained. "You see people running and jogging and working out, and, you know, sweating. You see people in a group, a couple encouraging each other, pushing each other. You feel that sense of not just unity. You feel that sense of people that you can identify with. We're on the same journey. We're all trying to get some place and try to get something out of your time in that gym, you know? It's an encouragement. The worship is always on for me personally. I have people all around me, but I lose focus on those around me. When I'm there, it's just to have an intimate time of acknowledging him, worshipping him. There's been times, there's been incidents where it's been very euphoric. Powerfully euphoric. Where I just put in all by being, body, soul, and spirit in uniting. There's like a connection there. I walk out almost like high. I'm lit up. I feel strength and super joyous. It's a combination of good attributes, good vibes, good energy. Well, people call it energy, but it's the Holy Spirit. You go into a different state, a different realm so to speak."

Intense. The emotional energy overwhelmed him so much that he could only attribute it to the Holy Spirit. It was a religious bliss that he chased over and over—like he once chased heroin's high. In this case he did not replace one drug with another, like using methadone instead of heroin. Instead, he replaced one high with another, a spiritual high for a drug high. He also replaced crime thrills with religious emotional energy. The sensations he felt during a sermon packed with people—the tingles, the warmth, the feelings of uncertainty and vulnerability—turned to thrills, especially after the ceremony.

Successfully letting God lift him up during song and then carry him through a sermon made for a thrilling triumph. That was the emotional high that kept Chico religious.

Heroin, though, was stubborn. Chico occasionally felt its tug; he experienced recurring pain that threatened to become full-on withdrawal; he experienced the mind tricks that told him that one jab of heroin would do no harm. He was vulnerable. The church did not hold daily services, and sometimes Chico's emotional energy from the most recent church service began to wane. He needed a recharge, fast. He found the answer: performing church rituals at home.

"I learned to experience what I experience in church at home," Chico explained.

"You feel those emotions at home?" I asked.

"Yeah, put some music on, and *wow*," Chico answered. "I'm not even in church. I'm at home."

"What kind of music?" I asked.

"Worship music," Chico answered. "That's my preference. It's kind of a slower worship. Some acoustic, some piano, for example. The reason for that is that it's instrumental and brings about this atmosphere that builds within you. That's like the divine inspiration of the Holy Spirit in the music. It moves that person. I put it on in my room and I'm like, '*Woooow.*' And I just get right at it. I just focus. I just go into a personal time with the Lord. And it's so powerful that it's even brought me to tears, Randy. To tears."

"By yourself?" I asked.

"Yeah, when I've been alone, it brought tears," Chico answered. "Just broke down. It did something to my heart, to my mind. It doesn't necessarily mean that I'm going through a tough time in my life. It's just that those tears could be tears of gratitude. Tears of appreciation. Tears of you making that connection with our Father under the inspiration of the Holy Spirit, of the presence of the Holy Spirit. Oh man, there's nothing like it."

How could Chico not believe in a Holy Spirit? The symbolism of religious music brought the sacred into his tiny state-funded SRO (single room occupancy) in the heart of Skid Row. Outside his facility, makeshift tents housed thousands of homeless people, many of them addicted to drugs and mentally ill. They sold and used drugs, traded money for sex, urinated and defecated, argued and fought, and sometimes stabbed and killed each other, all out on the street. Whenever I spent time at Chico's place, the stench, the trash—the government neglect—was horrendous. It could not get any more profane. But when Chico played Christian music, he magically fell into a trance, during which his surroundings vanished and his focus on God turned the moment sacred. Chico recharged his emotional battery. He felt love and joy, a beautiful combination that flooded him, soaked him, made him unable to bear the pleasure. He wept in bliss despite living in LA's little hell.

Weeping is integral to Christianity. Weeping occurs throughout the Bible, in descriptions of nourishing prayers, in portraits of a crying Jesus, and in the crying of those who loved Jesus.[11] The medieval Christian mystic Catherine of Siena argued that there was a progression of tearful experiences that reflected one's increasingly closer relationship to God: tears of pain (for nonbelievers); tears of fear (for new believers); tears of newfound compassion and awakening; tears of sweetness or happiness; and tears of peace that signal a oneness with God.[12] At this point Chico and his peers had moved beyond the tears of fear and awakening and now shed sweet tears full of God's love.

Such tearful, emotional moments also happened for Chico during Christian retreats. He often took trips sponsored by the church and private donors, retreats that took him far from the grimy area where LA contained its poor. He traveled to affordable resorts in Utah, Arizona, and Northern California, tranquil and forested areas that filled his senses with nature's sights, smells, and sounds.

Christian brothers and sisters surrounded him like the water that floats a buoy, bouncing him up and down and pulling him along with their collective effervescence, or emotional energy. Everyone smiled; everyone laughed; everyone treated each other with kindness and grace. Conference sessions featured sermons that touched everyone. Some congregants became teary-eyed and wept; others closed their eyes and focused on the emotional energy running through their bodies, which they interpreted as the Holy Spirit.

Even a get-together in someone's room could turn into an emotionally charged event. At one retreat, for example, Chico was in a room with Pastor Nito (a former Maravilla), Pastor Herman (a former lifer), and Joe (who had been imprisoned for fifteen years). They were doing their dinnertime "devotion," during which members shared their thoughts on a Bible passage or provided a personal testimony. Then the moment began.

"We were done with our prayers, and we opened up on some personal stuff that's going on," Chico recalled. "Even though Nito is doing pretty good, he has a son that's struggling with drugs. In fact, he's doing [prison] time right now. So Nito shared, 'Hey, I got something that hit me in my heart. My son.' And we all kind of had an idea already 'cause we're real close. So he shared. Then Joe shared a little bit about his daughter, who is doing thirty years in prison, and he said he understood Nito's pain. Then we started praying. We huddled together, put our arms around each other. We started praying for Nito and before you know it—boom! An explosion. Herman started praying and he bawled, he just—boom! He broke, man. Herman was just in tears. It's almost like he lost his mother and father and all his kids. But he was praying, 'Thank you [Lord] that we're here. Thank you that you care about us.' And it got deep. And boom! It trickled. It trickled to all of us. And we were bawling. Grown men, tough guys, Maravilla, prison politics, Herman was deep in it. He was a lifer doing time and now he's a man of God. You look at him tatted. These aren't just art tattoos. And he starts bawling and I started praying, and boom! It blew up on me. I caved in because the presence of the Lord was so thick, man. It was so powerful."

"So it started with a prayer?" I asked.

"It started with a prayer," Chico answered. "One person praying. Another person praying. And boom! He started bawling. It's almost like he couldn't even pray no more. That's how powerful the prayer was. I jumped in there and I started praying. And I bawled. I busted. I broke. And then Nito prayed, and then he broke. And all of us were right there crying, man. I mean, you couldn't even hear the prayer. Whoever was in the next room must've been tripping out, haha! 'What the heck is going on in there? Did they all lose somebody at the same time?' And we didn't care. We just prayed. And then, after it was over, you could feel like a calmness. It was such a relief. It was such a . . . I can't really describe that. It was just powerful. None of us said, 'Man, what was that?' We didn't trip out. We were just quiet."

The prayer ignited the emotional energy that engulfed the room. Pastor Nito's story about his son resonated with these men, who have their own sons or daughters, nieces or nephews, doing hardcore drugs and prison time. True, such matters evoke emotions that make one cry whether in prayer or not. In this instance, though, the prayer turned a personal grief into a collective grief. The prayer's message— that the Lord loves and helps them—energized them, inspiring each one to take the helm when the other became emotionally over-whelmed and could speak no more. It was the ultimate teamwork, the ultimate unity, a spiritual oneness that made them feel as though the Lord was right there in that room. The emotional moment had quickened, faster and faster, higher and higher, with many bursts here and there, until it reached a peak—*Oh Jesus*—and then gradually subsided. The exhausted men then dropped into calmness and re-laxation. And they would not ruin what had just happened by talking about it. They let the moment remain sacred.

The weeping led Pastor Nito to affectionately call born-again Christians "crybabies." He, however, was anything but a crybaby as a teenager and young man. He had done violence and sold drugs. He also spent five years in prison, which hardened him even more. It was upon his prison release that his life changed. Some born-again homeboys spoke to him about the Lord, which he respected but kindly brushed aside. Then one day, according to him, God spoke to him. The voice told him to convert, to accept God and Jesus in his life. The moment surprised him. Then it moved him to tears. He cried for three days and three nights.

He explained, "When I encountered the Lord, I stayed in my room for three days. For three days I was crying like a baby. I was crying like a baby because I met God. God visited my life and spoke to me in an audible voice, like I'm speaking to you. And I was in holy shock for three days. Any time an individual has an encounter with God like that, their whole life changes. If any man is in Christ, he is a new creature. The old things pass away. All things are new. And that's exactly what took place in my life. On January 9th of 1982, I was born again."

Nito eventually married a neighborhood church girl, who now accepted him because he had been touched by God. He then put all his energy—the zeal he had once put into gangs and drug dealing—into establishing a men's Christian home and a ministry that visited prisons. Most of all, he was no longer afraid. He was no longer afraid to show his emotions in ways that his homeboys thought only *chavalas*, or girls, did. He cried openly when he perceived that God put joy, love, wonder, kindness, and forgiveness in his heart.

"I had that encounter with God and I cried like a baby," Pastor Nito explained. "I cried like a baby, and ever since then I'm a crybaby. I can cry when I feel for people. I can cry when I feel close to God. Or sometimes I just think back on that day. Every single time that somebody asked me about that day that I met the Lord, I can't get through that story without crying because it takes me back. But it's actually explained in the Bible. God says when we are born again, he takes out the heart of stone."

"Amen," Chico affirmed.

"And he gives us a heart of flesh," the pastor continued.

"That's Ezekiel 36:26," Chico added.

"I believe so," said the pastor. "And that's what happens to us. He takes out our hearts of stone. We all think we're hard, right? And we've been hard in life with different experiences. God is love. We can possess love and we can experience love, but the Bible says, 'God is love.' And when he comes to reside in our life, then that love is expressed in a lot of different ways. And he created us with tear ducts, and there's different things that can cause those tear ducts to flow. And when we allow God to move in our lives at different times of our lives, it results in grown men crying like big old babies."

Pastor Nito believed that God's Holy Spirit softened people, encouraged in them what most consider vulnerability but Pentecostals consider proof of God's presence. Only God could make steely-eyed men who appear desensitized to violence, death, and misery—and who willingly do violence that causes death and misery—only God could make such human beings cry. Crying becomes an important measure of Christian success.

"I'll never forget the day I met Brother Herman in prison," Pastor Nito said. "He's already been there almost twenty years. He walked into that [prison] chapel while we were preaching. And he looked hard. He was one of those hard-looking dudes. And he came in and sat right in the front row in an empty chair, crossing his legs. He wants to listen to what these guys had to say. And all of a sudden I turn around and this guy, his mustache is moving. His eyes are watering and he fell off his chair. And he's crying like a baby right there in the prison chapel. And then he looked at me. Because I squatted down to where he was at and I put my arm on his shoulder. And he looked at me, and he said, 'Why am I crying?' And I knew the answer. And I told him, 'Because God is calling you, bro. God is calling you.' And he was just crying uncontrollably. And his life was never the same after that encounter. And today he's a big crybaby, too, after doing thirty-three years in prison. And now they call him Pastor Herman because he's a minister. Because God made a minister out of him while he was in prison."

Next Pastor Nito described a primal moment he experienced, one that humans have been experiencing for tens of thousands of years: awe for the galaxy, for nature, for all the things that seem mighty and incomprehensible, that make the earth seem like a grain of sand on a beach. Like many of our ancestors, Pastor Nito considered such awe evidence of God and the sacredness of inconceivable things. At the time he could not help but cry—a show of vulnerability, or perhaps the emotional equivalent of kneeling in submission—and was genuinely grateful for being made compliant.

"I remember going to Pismo Beach with my family," Nito recalled. "So it's about three in the morning and I'm up drinking coffee. I decided to take a walk on the beach. And there was nobody out there. And I just put the chair down. And right in front of me was the light of the moon and the ocean and the beauty of it. I looked up into the sky and it was filled with stars. And then one of those shooting stars pass by. And it got me thinking about his handiwork, his creation. And I remember standing up right there and lifting up my hands, and I just started to praise God. And tears started rolling down my eyes. Because you're in tune like that. And when you don't know God like that, you're not in tune. And it's hard to understand why a man would cry for the simplest things. It's because we're grateful, bro. We're grateful and we appreciate our salvation."

The Lord's Work: Maravilla Style

Again, church events only happened about twice a week, and Chico could not stay home listening to Christian music all day. He needed to experience the world. But he had to stay away from old temptations. "When I was using dope, I had to have a fix every day," Chico explained. "And I was gonna go find a [drug] connection. I knew they were out there. It was just a matter of jumping on the bus and going out there. For us [drug users], it's all that mattered. I also had to come up with fifty dollars. At one time, it was two hundred dollars a day to support my habit, Randy. You see that car right now? [pointing to a parked car behind me] See how the door's open? I would'a went by there and played it off like I was looking to see if anybody's in there. If no one was in there, within thirty seconds [snaps his fingers], I would open that door, look and find something, and I'm gone. I was always paying attention to my surroundings. Burglary in broad daylight if I had to. I was doing everything I could to get my fix four or five times a day."

The effort Chico once put into heroin he now directed toward Christianity. He needed to stay diligent with the Lord's work to keep his emotional energy high. "It's easy to become bankrupt spiritually," he explained, "so I have to replenish it. And one of the ways to replenish it is by going to all of the Christian-based activities." So he attended church services, joined Bible study groups, and volunteered at Christian-based charities. He kept busy, busy, busy to keep his emotional reservoir full, because when he felt spiritually broken, he could always draw on how he helped and inspired people. He then used those special moments to reexperience the emotional high and stay on the Christian track.

Chico was still tough. When friends jokingly asked him, "Where you from, ese?" he would joke back, "Whatta you mean, where I'm from? I'm puro [pure] Maravilla, ese." And, despite being in his late fifties, he would take an impressive boxer's stance: he properly stood sideways, holding his leading left fist at his front shoulder and his trailing right fist close to his chest, just like a professional. He was letting everyone know that he could still physically fight. Fistfights, though, were mostly behind him. (I say "mostly" because he once told me that he was unlikely to "turn the other cheek" if someone struck him.) He now focused on spiritual fights. Every day he tried to lighten the suffering of the people around him. And suffering was everywhere. Homelessness. Drug addiction. Alcohol abuse. Crime. The Lord's work never ended.

Chico, though, took an untraditional Christian approach to helping others. I never observed him trying to recruit people into Christianity. He simply listened to his down-and-out homeboys and homegirls. They did not have to be from Maravilla or Mexican, just someone who needed help, like the Black woman I once saw him greet on Skid Row. As Chico tells it, this streetwise sex worker, whom he had seen around for years, glanced his way once when he was on his way to church dressed sharp, old-school style. He made eye contact, then greeted her and spoke to her. They became friends. When he saw her now he would stop and listen to her; he listened to someone most people rejected. "So when she sees me," Chico explained, "she's like, 'Hi Chico.' And I say, 'Hi Shauna.' And that's her real name that nobody knows. Things like that, times like that, that's what I live for. Those are the kind of fixes that I get."

Chico used his hands-off approach on others, such as the homeboy window washer who relapsed into heroin use; the Maravilla recently released from prison after serving ten years, whom Chico invited to a Dodgers game with us; and the mean-looking youngster in his late twenties who had tattoos on his face, neck, and arms and wanted to start a new life. He offered all of them advice on housing and drug rehabilitation services. Not a word on prayers. Not a word on Christ or God.

"I'm not a Bible thumper, Randy," Chico explained. "I don't have to try to save souls or win souls. That's actually the ultimate goal because people need to be saved. They need more than just what they accomplished here on this earth. There's a life after. That's the ultimate goal. But it's not up to me to save nobody. I can be a light and guide them and introduce them to the way. But it's up to the Holy Spirit to draw them. I don't force people. I pray for people. I wish the best. Some get that mistaken. They feel like they have to evangelate [evangelize], they have to preach about Jesus 'cause their souls are in jeopardy. I have a different approach. There's a saying that I heard, and I've embraced this. It says: 'Preach to the Gospel at all times. Twenty-four hours a day. Seven days a week. Three hundred and sixty-five days a year. And when necessary, use words.' So, in other words, live it, display the love of God, the light of God, the wisdom of God, the good of God, the mercy of God, the truth of God—and when necessary, use words. And I've embraced that. That's kind of the model for my life, the way I try to live. Believe me, there's times when I want to say, 'Hey fool, don't make me backhand you!' [laughing] But that's not Christ-like. [laughing]"

Marcos took the same approach. He likened himself to a gardener who gently tended to those in need. "I plant a seed," he explained. "They know me, and they see my life. That's a seed planted, and then I give it water every time I see them and talk to them. They know me. Eventually they'll change and come to the knowledge and accept Christ. It isn't easy for them in the beginning. But now that they know somebody that's been there, it changes them."

Marcos even remembered "planting a seed" in Chico in the early 1990s. He showed that he—someone Chico respected as an ultimate gangster—changed his life. He also used his social capital, or personal networks, to get him into drug rehabilitation programs. But he only helped Chico if he asked. He took this approach with everyone, so when he attended a neighborhood barbecue and saw his homeboys drunk and high—hands off. No God. No Jesus. No talk of everlasting life.

"I don't judge," Marcos explained. "I can't judge. God judges. I'm just there to be an asset. A tool. An example."

"Do you approach people and ask them to change their ways?" I asked.

"No!" Marcos answered, laughing. "That's a no-no. If they want to change, they know who you are. They know where to go. They ask around. They know if they want it. Forcing religion on people is not having compassion. That's not being a big brother. You need patience. But God has mediums. He has me. That's where I'm at."

Christian Borderliners

Christian drug recovery was hard. It could take years for a homeboy to fully commit to religion. Several Pentecostal Maravillas, especially the newly reborn, still existed in a limbo. On the one hand, they believed that salvation came through obeying an Almighty God, and that Jesus Christ died for their sins. On the other hand, they still could not ignore heroin's commands and bliss. It was thus a battle between the emotional energy and rituals of religion and the ecstasy and rituals of heroin use. The morphine molecule held on tight.

Most Maravillas, like Chico and Marcos, were borderline Christians for a long time before their bodies accepted religious emotional highs in place of heroin. And I met many borderliners whose heroin addictions still had them up and running, never in one place for long. My best bet was to catch them during a heroin high while they stayed put. Once the pleasure wore off, they were gone. *Chale, homes—hold up!* Also, many of them dealt drugs, so they preferred not to speak to me while they worked. My square appearance might cause their coworkers to think that I worked for the police.

One borderliner was Saul, a homeless dope fiend. He was an old-timer that many Maravillas respected for his fearlessness around guns. He had shot several people and had been shot six times himself. And, despite being bedridden for a few months, he returned to action as though he had never been downed. In prison La Eme targeted him as a leader of the Maravilla resistance. He was stabbed in a prison yard but never snitched. He was stabbed in another yard, and still he did not snitch or go into protective custody. He stood his ground and continued where he had left off. Maravillas admired him.

I first met Saul over the phone several years ago. I told him that I wanted to learn about his life as a Maravilla. He gruffly—and rightfully—asked what was in it for him, telling me that I had to give him at least thirty dollars for his time. Unfortunately, I had no research funding, and I hesitated to set a payment standard that I could not always afford. We left it there. I still saw him around Whitter Boulevard and Atlantic Avenue, where a lot of heroin addicts hung out. Then he disappeared. Chico told me that Saul was in a Christian drug detoxification program. It was not his first time, but Chico prayed that Saul would finally surrender to God.

After about a year, Saul returned. I noticed his dramatic change, from stern to polite. As the years passed he greeted me happily and always promised to talk, but he never had the time. He still used heroin and sold drugs to support his addiction. I could only follow him through updates from others. When we did speak, it was only for about five to ten minutes after greeting each other. He was always accompanied by his girlfriend, a heroin user who was shy and barely looked up during conversations. But Saul spoke a lot—especially about God. He talked about God so much that I wondered why he was not yet a committed Christian. He knew Bible verses by heart, and, with his charismatic voice, he sometimes sounded like a seasoned pastor.

Once, on Christmas Eve, Chico and I encountered Saul while walking down Whittier Boulevard. He was with his girlfriend, who shivered in the cold under a sweater (it was just under sixty degrees, cold for Southern California). As always, Saul greeted me warmly. He then told us how he had been at church last night with Mr. Serna, who provided them and others with food. There was more:

"Then [Mr.] Serna came by this morning and blessed us with a hundred bucks," he explained. "I started crying. He knows our situation. We're sleeping in a camp area, where we set up a tent. He said, 'God touched my heart yesterday and this morning. I want you guys to go have breakfast.' It was a blessing. We got to buy some tennis shoes. God blessed us, bro. God blessed us in the night, and the night blessed us. Whatever God blessed us with, it's overflowing. Pressed down, shaken up, and overflowing. We got to share his blessings. That's what that means. Pressed down, shooken up, and overflowing. There's so much that we don't know about. We have no imagination of how much God could bless us. We have no idea."

Then Saul remarked on the cold weather, how the temperature at night dropped to forty degrees, and they only had three blankets and had to rely on each other's body warmth; how they covered the small windows of their tent with cardboard or paper, but the wind blew it all off; and how the wind also blew in dust, which they had to breathe in. The topic then quickly changed from the weather to blaming individuals for their suffering. Saul now acted as though he were on a pulpit. He preached about how personal responsibility explained one's misery, but only God explained one's success. Then he recounted the story of his conversion to Christianity. He had been in Chino prison when he first heard the words of Romans 10:8–10, which he recited almost verbatim: "But what does it say? 'The Word is near you, in your mouth and in your heart,' that is, the Word of faith that we preach. If you confess with your mouth the Lord Jesus and believe in your heart that God raised him from the dead, you will be saved. For with your heart one believes unto righteousness, and with the mouth confession is made unto salvation. You are saved."

These words brought him to Christ, but it was a struggle. "I had no idea that it wasn't my season yet," Saul preached. "I had no idea what that meant. When it ain't your season, it's not your time. And I didn't know what that meant until a few years ago. I was in a men's home for ten months, and I walked with the Lord for about three years consecutive. And I was really touched by God in a lot of different ways where he showed how he could use me. And he showed me the things that I have doubts of, and he proved me right about. And he showed me that all my prayers except for three of them had been answered. And the ones that he hasn't answered, I still thank him for them."

While Saul spoke, Chico looked over at Saul's shivering girlfriend and offered her his jacket. She respectfully refused. Given the street codes concerning wives and girlfriends, I immediately thought that Chico had just trespassed by concerning himself with Saul's personal relationship. Saul perhaps thought the same, because after watching Chico offer his jacket to his girlfriend, he lost his train of thought and struggled to get back on track. It seemed like the Word of Masculinity trumped the Word of God because what he said next became convoluted:

"So, we uh, we uh, we uh, we . . . we uh . . ."

After he rambled for about a minute, he got back on track by speaking about the wrath of God and about his fear of God. He ended this street sermon by stating that it was God's plan for him to suffer.

"But I know that God is working his way," Saul explained. "And I know that God has plans. And this is not a coincidence. There's a reason why God is doing what he's doing. And I could see it working already. I could see it working in my life. And everything I see, I see God in it. Everything that we go through, whatever trials and tribulations we go through, sometimes it's to make us stronger. It's not to make us weak. If we could see the good out of it, we could understand what God is doing. If we can't see the good out of it, we're going to constantly be thinking about fixing it when we can't. That's the way I attribute what God teaches me. Not what I know, but what God teaches me. What he blesses me with. The Holy Spirit that teaches me."

As a critical sociologist, I wanted to ask Saul about how he interpreted God's plan. What was God's intention of having him born and raised in a poor barrio; of having him join a gang; of having him shoot people and get shot himself; of having him become a heroin addict; of having him go to prison where he got stabbed; of having him live on the streets, where he did drugs, sold drugs, and lived in a flimsy tent. What was God's intention in having him live such a miserable life?

I never asked. It would have been a critique of Christianity, an attempt to topple the religious dominoes that he had lined up the best that he could. Also, I could not offer him a better alternative. He had unsuccessfully tried secular drug treatment programs, ones that treated him for short periods, which did not give his body enough time to heal and learn to resist heroin. As patronizing as it sounds, at least he believed that the Christian God was with him on his wretched journey. This was better than thinking that he had no moral guidance or authority, that he wandered the world alone. He had already spiraled downward; if he fell any lower, there would be absolutely no hope. I did not keep him any longer when he said that he and his "old lady" had to go.

"Alright, take care."

"God bless you, brother."

"God bless you too."

Borderliners believed in God, in Jesus, and felt the emotional energy, or the Holy Spirit, during Christian gatherings. And they loved it. It was beautiful—so beautiful that they could not put the feeling into words. But they also could not overcome their heroin dependency. The addiction kept them on the streets doing drugs and crime. They believed that God worked in mysterious ways, a saying that justified their long and hard journey into conventional life. Yet there was no mystery at all: it was a battle between physiology and spirituality. They often described the struggle as out of their hands, as the work of a higher being. At the same time, they blamed themselves, making themselves out to be moral disappointments who had experienced the Holy Spirit—knew its glory and splendor—but turned away from it at the thought of a heroin fix.

Chico: "I don't make excuses. I don't blame my life as a dopefiend on how I grew up in a poor community or how my parents were poor, or how the schools that I went to were no good. I don't blame none of that. Everything was on me. I made the decision to do all of the evil things that I did. No one made those choices for me. I made the choice. And I made the choice to stop doing those things. I made the choice to follow God."

Marcos: "God has a plan for all of us. Everything that happens to us is because of God. I can't explain why things happen the way things happen. Only he knows what he's doing. I'm just a vessel for his Word. I just go on the journey that he has set out for me."

Chico (again): "I believe that God has a plan for all of us. I don't know what that plan is, except to accept him and Jesus Christ. But God let us keep our personalities. He let us be who we are. That's what makes us all different. Then it's up to us to do the right thing and find the path to his glory. If we don't find him, then that's on us."

In all, their reasoning lacked a structural explanation. No economy, no labor market, no politics, no racism, no sexism, no history, no family influence, no drug market, nothing that could explain why someone's social circumstance influenced them in one direction or another. Just like anthropologist Kevin O'Neill found in his Guatemala research on forced drug and gang recovery through Pentecostalism, their reasoning blamed only the individual for everything that was wrong and credited God for everything that was right.[13]

Sometimes I felt bad for the Christian Maravillas like Chico, Marcos, and Saul. The conservative media, neighbors, schoolteachers, police officers, politicians, and family members told them—and they told themselves—that they were innately bad people. Their branch of Pentecostalism also told them that their misfortunes resulted solely from immorality. It stripped them of critical thinking; it constrained them in a straitjacket of individualism.

At other times I was happy for the Christian Maravillas. They were once the pariahs of the barrio: they did lots of drugs, violence, and prison time. Society stigmatized them; their communities shunned them. Only the house of the Lord opened its door. The holy light brightened their hearts and removed their former gloom. It welcomed them despite their faults. Former burglars, robbers, and murderers—all were welcome, all were born again, restarting their lives with a clean slate. And they could feel Christian emotional energy course through their bodies when they wept, sang, and prayed. How could they not love Jesus and God? They were thankful for being appreciated and for having a space to feel great.

They mattered now.

FIGURE 1. Low-rider car. Photo by the author.

FIGURE 2. Maravilla handball court. Photo by the author.

FIGURE 3. Whittier Boulevard. Photo by the author.

FIGURE 4. Mural in East LA with themes of empowerment and resistance. Photo by the author.

FIGURE 5. Participants still prefer to use the street's old name of Brooklyn Avenue. Photo by the author.

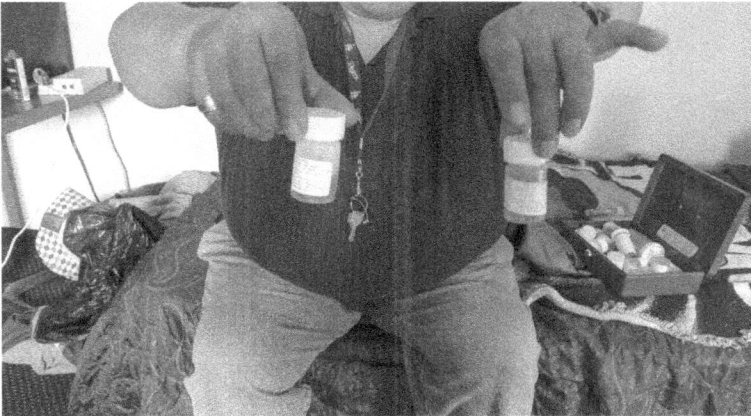

FIGURE 6. Emilio and his medicine. Photo by the author.

FIGURE 7. Emilio watching TV. Photo by the author.

FIGURE 8. Author before haircut. Photo by Lauren McDonald.

FIGURE 9. Author after haircut. Photo by Lauren McDonald.

FIGURE 10. Author looking at Whittier Boulevard sign. Photo by Jasminder Sekhon.

5   *The Streets*

Pentecostalism could not help all the Maravillas who were still tied to street life. Drug addiction often limited their conventional successes, which led them back to the streets. To matter again, they reimmersed themselves in the street logic that shaped their everyday interactions, which could turn perceived insults into an assault on their name. Violence would erupt as the men battled for honor and respect. Even Pentecostal Maravillas navigated East LA carefully. Their past gang affiliations, along with their neighborhood's past and present rivalries, dictated where they could or not go. In the end, some Maravillas tried to escape street violence. Others, however, embraced it and celebrated drugs and violence, which they thought made them matter as men.

Landing on the Streets

When I first met Emilio—whose mother introduced him to heroin at the age of thirteen—he was in his early fifties and lived out of his old car. It was stuffed with green trash bags storing his belongings. He parked it near the rundown home rented by his sister, a crack addict. When he was a trucker, she charged him five hundred dollars a month to sleep on her living room floor. When he lost his job and went on public assistance, she kicked him out. She only allowed him use of the wash sink in the backyard.

"This morning when you called me up, I used the deep sink in the back [of his sister's house]," Emilio explained. "I have my shampoo, my toothbrush, my deodorant. I went back there, washed my armpits, washed my hair, put [on] my deodorant, put my gel on, just to look presentable. Just because I'm not worth a million dollars doesn't mean that I can't look like I'm worth a million dollars, you know what I mean?"

Over the years Emilio characterized his sister as a selfish crack user who once "shook her ass," or did sex work, and failed to treat him like family. "She's a greedy bitch," he complained one day, drunk. "Once I couldn't give her the amount of money she wanted; she just kicked me out. Greedy bitch. Hay un dicho en español [There's a saying in Spanish]. It says, 'Después de tres días, apesta los muertos.' After three days, the dead stink. That's how she felt about me. She put me out on the streets. Now what better things do I know about the streets than to get high [on heroin]? Getting high is a way of forgetting. A way of not having to deal with everyday problems. I mean, not being able to buy yourself new shoes. Not being able to buy yourself new pants. You know, I've been going commando. You know what commando is, right? No calzones [underwear] for months. Because I can't buy myself underwear."

In addition to using his sister's sink, Emilio visited the local Jack in the Box (a fast-food restaurant) on Whittier Boulevard to use the restroom. He was there by 6 a.m. to beat out the other homeless men and women with the same problem.[1] The humiliation became crueler. "The other night my stomach didn't feel right and I had to go bad. It was late at night and I was in my car. I couldn't hold it anymore. I tried, I swear, Randy, I tried, but I couldn't hold it no more. I shitted myself. Here I am, a grown man, and I shitted myself. My sister didn't let me use her bathroom anymore, so I shitted myself. Fuckin' bitch.

I had to go to the back of the house and clean up. I was out there na-ked with my balls hanging out, washing my clothes with soap. It was at night, so nobody could see me. I'm embarrassed that this is what my life has become."

To feel important, Emilio often harkened back to his postprison life, which he always presented like a great American success story. It featured classic notions of working-class masculinity: indepen-dence, hard work, and earning a solid income to support a family.[2] His stories were also laced with smitten women—stories that contra-dicted his current state. At a height of five feet seven inches, and at an unhealthy weight of three hundred pounds, he could barely walk on his swollen ankles and knees. So he looked back to a glorified mas-culinity to lift himself from misery.

For instance, when he got home from prison in the mid-1980s, he found an aging father still on heroin and a younger brother who was being processed into the state's foster system because of his mother's death. In recalling these events, Emilio presented himself as a super-man who did good deeds and made women swoon. "So I get home from prison to obligations now," he explained. "I took custody of my younger brother through the court. I had a meeting at the school he used to go to. It was called the Los Angeles Child Guidance Clinic. It was for kids that had problems. They had a conference one day—and don't think I'm conceited [grinning]—and here I walk in, this stud. Here comes this guy [referring to himself] that's young and healthy, has been out of prison less than a month. And in that school there was nothing but women. And they seen me and I got nothing but *'wow!'* Did I turn heads. Miss Perez was the president. She had a PhD in so-ciology, psychology, or something. She was a doctor in a lot of differ-ent areas. She was one smart woman. Well, she offered me a position [in recreation] there, and I took the job. And I was *partying heavy*, man. I'd go to work from a party smelling like a brewery. But I'd give the kids five dollars. [Pretending to talk to the children] 'Here, shut up.' The teachers, Ms. . . . what was her name? Ms. Rodriguez and Ms. Castro. They'd go pick me up from home and we'd have a little love session before I'd go to school. I had a blast like for a whole year, man."

Emilio, though, began using heroin again. He was soon fired for missing work. With no job prospects, he called a former prison buddy, Joe, who had once offered him work. "When I had started using heroin again, I told myself I had nothing to lose, man," Emilio explained. "I didn't want to go back to prison. So, I call that guy Joe up. And I kid you not, Randy, he came to pick me up. He took me to a life that I had never been in, man. I was living in a two-story house with air-conditioning. His sister had trucks. They taught me how to drive trucks. Then I went to trucking school and started driving. It was an organization called SASSFA [Southeast Area Social Services Funding Authority].[3] And being that I was on parole, they paid for it. Over four thousand dollars. I did trucking ever since."

Then he met his future wife, Sara. She held a well-paying managerial job for another trucking company. "They would send her to North Carolina, Florida, to various places to have meetings," Emilio explained. "They'd buy her two thousand dollars' worth of wardrobes. She used to fly first class. Stay in five-star suites. They loved her there. And I swear to God, she had beautiful furniture. She paid over three thousand dollars just for the love seat and the couch. She loved the finest things. She was a lesbian before I met her. And lesbians have a beautiful way of living. Then she met me, and I turned her out [made her attracted to men]. We got together and she was buying me clothes. She was taking me to Disneyland, Knott's Berry Farm. She gave me [a] four-by-four Toyota truck. She showed me what life should be."

As much as Emilio fantasized about turning lesbians straight, he did turn Sara onto one thing: crack. According to Emilio, Sara had never consumed hard drugs. Then one day they visited her cousin, a crack dealer. "This guy is a wanna-be gangster," Emilio recalled. "He went to prison one time and became a bad boy. But I'll slap the shit out of him [scowling]. But anyways, we go to his house and I'm not feeling well [with heroin withdrawal]. And I say, 'Sara, I need a spoon [heroin fix]. I don't feel good.' She goes, 'Fuck, here we go again.' So she gave me the ten dollars and I tell her cousin that I need something. He shows me some crack. I go, 'Okay.' He puts it in the pipe and lights it, and I smoke it. And I did that and *wohooooo!* It was *wooow!* It was good! So I want another one.

"Then Sara comes up to me and goes, 'Let me try that.' I said, 'No, no.' So she looks at her cousin with that authority. 'Give me one!' He goes, 'Give me the ten dollars!' There's no morals with that family. Money is money. So she smoked it and took it to a level that I never imagined. From that day within five months, she lost her job, lost her Corolla, lost her Celica, lost the four-by-four Toyota, the apartment, lost every credit card she had. The crack, it grabbed her. Crack will grab you and you will never be the same again."

Emilio kept earning good money as a trucker. After about ten years together, the couple started having children, ending up with three girls, each about two years apart. Later Emilio had an accident on city property and won a lawsuit worth tens of thousands of dollars. With the windfall they bought a couple of cheap houses on one lot. Now the family lived a solid middle-class life. They bought a van and took trips to San Diego. They bought year-long passes to Disneyland. "We did the American dream," Emilio recalled proudly.

However, they spent most of Emilio's trucking income on drugs. Emilio resorted to sexist stereotypes, blaming Sara for both misspending money and their family disfunction rather examining his own role in their problems. "Don't give women credit cards," he said, shaking his head. "You don't do that. Sara was ordering everything— oh my God! Then she had a slip and fall. So the doctor gave her Soma, which is a muscle relaxer. It's not a narcotic, but it gets you messed up. So we went from crack to Soma. It was just horrible. So we used to call her Soma. 'Soma, what are we gonna do today.' She just lost touch with everything, man. But she wasn't on crack with that Soma. It got ugly and my kids had to see this. So, to make a long story short, she ran us into debt again with her credit cards. All I wanted to do was to be a good husband and good dad. She didn't let that happen."

In the end, the bank foreclosed on their property. Fortunately, Emilio had purchased his own truck and found a job. The company owner allowed the family to live in the warehouse. "We were there for almost three months," Emilio explained. "There was no refrigerator. We had a TV, a little room with two couches, sleeping on the floor, taking a shower with a water hose. Later we found motels and houses to rent. Man, we had it all and we lost it."

Then Emilio experienced a racialized emasculation: his wife left him for a Black man. Emilio's father had taught him that white and Mexican women in relationships with Black men were worse than insects. He called them *mayateras*. "Here they call a Black person a mayate [a black beetle that feeds on feces]," Emilio explained. "And they call a woman that goes out with a Black dude a mayatera. That's heavy. That's an ugly word. And my father was born prejudiced. He hated Black people. We could be on the streets with the family, and if he sees a white woman with a Black man, or a Mexican woman with a Black man, he would stop the car and start cussing her out. 'You fucking no good piece of shit! You fucking mayatera!' Wherever we were at, he would just start. He hated Black people with a passion. So, of course, he influenced me."

Ashamed, Emilio sought ways to bolster his manhood. He portrayed himself as a faithful man who honored his family. He also constructed Mexican men as superior to Black men while demeaning Sara's Mexican femininity: she had polluted her mestizo body—indigenous and white—by sharing it with a Black man.[4] "I was with my wife for a long time and she left me for another man, and I was the pendejo [sucker] because I was faithful. I never went to bed with another woman. And when she left me, she left me for a Black Puerto Rican. And what was funny was that she hated Black people. She used to use that term 'nigger.' And this guy is blacker than midnight. But she still holds her head up high and says that he's not Black, but he's Puerto Rican. I don't know what the difference is. The color is the same. So my ex-wife ended up marrying him.

"So now they're at the crossroads of their marriage. She told me that she woke up at night and he was on the phone looking at a [porn] flick. And he denies it. And she says, 'What kind of shit is that? He got a woman right next to him and he's going to do some shit like that?' Randy, he doesn't know what to do with a woman. That's what she left me for? To be with a Black Puerto Rican who doesn't know how to take care of her right? And I don't care what she says. He's Black. He's Puerto Rican, but he's Black. She can't deny it."

Despite his racist and misogynist attempts to matter, the moment crushed him. He was left alone with his three daughters. He used heroin again. Driving a truck under heroin's influence, however, proved dangerous. Emilio got into three accidents because he dozed off. The trucking company demanded that he take a drug test. After refusing the test, he was fired. Adding to his humiliation, the roles were now reversed at home. His children became the parents; he became the child. They scolded him for his drug use.

"My kids, they were on me," Emilio explained. "A lot of horrible things were said. A lot of horrible truths were said. I got up sick every morning at five o'clock 'cause I needed a [heroin] fix. Sometimes they would wake up, 'Where you going, Dad?' My oldest daughter, she has the biggest heart of all of them. Sometimes she would just throw me a twenty-dollar bill. The same thing I used to do with my mother when she was sick. 'Here, I rather have you home than have you sick.' That's what kept me from going stealing, hustling, or panhandling."

Then, tearfully, Emilio described how his heroin dependence made him betray his children. "One of my daughters got a job at a clothing store for big women. God, she was happy. Then my other daughter got a job there, and they were both happy. One of them bought me a cheap car. I'll never forget that [he tears up again]. Then she paid the rent one month because I couldn't do it. And yet I had the audacity to wake up sometimes early in the morning, man—*woof* [he expels a deep breath and tears run down his face] . . . and go into her fucking purse and her wallet and take her ATM out and run to the fucking Arco gas station up the block and take a twenty out. Come back, sneak back, and put it in [her purse]. Then pretend like I was sleeping. And I did that not every day, but more often than I like to think of. [Struggling with his words]. Then I . . . then I did it to the other one. And I don't think no matter what I do with this life, that's something that I could never come clean with. I would never be able to face that, how down and dirty I became."

In the end Emilio's daughters grew tired of his drug use. Soon they transitioned to living by themselves or with extended family. Emilio moved in with his sister, who, again, later kicked him out. This is how Emilio came to live in his car, where I found him struggling to matter and alone.

The Unhealthy Streets

Living out of his car, Emilio felt lost. The only structure in his life came from the medical appointments that filled his weeks. He suffered from heart and liver problems. He suffered from insomnia and anxiety. He suffered from obesity, which inflamed his feet, ankles, and knees. He wanted compassion. He wanted love. He got them from doctors and nurses who begged him to change his life lest he die. Then he suffered when busy medical staff treated him with indifference. For instance, one afternoon, I took Emilio to a bakery for a bite. He described his last medical visit.

"I was ticked off because I get there at 8:45 in the morning, and that's early. They don't see me until more than a half hour later. Then they gave me the injection so that they can put me like in an MRI machine for a scan, to take [images of] all your bones. And I'm telling the woman [nurse] that I'm an ex-hype [former heroin addict], and I tell her, 'Right here, you can hit me. I got a good vein right here. I use it all the time.' Making a joke, right? She goes, 'Don't tell me how to do it. I know how to get it.' She just had this bad attitude, man. I was just joking and she just had this face like she didn't want to hear it. She's a different nationality, you could tell. And I ask her, 'What nationality are you?' She says, 'That's my business.' What the fuck does that mean? She just started off wrong. She was acting like a bitch. Then I stood waiting in the lobby until 3:30, until the dye took place in my system. Then they did [the] X-ray."

I felt bad for Emilio. He had tried to be social and funny, but the no-nonsense nurse rejected him. He failed to think about how the nurse might deal with patients who complained about her skills or made racist remarks. Instead, he questioned his own existence.

"Then, after all that, I took the bus and I'm just thinking that things are getting like . . . I know it takes a lot of patience. But it's like, why am I not getting the medicine that I need? Why am I so struggling to get my prayers answered? Why isn't God helping me? Why am I freezing in my car? Literally, in the night it gets so cold, and I cover myself and I'm still freezing. And my feet get fat [swollen]. What's happening there? I tell you, I see people out here that are going through the same thing. And they can't afford to live like this. I don't understand it because I am looking for help."

Emilio's health worsened. When I met him in the morning, he often started the day with cheap cans of malt liquor. He drank more when we hung out by a liquor store with his homeless alcoholic friends. His weight ballooned. He could barely walk. I felt a moral crisis: I sometimes gave Emilio ten to twenty dollars to help him out, but he used the money to buy beer. Did I aid in his destruction? I just did not want him returning to a life of crime.

One day I asked him about what led to his health issues. He then provided a critical analysis that had little to do with individual fault. He blamed his parents and the government. "Like I told you, I was exposed to drugs at an early age," he explained drunkenly. "I saw my mom and dad doing heroin frequently, so I never knew that I was addicted until later on. And a lot of the homies here are dying off. This is my theory. I had someone that collaborated [corroborated] my theory—my doctor in fact. When you're coming up in the barrio, especially here in East LA, you always have liquor stores just about on every corner over here. Accessible. We got drug dealers everywhere. I could go find you whatever you wanted right now. We have beer, King Cobra and [Steel Reserve] 211, that's higher in alcohol content, but it's cheaper in price. And my theory has always been that the government pushes that into the barrios and know that we're going to kill ourselves off."

"But never had I realized that until now. I seen homies biting the bullet because somewhere along the line they have cirrhosis. That's attributed to all the drugs and the alcohol. 'Cause a lot of the homies are into drinking. I went on a three-month binge of drinking. Every morning I go get my methadone, hit the liquor store. The [King] Cobra. Started gaining weight. My feet started swelling. Took a lot of [medical] tests and all my tests came back abnormal. So I'm in a critical state right now. I got the choice. The doctor said, 'Keep on drinking, you may not make it till next year. Please stop.' And a lot of the homies are going through that. A lot of them give up now. They sircum [succumb] to death because they can't deal with it no more out here. 'Cause they've given up, man. They've lost hope. They feel that there's . . ."

Emilio then closed his eyes. It seemed like he was enjoying the high produced from combining methadone and beer. Then he resumed. "In the last few months I've had three or four homies die of cirrhosis of the liver. And I look at it, and they were drinking that cheap stuff that has a higher alcohol content. [King] Cobra—a dollar! The same size can of Budweiser would cost you a dollar seventy-nine. Why is it that this [King] Cobra is higher in alcohol content but yet it's cheaper? You know why it's like that? Because they know that the drug addicts and winos, they could afford them. And they're going to kill themselves off eventually. Go into the Black neighborhoods—what do they have? Old English 800. That's what they buy, Colt 45. You go to a lot of nicer areas, you don't find them in liquor stores. You don't find that low-quality beer. 'Why is that?' I've asked myself. And then I came to the conclusion that they know that we're gonna kill ourselves off."

I saw the self-destruction at the health clinic that dispensed his methadone. Sometimes Emilio hung out there to catch up on neighborhood news. A lot of the clients used drugs in front of the clinic. They smoked medical marijuana on the sidewalk and in parked cars. They also drank beer in plastic cups to avoid police attention. In fact, I was often offered drugs by Emilio's friends. He then told them that I was a professor writing a book about Maravilla that featured him. In those moments he looked so happy and proud.

My presence, though, did not stop the action. Perhaps it was because a gastrointestinal issue had caused me to lose sixty-five pounds in five months. I had been diagnosed with Ménière's syndrome, an autoimmune disorder. Whenever I ate, fluid filled the endolymphatic sac in my inner ear. The sac then became so enlarged that it touched the nerve responsible for balance. As a result, eating gave me vertigo, causing the room to spin around me wildly and forcing me to lie down for several hours to recover. To function, I stopped eating. In fact, I survived on about two to three hundred calories a day. When my weight dropped to just below 130 pounds, I was bony and emaciated, easily mistaken for a drug addict. (In fact, a Mexican student I mentored admitted that he thought that I had become a crack user.) So even if I was a "professor," I looked as if I could be a drug addict. I knew that this drug-related atmosphere could lure Emilio back to heroin. I asked for his analysis of what was going on.

"People just want to get more high," Emilio explained, " 'cause you do get high off of that [methadone]. Beer enhances it. And they tell you, 'Don't drink beer.' But we want to get high, man. That's all we've done all of our fucking lives."

"When you say that it enhances it, what do you mean?" I asked.

"You get feeling good, man," he answered with a smile. "It'll bring back somewhat that sensation of heroin again. It'll get you nodding. Oh, you're co-o-o-o-o-l. Sometimes you'll get drunk. But it enhances it. It speeds up the effects. That's what we believe. We might be just getting drunk. I typically don't know which comes first, getting high or getting drunk. And it's sad, Randy. A lot of the homies go to the hospital because they're throwing up blood, pieces of their liver. I've seen it. They come out of the hospital and they look healthy, man. They look good. And then that same evening, you'll see them with a beer in their hand again. [King] Cobra or 211. I've just lost three friends in a matter of months. Caballo died. Bobby Taco died. Carlito—all of them, cirrhosis, drinking that cheap stuff that's fed into the neighborhoods."

Mattering through Violence

On one of my returns to Los Angeles from Toronto, I noticed that Emilio no longer hung out at the clinic. He only went there to pick up his weekly methadone doses, which he then took daily on his own. Although the clinic scene fascinated me, I stopped asking him to take me there. I wanted him off drugs. More important, I saw that he had gotten a part-time job. For a few hours a day he helped a young woman recruit people to get tested for sexually transmitted diseases. It was an informal arrangement that earned him five dollars for every person he enrolled. The enrollee received ten dollars for their first test and five dollars for each follow-up visit. Emilio looked so proud. He helped his employer screen heroin users for life-threatening STDs—and helped his friends earn some quick cash.

Nevertheless, his best friends were heroin users, so he still abided by street codes that could harm him. For instance, one day he recruited his sister and two Maravillas, Henry and John. Since I wanted to respect their health privacy, I waited in my car as they got tested. I later learned what had happened inside the clinic. After everyone was tested, Emilio's employer gave him money to distribute to the enrollees. His sister was over fifty-five years old, which disqualified her from the program (she was too old), but she still got five dollars for the trouble of showing up. Henry received ten dollars since it was his first time being tested, and John received five dollars since this was a follow-up visit. John protested. They took the argument outside. I left my car and caught the following:

"Nah, fuck that!" John shouted. "Give me my fucking ten dollars! Stop fucking with me!"

"But I'm trying to explain that you're a follow-up visit," Emilio said, staying composed. "You're not listening. You already got your ten the first time. When you do a follow-up, you only get five."

"You said that it was ten when we were coming!" John yelled. "Don't fuck with me!"

"I didn't know that you had already taken a test," Emilio's employer explained. "You're a follow-up, so you can only get five dollars."

"Emilio, I'm gonna tell you now: don't let me find out different," John said angrily.

"Find out what the fuck you want to find out!" Emilio shot back. "I'll tell you how it really is right now!"

Emilio and John stared at each other. John walked off, muttering, "I'm gonna find out."

Still fuming, Emilio apologized to his young employer: "I'm sorry the old Maravilla had to come out of me. I don't like that part of me to come out again. It's that he already knows how this worked. He's just trying to get over. That's how some of the guys out here are. It's sad. They're always trying to get over. He's lucky I didn't put him in his place. I'll slap the shit out of him."

Eventually Emilio calmed down. He and his employer then took his sister and Henry to their homes. I also headed home since they were recruiting people for the next few hours.

A couple of days later Emilio called me, telling me to meet with him so that he could tell me about something important. I raced to Maravilla. When I got there I saw that the two driver's side windows of his car were smashed and bandaged with duct tape. "What happened?" I asked, shocked. "Don't worry. I'll let you know when we find a place to sit and talk," Emilio said, appearing to enjoy the suspense. We drove to a park and found an empty picnic table. He then recalled how, after the incident with John, he and his employer drove around afterward.

"After we finished, I have her [his employer] leave me off where I park my car at. What do I see? Two windows in my fucking car busted. I'm having a hard time as it is. You know, I'm living in my car. I don't have a license. I don't have [car] tags. I don't have insurance. Now I have two broken windows that are bandaged up. That draws more heat [attention] to me. So now I know who did it. He's the guy that had the only reason to do it."

"So on Saturday I went to go get my methadone and I walk in [the clinic] and see one of the homies and he comes up to me and goes, 'What's going on, man?' I looked at him and said, 'Nothing.' And he says, 'Nah, what's going on?' And I said, 'Nothing.' He goes, 'I heard they broke your windows.' And I told him, 'The word is already out there?' And I got upset because the only guy that knew was John. He goes, 'John told me that he broke them.' So now I got the proof. But he says, "Don't go say I told you.'

"So as we're walking out of the clinic, guess who's walking down? John. So I told my friend, 'I'ma go get my shoes in my car.' Then I thought about it. I said no, I can't walk away like that. I said, 'Fuck this.' I went to go confront him and I told him. 'You think you gonna break my fuckin' windows for five dollars?' And he comes out like stupid, like, 'Aw come on, you think I would break your windows?' And his hand pushed me. And I told him, 'Don't put your hands on me!' And then he literally pushed me. And told him, 'Don't touch me!'

"I'm in my slippers, bro. I got my glasses, my phone with me. So I pushed him and he had a bag, a bunch of colognes in them. He starts swinging that bag at me. And he's hitting me and I'm just trying to move out the way. So, you see that cut I have right here? [above his eye] He hit me one time with it where it literally dazed me. And I just said to myself, 'You got to stay up.' And I put a whipping on him. I busted his face up. I busted him up. And I'm not talking and saying that to be bad. But I busted him up. Even my homeboy said, 'You got him good.' And all of this happened for five dollars."

Yes, the fight happened over what seemed like a measly five dollars. Five dollars, though, means a lot to homeless heroin addicts: it is half the price of a ten-dollar heroin bag. But the fight was also about protecting one's honor. John claimed that Emilio and his employer cheated him. When dealing with homies, however, one cannot seek help from legal authorities. One must either let the problem go and suffer from being seen as weak, or use violence to settle matters. John chose violence.

Randall Collins would argue that John's attack was a weak form of violence.[5] John shattered Emilio's car windows rather than inflicting bodily harm. Perhaps John wanted to harm Emilio financially, to turn a five-dollar dispute into a loss of several hundred dollars. But when he revealed himself to a homie as the culprit, he must have known that Emilio would find out. The time between breaking the windows and the eventual showdown must have been emotionally intense, a buildup of tension and fear—waiting, waiting, waiting— that cleared a path toward a violent confrontation. It was up to Emilio now to move forward or stop in his tracks.

Emilio went forward. He and others knew that John had smashed his windows. He and others also saw John appear within his sights. He could not back down; his reputation was at stake. He confronted John, who denied wrongdoing—*Aw come on, you think I would break your windows?* Perhaps John thought that sneaky, behind-the-back violence might be seen as unmanly or weak. Or perhaps he enjoyed the thrill of tormenting Emilio as he tried to figure out the culprit. Yet John still initiated physical contact by pushing Emilio, letting Emilio and others know that he was unafraid. Emilio felt compelled to push John back, and then the fight started.

It did not matter that these were older, unhealthy men. They had spent a lifetime living by street codes.[6] Violence was still something to be proud of, something that, like a religious tenet, was to be believed in. "See, I'm fifty-six years old, Randy, and I'm 310 pounds," Emilio explained. "This guy [John] is forty-something years old and 170 pounds. He should've outdid me and maybe put it to me. I've always said that I ain't gonna let no young man whip my ass. But that's just my ego talking. Because you got some bad boys out there. It was sad, man. But I had to do it anyways. 'Cause one of my homeboys goes, 'I'ma tell you, dog. You getting kind of soft. I understand that you're doing the Christian thing, but you got to remember where you're living at. You're living in the jungle, brother. The homeboys see this, your softness, they gonna throw you out the neighborhood.' I can't let people see me get soft. I ain't gonna get thrown out my neighborhood."

No one—not Jesus or God, not friends or family, not me—could dissuade Emilio from violence. He could not let a perceived wrong just slide by. Weeks later he still thought about the fight. He wanted payback. He wanted to show that he still mattered on the street.

"You know how bad that was—that for five dollars I was really gonna get him," Emilio explained. "I was thinking of giving this boy a hotshot [a deadly dose of heroin]. How would I have lived with that? Because here I am trying to walk this [Christian] walk. I try to straighten things out verbally. But I still have that in me. 'I'm gonna kill big boy. I'm just gonna go and stab or shoot somebody. I'm gonna give him a hotshot.' I want that old Emilio to be gone. I want him to be dead. I try and try, but it's still in me."

Worse, Emilio drank a lot with his homies, which kept him in the neighborhood state of mind. He retold old war stories, drunkenly slurring his words as he described his courage and violence—how he was the first homeboy in his peer group to murder someone; how he almost strangled a man to death; how he was involved in robberies and shootings; and how he did violence in Soledad, the "gladiator" prison. He often told these stories around Diego, a homeless heroin user whom he knew as a teenager and hung out with in prison. Emilio and other participants had told me of Diego's violence and respect on the streets. Emilio enjoyed acting tough in his presence.

For instance, one day we hung out several yards from a liquor store, where he and Diego downed tall cans of malt liquor beer. When Emilio went back to the store for more beer, Diego started a story about his teenage violence. A few minutes later Emilio returned and rudely interrupted us. "You heard that I fucked up John," Emilio blurted out, slurring his words. He then retold an embellished version of the fight story that made him appear ultramasculine. Diego enjoyed it, laughing hysterically at many points.

After Diego left to meet someone, a drunk Emilio was upbeat. Retelling the fight story had reenergized him, allowing him to relive the emotions he had felt during the actual event.[7] That emotional high competed with the emotions that he felt in church. He lived a terrible existence—but not when he remembered his violent triumphs. He felt depressed—but not when his homies respected his violence. He was on top of the world.

Then, in a heightened mood, he spoke about Diego glowingly.

"You see Diego? This guy would give his life for me. He would go with me and back me up. And he's not gonna fuck with me. I know that whatever would be said, it's not gonna be spread around. He's not a noticero [newsperson]. He's not a 'Hoy, en la noticia, que esto y esto paso [Today, in the news, this and this happened].' He's not that guy. You know, he's been in the streets, literally living on the streets, for years. He's as firme [solid] as they come. We've been through a lot together in prison. He had my back and I had his back. We got a lot of love for each other. That real Maravilla love."

Diego was not only as solid as they come, but also as violent as they come. One time, when we were alone, he told me a story about how, as a young man, he once shot someone, and after the victim dropped to the ground he pulled out a knife and stabbed him a couple of times for good measure. Sure, he was nervous before he did it, but he showed courage by overcoming his tension and fear. He was once a vato loco (crazy gangster), a reputation he still held at his older age. Moreover, he upheld all neighborhood codes: no gossip, no snitching, no slander, and no disrespect. Diego was the street code in living form.

For instance, one afternoon I hung out with Emilio, Diego, and several other old-school Maravillas outside a strip mall. They all drank beer gifted to them by Emilio, who bought it with the fifteen dollars I had just given him to help him get by. Today he criticized the new generation of Maravillas, claiming that they accused homies of being "rats" without evidence.

"You see this guy?" Emilio said, motioning to Diego. "We grew up together. If I did something wrong to him, like if I put a jacket [an accusation] on him—"

"You do something wrong to me, they'll kill your ass, fool," Diego said assuredly.

"He would kill me or his homeboys would kill me," Emilio said, yielding to Diego.

"He does something to me and they'll kill him," Diego said again. "He knows all about it."

"I'll slap all those guys from your neighborhood," Emilio said, joking.

"He ain't gonna slap nobody," Diego said. "Even the smallest one will kill his fucking ass. He ain't going to do shit to me."

"Okay, okay, okay, I'm sorry," Emilio apologized, sensing that Diego took the comment seriously.

"He ain't gonna do shit to me," Diego said again.

"Okay, okay, I am sorry!" Emilio said loudly but in a joking way.

"You'll be sorry, hahaha," Diego said.

"When do the prison politics end for you guys?" I asked, trying to change the topic.

"They don't," Emilio answered.

"When does Washington, D.C. [politics], end?" answered Diego, making us laugh. "How you like that for an answer? It's the same thing. You got your Democrats and Republicans. They're always going to argue."

"Even as you get older?" I asked.

"You get more respect when you get older," answered Emilio. "'Oh, he's older. Leave him alone.'"

"So, what's the age that you would say that politics don't matter anymore?" I asked.

"I'm over it now," answered Diego.

"There's one thing before," added Emilio, "I could go around telling somebody, 'Hey, did you know that that fucking Diego is a fucking rat?' 'Nah, it can't be, chale.'"

"You know what would happen if he were to say this about me?" asked Diego. "He'll get killed."

"Back then," continued Emilio, "they'll say, 'You know what? Show me the fucking paperwork.'"

"They wouldn't agree with him because I'm not a rat," Diego said. "I showed that several times. I've been put down for fucking murders that I didn't even do."

"They'll say, 'Show the fucking [police] paperwork,'" Emilio continued.

"I've proven it already," Diego said. "The homeboys know my solidness."

"Now, with the way things are," Emilio said, "you go around saying, 'Oh, he's a rat,' and they run with it. There's no paperwork. Before you had to have paperwork."

"I don't worry about that part," Diego said angrily. "You better pick a different example when it comes to me because don't ever call me a fucking rat. Because I will fuck your ass up. I don't give a fuck who you are. Don't ever call me a fucking rat."

"That's not what I'm saying, though," Emilio answered, confused. "That's not what I'm saying."

"I take it really fucking personal," Diego continued angrily. "Don't ever call me a fucking rat, ese."

"That's not what I'm saying, though," Emilio said again.

"You heard what I said!" Diego said, yelling. "Don't ever call me a fucking rat! I never have been and I never will be one!"

"That's not what I'm saying, though," Emilio continued.

"I don't give a fuck," Diego said. "You heard what I said."

"Okay, okay, you don't have to get like that," Emilio said, drunkenly slurring his words.

"What do you mean don't get like that?" Diego said with a mean expression. "I don't like that fucking word."

"No," Emilio said, pleading, "I'm telling you is that if they said—"

"You want me to show you?" Diego asked.

"No," Emilio said, worried, "I'm saying that if somebody—"

"You want me to show you?" Diego yelled.

"Why you coming at me like that Diego?" Emilio asked, seeming hurt. "You're taking it out of context."

"Let's go over here," Diego said, walking a few yards.

"You're taking it out of context," Emilio said, following him.

"What happened?" Quete asked while walking over to me.

"Emilio was using a hypothetical situation to explain how people today don't look at paperwork anymore when somebody's accused of being a rat," I explained. "He said, 'Suppose someone called Diego a rat,' and Diego took it serious, like if Emilio was calling him a rat."

"Don't call me a fucking rat!" Diego yelled in the background. Then boom! He punched Emilio in the mouth. Emilio looked shocked. Boom! Diego punched him again, this time on the cheek.

"I didn't call you a fucking rat," Emilio said.

"Guys, don't do that," pleaded a homeless woman hanging out at the outskirts of our group.

"Why you gotta do that, homie?" Emilio asked, "Why you gotta do that for, homie?"

"Fuck you!" yelled Diego. "You called me a rat, motherfucker!"

"I didn't call you a rat," explained Emilio. Suddenly, Diego swung wildly at Emilio.

"I didn't call you a rat," Emilio said. Diego ignored him and began punching in a rhythm: left, right, left, right, left, right, left.

"I . . . didn't . . . call . . . you . . . a rat," Emilio said, cutting his words as he tried to avoid the blows. "The way you fucking backhand me like that, homes," he said while Diego paused for a better punching angle. The blows started again. Emilio put on an angry face and said, "That's straight up, motherfucker! You want to go straight up, motherfucker?" He swung back: left, right, left, right, left, right. "You want to go straight up?" Punch, punch, punch. "Let's go straight up!" Punch, punch, punch.

"Let's stop the fight," I said to Quete. "I don't want them to get arrested if the police come by."

"Nah, you gotta let it go, man," he said. "Just let them fight it out. Get their anger out."

Emilio and Diego stood in front of each other, swinging—left, right, left, right—like robots, moving little. Their terrible health and old age showed; they hardly hit each other. One punch did land on Emilio's jaw, knocking him back against a white van. He then gathered himself and resumed swinging.

Then, after about a minute of fighting, they ran out of gas. Huffing and puffing, they glared at each other. Emilio's mouth bled from a busted lip, which he nursed lightly with his fingers. He looked confused again.

"You both all alright right now?" asked Quete.

"If you ever call me a fucking rat again, I'll kill your ass!" yelled Diego.

"You guys are all right now?" Quete asked again. "Forget about it, man."

"This fucking fool called me a fucking rat!" Diego explained. "Fuck him!"

"Just let it go, man," Quete said. "Just let it go. We're from Maravilla. We shouldn't be fighting each other."

"I know where we fucking are," Diego said. "He don't have to call me that."

"You took it the wrong way, homie," Emilio said.

"How you expect me to take it?" Diego said. "You called me a fucking rat."

"I didn't call you that," Emilio said. "I was just saying that if anyone says it, people run with it without looking at the paperwork."

Diego and Emilio then kept debating whether Emilio had called him a rat or not. Throughout the conversation, Diego seemed energized while Emilio seemed deflated. Emilio tried to project toughness by crediting Diego for busting his lip. Diego, though, kept emasculating him by claiming that Emilio was lucky that he was not knocked out. It seemed as if Diego detected Emilio's weakness and wanted to fight again.

"All right, let's get over it, guys," Quete said, sensing Diego's heightened mood.

"You got me good," Emilio said, extending a hand to Diego. They shook hands and partially embraced.

"You see, that's what I like to see right there," Quete said, happy.

"Alright, don't worry about it," Diego said to Emilio. "He knows not to fuck with me, fool. I fought for five Golden Gloves, mother-fucker. He should have known better, hahaha."

"All right, guys, let it go, let it go," Quete said.

"Man, you fucked up my lip," Emilio said, not letting it go.

"Hahaha!" Diego burst out laughing as he addressed me. "So that's what we're all about. Now, you know to put that down in your book. There were some stupid old motherfuckers. You could write about how these two big old, semi-old bastards started fighting, hahahaha!"

"Okay man, let it go," Quete said gently. "Let it go."

"No, man, he's gonna put it in his fucking book," Diego said. "He's gonna put it in his goddamn book."

"Okay, he's going to put in his book," Quete said. "He could put it in his book. But it's over. You guys are friends."

"We've known each other for a long time," Emilio said.

"I know," Quete said.

A firework suddenly went off, making a blasting sound. "Ah, you shot me you dick!" Diego said, joking. Another firework blew up, making a car alarm go off. Diego then left to investigate who was lighting them up. We watched him walk down the block and then cross the street. He returned. "I still don't know where the fireworks are coming from."

"Hey, hey, hey, homie," Emilio said, addressing Diego. "Whatever happened here, happened here. It's done. Let's not let that affect us."

"Let's just do each other a favor," Diego said. "Drop it."

"We took care of it," Emilio said. "It's gone."

"Okay, drop it," Diego said again. "It didn't even happen."

"What happened?" Emilio said, joking.

"Nothing," Diego answered.

"I didn't see nothing!" Quete said, joining in.

"Nothing happened," Diego said firmly. "Drop it."

I felt bad for Emilio again. He thought that his strong bond with Diego shielded him from street codes. But even I became concerned when Emilio had hypothetically called Diego a rat. *Emilio, estás loco?* Diego was not a born-again Christian. Diego had not transformed into a working family man. Diego still went to prison and played politics. Diego still chased heroin and did violence. Diego still acted hard. Diego *was* still the streets. So, he projected a violent identity even when interacting with a friend.

Emilio, though, had shown softness. True, he had valiantly fought Diego. After the fight, however, he continued to try to explain himself. According to street codes, he seemed pathetic, emotionally weak. In contrast, Diego maintained a violent masculinity, even ordering Emilio to let it go, not yielding an inch. He even asserted that they consider that the fight never happened, a masculine assertion that physical violence was no big deal. He was a seasoned violence-doer. Therapy-like sessions to solve conflicts: chale! Problems were solved with fists.

Worse, it appeared that, during the fight, one of the homeless Maravillas had stolen Emilio's walking cane. He looked pitiful as he limped around, searching for it on the sidewalk and behind parked cars. *Where's my cane? Has anybody seen it? I need it 'cause I can barely walk.* Even Diego showed concern by asking if he left it home or in the liquor store. *Híjole!* Someone stole Emilio's property in his presence. The streets saw him as weak.

Later, as I drove him back to his parked car, he quickly brought up what bothered him the most: Diego.

"That first punch," Emilio said, "he really hurt me. I didn't expect it."

"It was a misunderstanding," I said.

"It was a misunderstanding, but see, I didn't expect that first punch. I thought we were going to go talk. I was trying to tell him that the way people are now is that you put a word up [an allegation] and they run with it."

"He misunderstood everything you were saying," I said. "I was going to break it up, but then they told me to let it go, not to get in."

"No, no, no, you don't get involved," Emilio said. "You never get involved. If you ever see any problem, you just stay away. It won't happen again. You know, me and Diego got a lot of love for each other. It was a misunderstanding. We were drinking a lot of alcohol. But like I tell you, that first punch, that threw me off. I hit him a couple of times. So it's all right.

"You know what, Randy?" Emilio continued. "I really hate to lose a fight. I hate it."

"But I thought it was even," I said, trying to make him feel good.

"No, he hit me good. He got my lip good. The first punch because I didn't expect it. I never thought my homeboy would roll off on me like that. I never thought that he would just, boom, hit me, you know what I mean? And like I tell you, my health isn't good. I'm not in the best condition. Which is no excuse. But still that first punch. It was like, wow. Other barrios seek revenge. I won't seek revenge because that's my homeboy."

We stayed silent until we got to his car about a minute later. "But that's the way shit happens," Emilio said, still thinking about it. "God bless you. I'll see you tomorrow."

Oh Emilio, I thought, as I drove on the freeway. *I wish I could make things right.*

Spatial Problems

Historically, the Maravillas have abided not only by street codes but also by spatial codes. In his groundbreaking book *City of Quartz*, Mike Davis documents the rich history of spatial exclusion in Los Angeles.[8] In the past, it was common for privileged whites to create spatial boundaries and use real estate laws and agents to keep Black and Brown people out of their neighborhoods. If minorities entered their neighborhoods, whites confronted them or called the police to force their exit. In the 1950s some young white men even formed the Spook Hunters, a group whose goal was to beat up African Americans and keep them from entering white residential spaces.[9]

And when upwardly mobile African Americans moved into white neighborhoods, they were met not with baked pies or cookies but with racist slurs, signs, notes, burning Klan crosses, and protests outside their homes.[10] Whites claimed the space; whites told everyone where they belonged. In Los Angeles, African American boys responded by forming neighborhood-based clubs, and later gangs, for protection.[11] Mexican residents also experienced forced racial segregation, and boys formed neighborhood-based athletic clubs, which later evolved into gangs that identified with their street.[12] Young Black and Mexican men now claimed a space. They now told everyone where they belonged.

In East LA the Maravillas created spatial identities that followed them. If they were from Lopez, a slice of northwestern East LA was their space. If they were from the Rock, the public housing area was their space. If they were from Marianna, then almost the entire southeast area of East LA was their space. When they walked outside their neighborhoods, other gang members "hit them up," or interrogated them by asking the potentially fatal question, *Where you from?* That seemingly benign question was a demand that meant *Tell me what gang you represent!* As the sociologist Robert Garot notes, the gang member commanding an answer showed their willingness to confront rivals and protect their neighborhood.[13] They also gained status for confronting a potential gang member who might have a knife or gun. They felt power when they made both gang members and non–gang members alike seek safety in the weakest response: *I'm from nowhere.*[14]

I always thought that the demand "Where you from?" was a young person's concern. Surely once gang members aged and became inactive they could walk the streets without worry. I was wrong. The aging Maravillas still scanned the streets for hostile faces, worrying about other old-timers who never forgot past rivalries. They could also come across youngsters currently warring with the young men in their neighborhoods. Sometimes it did not matter if one had gray hair or a feeble walk. One's spatial identity represented a whole history of neighborhood relations. The Maravillas still worried about safety on the streets.[15]

I first learned about these spatial problems while hanging out at the Maravilla handball court. One day I helped a Maravilla, Robert, who was in his late thirties, clean up. He had given up gang life about ten years before and rarely spoke about his past violence. Our conversation revolved around bringing young people together through peace talks and sports. As we finished up, I remarked on how some old-timer Maravillas came together to improve the community.

"It's all good that we left that violence mentality behind, that neighborhood-against-neighborhood mentality," Robert said. "For example, if Chico and Juano wanted to, they could tell me that I can't be here [at the handball court]. I'm only here because they haven't said that I can't be here."

"What do you mean?" I asked.

"This isn't my neighborhood," Robert explained. "I'm from another neighborhood that right now don't get along with their neighborhood. The youngsters in their neighborhood have conflict with the youngsters in my neighborhood."

"But that's the youngsters from both neighborhoods that have problems," I said. "It has nothing to do with you guys. You're all older and not involved in any of that stuff anymore."

"You're right, none of us are involved in that conflict," he said. "But it doesn't matter. If a youngster that's like their nephew or something gets killed, they could hold it against me. They could get mad and tell me not to come back to the handball court anymore."

"Can they do that?" I asked, surprised.

"Yeah, they could do that," Robert answered. "They could do that because the handball court is in their neighborhood. If they tell me I gotta go, I have to respect them. I gotta go."

Whenever we spent time on the street corner or the nearby public park, Robert was hyperalert. As sociologist Michael Walker would say, he was *bracing*, on the lookout for danger.[16] He looked around nonstop, checking out anyone approaching, even those walking or standing at a distance. Sometimes he got into a prison-style squat or crouch, and his eyes scanned the area as he spoke about creating peace among youths. He seemed paranoid about being victimized outside his neighborhood.

Chico felt Robert had good reason to be cautious. "By hanging out at the handball court, Robert is putting himself in danger. Where he's standing on, at the handball court, he's on enemy territory. It's almost like me going into his neighborhood," Chico continued. "I'm a lot older, but still, I'm very aware of who I'm walking towards."

"Can you tell Robert to leave the handball court?" I asked.

"Yeah, if we told him to leave, he would have to leave," Chico answered. "He would have to respect us. But maybe we could be telling him to leave because we want to save his life. We can say, 'Hey, Robert, you should split. Right now is not a good time to be here. I don't mean anything by it, but I'm just looking out for you.' Like somebody could just be saying for information purposes, 'Yeah that vato [Robert], he's from that neighborhood.' And then someone could overhear and say, 'Who's from that neighborhood?' and then make him a target. Robert's young. He's under forty, so he's close enough in age to probably have done something or to be active. He's a target."

Chico then recounted an incident at a car wash, a fundraising event at which neighborhood members washed cars to raise money for funeral costs. Chico talked with some old-timers there who knew him from their prison days during the greenlight. They felt comfortable having him around because of his Christian identity. However, one of the neighborhood's younger members went up to Chico and asked, *Where you from?*

"The sparks are flying between the youngsters from my neighborhood and their neighborhood," Chico explained. "So one of the gung-ho youngsters from their neighborhood walked up mean-looking. He had a chip on his shoulder. 'De dónde eres? [Where you from?] Quién eres? [Who are you?],' he asked just like that. I shook his hand and introduced myself as Chico from ——. And I could see his body language, like, stiffen up. He left and I heard him ask someone, 'What's he doing here?' And someone told him that I came to pay respects for the homie who passed away. They told him to back off, 'Cálmate [calm down].' And I sensed right away that this youngster got an issue. I'm surprised that he didn't try to swing on me or get crazy with me."

"But I don't understand," I said, "I know that there's neighborhood beef, but he knows that you're not involved in that."

"He might have gotten beat down or chased down the day before," Chico answered.

"But he knows that you're not active," I countered.

"That's how deep it is," Chico explained. "It's not about who I am. It's about the body of what I'm representing. Because that's the intensity of the barrio that I represent. It doesn't matter if I am an older guy. I knew that it bothered him. But he had to catch himself. I know that he struggled with it. The other guys saw him and they had to let him know. 'This one, he doesn't count.' It's a strong identity. Even with myself, when someone asks me where I'm from, I say, 'Soy de Maravilla.' Jesus was a Nazareth—he was from Nazareth. So you can't take Maravilla away from me, hahahaha."

From my experiences in East LA I knew that youngsters were suspicious of outsiders. Once, when I was walking with Chico and Giant, three youngsters in their early twenties approached us. They greeted Giant, whom they knew, but asked Chico, who now spent more time in church than in the neighborhood, *De dónde eres?* [Where you from?] He then explained his neighborhood roots and learned that he was homies with one of their fathers. Then they asked me, with suspicious faces, *De dónde eres?* Before I could answer, Giant told them that I was a social worker writing a book about the neighborhood's old-timers. They sized me up and then shook my hand. *Mucho gusto.* Then they took off.

Another time I hung out with Emilio and Diego outside a strip mall. Three neighborhood youngsters strolled by mad-dogging us, or staring at us with hard looks. Diego, who knew them, shook their hands. They then shook everyone else's hands, including mine. *Mucho gusto.* Then one of them stepped back and stared at me. Hard. I got uncomfortable and avoided eye contact, yielding to his emotional dominance. Then he broke his stare, said a few words to his homeboys, and they left. Diego came up to me and said, "Don't worry about the hard looks that these youngsters were giving you. They're like that with people they don't know." Even he had noticed their behavior.

Other old-timers traveled to other neighborhoods only if necessary for medical appointments or grocery shopping. If someone asked them who they were, they just said their name, withholding information about their neighborhood. However, if asked *Where you from?* they could not help themselves: they revealed their neighborhood even if it could lead to violence. For example, Marcos once described his problems when navigating East LA.

"Back then, when there was the [greenlight] unity, we could go down to Whittier Boulevard [Marianna territory] with no hassle. It was a lot easier. Like I said, we got along. Now it's all messed up. I don't want to go there now because I don't want to disrespect that neighborhood. That's the only reason that I don't do it. [I'm] talking about respect for their pride. That's their neighborhood. About two weeks ago, I was asked to go to a barbecue [in another neighborhood], and I got into prayer. The Lord said, 'You know what? Don't go.' The reason why is because you have to respect. Even though they invite you, I gotta respect that maybe there's somebody in the bunch [that says], 'I don't like him.' They look at you, reckless eyeball you, whatever you may call it. I just didn't go."

Chico and Marcos were born-again Christians who rarely got caught up in neighborhood drama. Other Maravillas, however, immersed themselves in the street. If they used heroin, they got caught up in personal rivalries that turned into spatial affairs. Then they could be harmed for simply standing on territory not considered theirs.

For instance, one of Emilio's friends, Julio, a heroin user, was from an area just south of East LA. Despite being from a different neighborhood, he dealt heroin in Maravilla. One day a drug client phoned

Julio to tell him that a Maravilla wanted to sell him (the client) drugs. Julio then told him to tell the Maravilla dealer that he could not sell drugs in the neighborhood. Emilio became upset. He announced to others that Julio was from another city, so he had no right to order a Maravilla to stop dealing drugs in East LA. Now Emilio became involved in a dispute over spatial identity. He then recounted what happened several times over a few weeks, especially when he was drunk.

"You already know how I take my car and go look to different parks to get away from everything," Emilio said one day while in a stupor. "I lay my blanket and my book down and go to sleep. Waiting for nighttime to come and fall asleep at night. Well, I'm over here in the park in ——, and I get up 'cause I had to go use the restroom. And I'm walking, and I tell you, I try to be aware of my surroundings, where I'm at. I felt pretty safe there because I know the police station is there. It takes a pretty goddamned fool to do something right here. So I'm walking to the restroom and I see that there's a bunch of guys, about twelve of them. And four of them start walking towards me. I don't got a knife. I don't got my strap [gun] with me. I don't got nothing. I loosen my belt and then one of them tells me, 'Emilio can I talk to you?' I said, 'Do I know you?' He goes, 'No, but I'm Mito.' I go, 'What do you wanna talk about?' He says, 'You can't be coming here no more.' This got me mad. I said, 'Who in the fuck do you think you are, gonna tell me where I could step and can't step? Let me tell you something. I put my work in. I did what I had to do. And not you, them guys over there, your homies, or anyone's gonna tell me where I can step.'"

Emilio then claimed that a youngster holding a skateboard threatened to hit him with it. "I told him, 'If you hit me, homie, you better knock me out. 'Cause I will beat the fuck out of all you motherfuckers right now. And there's [a Parks and Recreation] office right there and there's people right there. So let's go in the restroom.' But they didn't want to go in the restroom."

According to Emilio, he then gathered his belongings and got into his car. As he drove down the street, he saw a couple of the same guys walking. "I see that little fat sucker with the sweatshirt talking about 'Kill the fucker, hit him, this and that.' I put my car in neutral and they stopped. I said, 'Come on, now! Come on, cross the street—it's green! Who's bad now motherfuckers? Come on!' And they took off. They ran in front of my car and *errrh!* I swear to God, Randy, by a couple of feet, I would've hit both of them. I put that on my mother's grave, on God that I love so much. I almost hit them. Then they went the other way. Then I acted like I had a gun. I was reaching down. I was like, 'Come on, who's bad?' And they were hiding behind cars and this and that."

I do not know if Emilio showed the bravado that he claimed. When drunk, he always acted tough and threatened to "slap the shit" out of anyone doing him wrong. But others familiar with the incident corroborated the following points: an outsider acted like it was his own Maravilla neighborhood; Emilio called out the disrespect; the outsider then banned Emilio from his neighborhood. All of this was about expanding or restricting someone's movements based on spatial identity and disrespect. In other words, where one was from mattered in what they could say and do in a certain space.

Streets for Life

Many Maravillas wanted to leave the streets. They looked for housing support and refuge in the homes of family and friends. Still, some Maravillas wanted to stay on the streets. They preferred to up and run, a life that destroyed their health but nevertheless gave them meaning. They knew the street talk and walk; how to hustle for drugs and money; and how to do violence. And their peers respected them for those things. As the sociologist Pierre Bourdieu would say, they dominated this specific social field (the streets); had the proper cultural capital (street smarts or know-how); and gained symbolic capital (street and prison fame).[17] It was hard for them to give it all up.

The Maravilloso Giant was one such person. He wandered around his neighborhood, hung out in strip malls and at gas stations, and slept outdoors. He spent entire days high on heroin and did crime to feed his drug habit. Even under heroin's influence, he exuded confidence, slurring his words in a cadence and rhythm that reflected past East LA slang. The history of the pachuco's Caló flowed from his mouth: *Simón*; *chale*; *simón que sí!* The Mexican Spanish inflection, or the lengthening of syllables, found a home in his urban slang: *You kno-o-o-w what I'm sa-a-a-ying?* The streetwise sayings never ended: *The only thing I could tell you, bro, is that I'm one of them eses that have done so much with so little, for so long, that I could practically do anything with nothing. You just keep that in mind, you kno-o-o-w what I'm sa-a-a-a-ying?*

He also used crystal methamphetamine, or crystal meth, which he claimed added a spike of energy to his heroin high. I never encountered him under crystal meth's influence, so I never saw the ebb and flow that comes with simultaneously taking a drug that slams you down and one that picks you right back up. I suspect, though, that it encouraged his talk about an underworld. He claimed to have seen goblins, elves, and imps, who urged him to follow them underground. Whether crystal meth had him hallucinating about the latter, I cannot say. I can say that his hallucinations were real to him. He tried to explain them in vivid detail, but he often failed because of his heroin high.

What *was* real was the appreciation that homeboys had for him. When I walked with him drivers often honked their horns or yelled out his name to greet him. Despite being in his mid-fifties, he hung out with youngsters, imparting wisdom, retelling war stories, preserving Maravilla through oral history. The streets loved him. He loved the streets back.

The streets almost took him out. One day Giant felt a sharp pain in his back that almost knocked him to the ground. His back swelled and stiffened, and he could barely move. His hands and feet also swelled, making it look like he had mittens for hands and balloons for feet. His homegirl, Gladys, begged him to get medical treatment. Stubborn, he ignored her—*Chale!*—preferring to keep chasing heroin. Two weeks later he was incapacitated. His homies and homegirls had to gift him heroin. One of the youngsters became concerned.

"My younger homie goes, 'Aye, homie, I don't want you to die,'" Giant recalled. "'You better call the fuckin' hospital or call the ambulance. If I pass by here and I see you out here, I'm calling the fuckin' ambulance on you, man. I don't give a fuck what you say.' I go, 'Yeah, homes, I gotta go to the hospital. I can't take it no more. I'm pissing on myself and I don't even feel the piss come out.' I pissed on all my fuckin' pants and shit. And after that I said, 'Chingao! I pissed on myself.' I never fuckin' pissed on myself. Not even drunk. And finally, a homie, he was gonna give me some dope, but he seen the way I was, and he didn't give it to me. He had his son secretly wait there until he split. His son goes, 'Come on, I'm taking you to the hospital.' He stole a wheelchair from somewhere and he pushed me all the way and I rolled myself in.

"When I rolled myself in, I was in pain. The next thing you know, some technicians came, youngsters, like Jewish people. They go, 'You need surgery. You're going to surgery in the next ten minutes.' That quick. Imagine that? I never got surgery before, so, me puse todo Perry Mason, man [I got lawyer-like]. 'Wait a minute. What you gonna do?' 'We're going to open your back. You got an abscess in your spine. You go another day with that, that thing is going to set off all kinds of poison through your veins and shut down your heart and that's it for you.' So I would've been a dead puppy, man. Eso! [That's right!]"

Giant told this story to Chico and me when we visited him at the hospital. When we got there he lit up, happy to know that we cared about him. Surprisingly, he talked of not using heroin again.

"Hey, Giant," Chico greeted him.

"What's up, my brother!" Giant said, smiling. "Hey, Randy, how's it going, man?"

"Everything's alright," I answered.

"I got you your chanate [coffee]," Chico said, setting the coffee down on a small table.

"You made my day, man," Giant answered gratefully. "I'm happy to see my raza [race]. That's what I like to see, man, Latinos like you, man, that care about other homies, you know what I mean?"

"How you doing?" I asked.

"They were going to check my corazón [heart], but they didn't do it," he answered. "They canceled it. Yeah, man, they messed up my breakfast. Iba tirar charcas fritos [I was going to get fried food]. The way that they had me yesterday, they were treating me like a king."

"Did they tell you how you got the infection?" I asked.

"Yeah, they said the dirty needle," Giant answered. "Sharing needles sent an infection to my spine. And then it started collecting pus."

"I've seen abscesses on arms in photos," I said, remembering Phillippe Bourgois and Jeff Schonberg's book *Righteous Dopefiend*.[18]

"I never got one of them!" Giant exclaimed. "I've seen those, some gacho [bad] ones."

"You got good brazos [arms], homie," Chico said supportively.

"That's one thing," Giant said proudly. "I got good genes in my arms and my hands, that I have never gotten an abscess in my legs, in my feet, in nothing. I always slam in my arm. Probably in my neck once in a while. But man, it's a bunch of quemazón [burning], man. You know what I mean? Chingao [fuck]. Then on top of that, it's mas cabrón [much worse] when your old lady is a drug user too. So you know, it's like a catch-22. You know, if you're right there, todo sano [all healthy], y ella se ta piloriando [and she's injecting], aye, man, your nose is going to open up. But see, the thing is they already told me, 'You gonna die if you get out there and start using. Don't think that that shit won't grow back in your damn spine again 'cause it will.'"

"You gonna make it, homie," Chico assured him. "It's gonna take work. You gonna have to put on your guantes [boxing gloves], homie, and fight your way through."

Then a young woman doctor appeared and informed Giant not to eat anything right before his medical procedure in a couple of days. After some small talk, during which he introduced us to her, Giant could not help but attempt to display his lady-killer masculinity.

"She's the prettiest doctor in the whole hospital," Giant said. "I'm the luckiest patient in here to have a doctor so pretty."

"That's the medicine coming out of him," Chico cut in, realizing that the remark could make the doctor uncomfortable. "You better leave before he makes you blush."

"I'm not saying nothing that's not true," Giant said with a smile.

"Right, so I should go, haha!" the doctor said. "Alright, I'll see you later!"

"Okay, thank you doctor," Giant said as she walked out.

Giant then turned his attention to his sugar cravings. He had acquired a sugar addiction over the decades, surviving on cheap food like potato chips, soda, and chocolate bars.[19] A nutritious diet would have left him with less money for drugs.

"I need some Chuchulucos [chocolate bars] and haven't eaten those in a while," Giant said, opening the bag of chocolate bars that I brought him.

"No wasting time, aye?" Chico said, smiling.

"I been missing out," Giant said, now unwrapping a chocolate bar and taking a bite.

"Quieres café [want coffee], homie?" asked Chico.

"Yeah," Giant said, taking the coffee from Chico. "Thank you for the Chuchulucos, Randy."

"No problem," I said, watching Giant relish every bite, as though he were a wine connoisseur savoring a perfectly aged wine.

Chico then explained how he had already looked into information about Giant's care after his release from the hospital. He had found a housing program that helped homeless clients with meals, cleaning, laundry, and other services. He wanted Giant to get off the streets, to get off heroin. Giant knew, though, that he could not do it alone. He included Chico in his plans.

"I don't want to go to someplace where they gonna be messing around with me just to get my money and shit like that," Giant said, showing an alertness to mainstream hustles. "I want to get somewhere where I could get situated as fast as possible for myself. That way, you [Chico] can stay with me to help me. You can be my PA [personal assistant]. You know what I'm talking about?"

"Yeah . . . yeah . . . yeah," Chico said, seeming hesitant.

"You know, that way you can get something," Giant explained, meaning that Chico could earn money—a hustle—while helping him. "That's the way it works, man."

"Yeah," Chico said, again seeming unsure.

"Everybody workin' it like that," Giant continued. "That way, at least, you'll have a techo [roof over your head], homie."

Giant continued speaking about different subjects until the morphine made him tired and he fell asleep. Chico and I left. I walked out excited that Giant wanted to stop using heroin. He was the ultimate gangster, a Maravilloso whose experiences with violence never scared him straight. But the spinal infection made him reflect on his vulnerabilities. It was one thing to do violence while knowing how to emotionally deflate an opponent. It was another thing to fight invisible bacteria. Worse, he was an aging heroin addict, which increased his health risks. It seemed like his *tecato*, or drug addict, life was coming to end.

I was wrong.

Old Head—O.G. for Life

About two weeks later Marcos and I visited Giant at Ranchos Los Amigos National Rehabilitation Center, a hospital that helped patients with catastrophic injuries and illnesses. Marcos had been a patient there about thirty years ago, when a shooting had paralyzed him from the neck down. When we got there, Giant told us that the first hospital had discharged him early because his homies had brought a radio and played the oldies music too loudly. The nurses complained, claiming that it disturbed other patients. He was out.

Here, though, Giant seemed changed. He was energetic, as he had smaller amounts of morphine in his system and more steroids. After we talked for a while, he suggested that we go outside to get some air. "They gave me a steroid and it makes me go, *phsssh!*" Giant said as I pushed his wheelchair. "Crazy times. But how you doing, man? Randy, I'm so happy to see you, my brother. Tú eres como familia [You are like family]. I'm glad you keep coming to see me, man. I'm just getting through this. I don't care if I'm in this situation, man."

"Yeah, you have to keep it going," I said.

"The good thing is that my dick still gets hard, you know what I'm saying?" Giant said, making me and Marcos burst out laughing. "So it ain't over. De verdad [for real]! You know what I mean?"

An elderly Latino came up to us and asked for help getting his sunglasses from the bottom of the bag he held. Just then, some teenage Latinas showed up in cheerleading uniforms. Giant asked me to wheel him closer to them.

"How you girls doing?" Giant greeted them. "I just need a picture with you. I need to take a picture with my raza [race] right here. Come on, homegirls, that's right. Just get around me. [To Marcos, who was taking the photo] Just make sure to get that rubia [blond] right there."

"You girls look so cute," said a woman walking by.

"Thank you!" said a smiling and giggling cheerleader.

"You guys aren't cold?" the woman asked.

"We just performed, so we're hot right now," said another cheerleader.

"I just got warm all of sudden, hahahaha," said the elderly guy. The woman shot him a mean look and walked away.

"You got it?" asked Giant, referring to the photo.

"I got it," replied Marcos.

"Alright, thank you very much," Giant told the girls.

"You're welcome. Take care!" responded one of the cheerleaders while the other ones giggled.

"Making my nature rise, hahaha," the elderly guy said, laughing at his own lechery. "You guys take care."

"Alright, man, take it easy, brother," said Marcos.

Giant then spoke nonstop, going from one topic to the next. He talked about the pain of physical therapy: "Aye, that therapy está cabrón [is a fucker]. I thought it consist of Victoria Secrets bubble baths and massages. Chale! They make you walk, twist your feet around . . . it's a pinche pedo [a fucking problem], you know what I mean?"

He then criticized my masculinity: "It's never good to be a plain potato chip, Randy. You always want flavor in your vocabulary, if possible. Even in your body language, you know."

He then highlighted his ethnic identity by complaining about the volunteers making hospital rounds: "The charity here, [es]tá cabrón [is fucked up]! They comes early. I say, 'Chingao! [Fuck!] At least let me eat my breakfast first.' You know us Latinos, man. We gotta get up, wash up, use the restroom, come out and eat breakfast, and then go brush your teeth. That's like an hour and a half of moving around."

He then demonstrated his sexual masculinity: "Right here, man, there's so much sweetness with all these jainas [women nurses]. When they come in, I get a sugar rush just looking at them. Especially the ones that just got it, dog. If I hook up with one of them, I won't even introduce her to nobody. Keep her to myself, man."

Then he tried to improve my street talk, taking another shot at my masculinity.

"I got to do my physical therapy to get out of here, be on a successful road to recovery," he said.

"Simón," I agreed, using Cálo language.

"Yeah!" said Giant, excited that I spoke old school. "Simón que sí! Yeah! But it's not really 'Simón.' You would [have] to say, 'Qué bárbaro!'"

"Qué bárbaro!" I said, testing it out.

"Yeah, that's right," Giant said approvingly.

"Bárbaro means, 'Wow!'" explained Marcos.

"Like, 'You ain't lying,'" added Giant.

"Like, 'Awesome,'" Marcos said.

"Say it, let me see," Giant urged.

"Qué bárbaro!" I said with enthusiasm.

"Yeah!" Giant said proudly. "See, you got it! You ain't talking like a car worker in a Dodge [dealership] selling cars."

Giant then celebrated a vato loco masculinity, a necro-living that championed violence and welcomed death. His street orientation was back. "I lived a lot of life, man. So I can die tomorrow and I don't give a fuck. Serio [serious]. Because when I was dying, shutting down with this shit, half of me wanted to go to the other planet. Serio! I felt I did everything I wanted to do here. Have kids, got grandchildren, you know what I mean? Knocked people in the head, got myself knocked in the head too, vice versa. Because what goes around comes around. I'm a strong believer in karma. Hey man, I beat up people and got beat up. But you know what? The people that beat me up, I'll tell you something: we became the best of friends. I actually became best friends with a few of them. So everything they used to do on me, I used to pick up game and do it on other motherfuckers. Iron sharpens iron, you know what I'm saying? So I don't give a fuck what happens. I'm ready to go [die] if I have to go."

Back in his room, though, Giant became pensive and caring. Here he acted like a father figure, like an "older homie" who wanted to teach young men how to overcome life's obstacles on the street.[20] "I'm gonna introduce you to a youngster," he told us in a serious tone. "He's staying in that bed [pointing to an empty bed on the other side of the room]. I'm gonna try to teach him as much as possible. Porque está muy tapado [Because he is too ignorant]. You know what that means? That he's too stupid. When they're that age, they think they know it all, but they don't. They don't know shit. You know what I mean? Even though he has kids, he don't know shit. I told him that too. I told him, 'You don't know nothing, man. You're just a bebo in the beast.' I gave him these tennis [shoes] since he ain't have any. I blessed him with them since I have a brand-new pair. You know, what goes around comes around. I believe strongly in karma.

"I told this to him, 'Sabes qué, homie? [You know what?] What happened to you está muy cabrón [is too fucked up]. But you know what? Some motherfucker tried to kill you. That same person ain't dead. That same person puede mandar un asesino aquí dentro [could send an assassin here]. Te puede entrar un pinche hotshot en tu suero [He could inject a fucking hotshot in your IV bag] to take you out. You just let people [on the outside] know that if anything, "I'm in a coma."'

"Qué le pasó a el vato? [What happened to the guy?]," asked Marcos.

"They shot him in the back," answered Giant.

"He's paralyzed?" asked Marcos.

"Yeah, his own homie shot him in the back," Giant answered. "And he's from [a gang neighborhood]. But he's just a young guy. And then he has a little baby. Then his ruca [girlfriend] comes to visit every day, and she's young too. But she gots other kids too. His mother came yesterday and comenzaron un drama [they started a drama]. Peliaron aquí, y estaban tirando chingasos [they fought here and were throwing blows]. I said, 'Fuck man, I'ma have to be on call.' When all the plebe [rabble] left, I told him, 'You alright little brother?' He goes, 'Yeah.' I say, 'Ay, man, in case of emergency, all you gotta do is dial 911 Giant, and I'll put on my Superman suit and I'll fly over there.'"

"Batman, homie," Marcos said, smiling.

"Yeah, but since it was familia, yo no me quiero meter [since it was family, I don't want to get in]. Me pongos la brecas, put on the emergency brake."

Giant then took us to the rehabilitation room. The young man lay paralyzed on a mobile bed. "Hey baby boy!" Giant said. The young man broke into a smile. "These are my homies, Marcos and Randy." Then, pointing to me, he said, "He's a writer. He's writing about our raza. He already wrote about New York City. That's where he's from." I then waved my hand in greeting. Giant also introduced us to the nurses and physical therapists. "I hope these beautiful ladies are treating you well, homie. Stay strong. Ya sabes [you already know], if you need anything, let me know. We're all raza, homie, and we're here to help each other out." Then we made some small talk with a woman with neck problems, and later with the staff, who seemed to get a kick out of Giant.

Then we left.

I was sad. That was the first time I ever saw first-hand someone paralyzed from the neck down. The young man looked no more than twenty years old. I thought about his smile when he saw Giant. Although Giant had children of his own who did not know him, he took his role as an old head seriously and wanted to guide young men toward doing the right thing. Of course, the right thing on the street, such as earning respect and income through violence and crime, could be the wrong thing. But he worked within people's circumstances, giving sage advice on how to survive in jail, in prison, and on the streets.

Later we strolled the grounds, taking in the gardens. A church lady stopped us to talk about Jesus Christ. Marcos immediately engaged with her, happy to speak about religion. Giant looked displeased. "Come on, Randy, let's get away from this lady," he said loudly. We moved about five yards away and spoke about his medical condition, then about his love for his neighborhood. He had forgotten his thoughts about leaving the streets.

"Look at me," Giant said as he moved his wheelchair back and forth, making hard starts and stops. "The barrio, I won't let it down. Just because I can't stand, I can't walk, that don't mean that I won't blow a motherfucker away! I'll put a shotgun underneath my butt, homie, and if someone comes attacking my barrio, I'm gonna jump on them! Wheelchair or no wheelchair. It's just my nature, you know what I'm saying? It's just *who I am*. What I breathe. Call it a negativity. Call it a brujería [witchcraft]. Call it what you want to call it. It's a substance. It covers all of us. It's a blanket. Whenever you're cold, cover yourself with that, man. If you need it, it'll be with you, somehow, somewhere."

"But suppose someone thinks to themselves," I said, "'well, if you know that going back to protect your neighborhood with a gun will put you back in prison, why would you do it?'"

"Lookit," he answered thoughtfully, "The thing is that the elements that put you back in prison, they won't put me in prison because they put me in prison already, and I'm too trucha [clever] to go back. I know how to get over on that. Aye, if I can't strike you out with my breaking ball, I'ma strike you out with my curveball. If my curveball ain't getting you, I'ma put a slider on you. But you know what? I'ma try my hardest that you ain't gonna get no grand slam on me. You get what I'm saying? There's many options, brother. You're not just throwing that fastball where they're fuckin' hitting home runs over your fuckin' head every day."

"I never heard it put that way," I said.

"Well, I'm just trying to use the terminology, brother, so you can keep an understanding, man, me and you. I like you, Randy, man. That's why I break things down like that, you know? I try to. And you know what? I'm actually happy that you actually understood me on that terminology. Because some vatos don't know nothing. I tell them straight out, 'Hey man, high school for me was getting tried as an adult and getting sent to California Youth Authority. From there I graduated and went to the University of San Quentin.' I tell that to this guy and he goes, 'Oh, you went to college?' And the other guy caught on and said, 'San Quentin ain't no college. That's a prison. That's what he's talking about.' You understand what I'm saying? Well, maybe a tenth of who's hearing you [now speaking loudly and sternly looking at the church lady]—or *maybe the person who's ear-hustling and burglarizing your conversation*—when he hears stuff like that, he'll probably be the only one that caught on. He's gonna be laughing within himself. 'Cause always remember, there's always somebody watching you. Keep incognito. Keep it in the dark where people don't see it too much."

"So don't reveal too much about yourself?" I asked.

"Never do that!" Giant admonished me. "That's crazy! Only bitches do that, man. Like, when I came out here, there's another guy in a wheelchair too. We're talking. He goes, 'I'm so and so from [neighborhood].' I go, 'I'm from Maravilla.' I ain't tell him my movie star name. I told him just my real name. Nobody knows me by my real name. He goes, 'Aye, you guys got that greenlight off of you guys already?' You see the mentality? I go, 'Oh, a long time ago.' He goes,

'Yeah, man, your little homies are fucking up.' So that showed me what side of the fence he's on. But I don't take it like he's saying, 'Your little homies are fucking up.' I take it like he's saying, 'Your big homies are fucking up.' So I already knew what side he's on. I had to watch out for him, you know what I'm saying?"

"Órale," I said.

"That's right, Randy!" Giant said, proud of my lingo. "Órale—simón que sí!" He then looked over at Marcos and the church lady. "Let's go get some Chuchulucos [candy bars]. That way we get away from this lady."

"Yeah, let's go," I said.

"Aye, Marcos, let's split," Giant called out. Marcos bid his Christian sister a farewell—*God bless you*—and we headed to the vending machines. I got Giant a couple of chocolate bars, which he savored. "Randy, man, thank you, homie. I needed some of this, man. You're like familia to me, you know what I'm saying?"

A week later I went alone to visit Giant at the hospital. I found out that he was gone, unofficially discharged. A couple of days later Chico told me that Giant was back in the neighborhood. I drove around with Chico and found him. He sat in his wheelchair, unshaven and unkempt. He could barely put words together under the waves of heroin that pulsated through him. He paused often, slurred his words, closed his eyes, and dropped his head back in pleasure. His friend Gladys, who was also a heroin user, took care of him. She fed him bites of a hamburger and had him sip from a large cup of soda whenever he came to his senses. Despite the circumstances, it was beautiful. A caring community of *tecatos* showing love for each other.[21]

It was also disheartening. The lively Giant was gone. "H-e-e-ey, Rand-y-y-y, man, it's go-o-o-od to see you," he said, slurring his words. "Ch-i-i-i-co, que p-a-a-a-sa, homie?" After some small talk, Chico asked him about his hospital escape. In between heroin nods,

Giant recalled how he had taken his wheelchair out on the hospital grounds. When he saw a chance, he kept rolling onto the street. He got on one bus, then another, which left him somewhere in South Central. Then he got on another bus, and then another one, which finally took him to East LA. He was still in pain and could not walk, but he was back home. "You se-e-e-e, this is my neighborhood, y-o-o-o-u kn-o-o-o-w what I'm s-a-a-a-aying? I alw-a-a-ays got to be with my h-o-o-o-mies from Marav-i-i-illa. Born and built here, yo-o-ou kno-o-ow what I'm sa-a-a-yi-i-ing?"

The street was going to see more of Giant. He loved being needed by his younger and older homeboys. He loved being a star.

6   *Make East LA Great Again!*

Whether Maravillas bettered their lives or not, they still tried to matter in the world. But they wanted to matter beyond their legendary status as greenlighters. They tried to matter for the nation and East LA. They did so by distinguishing themselves from Mexican immigrants, often sounding like the white nativists who tried to expel their Mexican parents and grandparents from the United States. They were not alone. In my first East LA visit, I met several non-Maravilla second- and third generation Mexican Americans who volunteered complaints about Mexican immigrants. They claimed that immigrants rudely blasted *corrido* (Mexican country music) and littered everywhere. With few exceptions, the Maravillas I met later felt the same.

Ironically, most of the Maravillas adopted what anthropologist Leo Chavez refers to as the *Latino threat narrative*.[1] Throughout this nation's history, white nativists have constructed immigrants as its gravest problem, and Mexican immigrants became a target early on. Even though US capitalists lured Mexican labor, nativists framed Mexican immigrants as criminals because they entered the country illegally. Soon the term "illegal alien" became synonymous with criminality.

Chavez also shows how by the 1970s, white nativists likened Mexican immigration to an invasion. Alarmist conservatives and news sources, including *U.S. News and World Report*, projected a coming secession, or separation, of Mexican-dominant areas from the US or, worse, the return of those territories to Mexico.[2] By the 1990s, more scholars, journalists, white nationalists, and far-right politicians warned of America's doom at the hands of Mexican immigrants.[3] The retention of Spanish, bilingual education, Mexican culture, and a growing Mexican American population—all of these, they argued, would make Mexican descendants disloyal to the United States. In 2001 *Time* magazine even featured a cover with the headline "Welcome to Amexica."

Not surprisingly, the anti-immigrant rhetoric paused briefly during an economic boom in the early 2000s. As Chavez shows, however, it returned with fervor after the great recession of 2007–2008. Now the rhetoric was that the Southwest would be reconquered through forced cultural conversion by Mexicans.[4] Some conspiracy theorists added that the Mexican government secretly influenced Mexican Americans to retake the US Southwest. These conspiracy theories reflected and reinforced the fears of some white Americans. For them, a brown America was not a true America. They also believed that US citizens were being forced to live a Mexican way of life.

Rather than reject such white hatred of Mexicans, many Maravillas became what the critical educator Paulo Freire calls *suboppressors*. Freire highlights how the oppressed often internalize the reality created by their oppressors, or see the world through the logic of domination. Thus, the oppressed, who have yet to gain a critical consciousness, often seek victory by becoming dominators themselves. Freire states the following about peasants in Latin America:

> Their ideal is to be men; but for them to be men is to be oppressors. This is their model of humanity. . . . Their vision of the new man or woman is individualistic; because of their identification with the oppressor, they have no consciousness of themselves as persons or as

members of an oppressed class. It is not to become free that they want agrarian reform, but in order to acquire land and thus become landowners—or, more precisely, bosses over other workers. It is the rare peasant who, once "promoted" to overseer, does not become more of a tyrant towards his former comrades than the owner himself.[5]

This phenomenon reflects how many Maravillas internalized the white hatred of Mexicans and then externalized it through their own hatred of Mexican immigrants. In other words, they became Mexican sub-oppressors through their identification as Americans. To accomplish this, they did what Michèle Lamont refers to as *symbolic boundary work*, or the creation of ethnic-based moral distinctions.[6] Here, it is an intraethnic distinction in which some Mexican Americans claim that immigrants are immoral and culturally backward. In doing so, they reinforce the Latino threat narrative while distancing themselves from it as Mexican Americans and claiming that Mexican immigrants are the real problem.

Once the moral distinction is made, though, the Maravillas must rationalize their hatred of Mexican immigrants. I found that they used the following classic techniques of neutralization: blaming the victim (it is the immigrant's fault); condemning the condemners (claiming liberals are the hateful ones); and appealing to higher loyalties (one must follow God above all).[7] So once the Maravillas absorbed the Latino threat narrative, they blamed others for the reason they vilified Mexican immigrants.

Maravillas as Nationalists

In East LA I met many Maravillas who became immigrant-bashing nationalists. Like the Mexican Americans in Irene Vega's research, the Maravillas portrayed themselves as moral and proud Americans who were angered by widespread immigrant deceit and crime.[8] They also claimed to support legal immigration but not "illegal aliens," and they complained about how Mexican immigrants had turned East LA into a dirty "little Mexico" or "little Tijuana."

For example, Chico and I once hung out with some older Maravillas, a deeply religious one, a city worker, and a retired blue-collar worker. Without prompting, they called Mexican immigrants ungrateful job stealers who undeservedly received public assistance and healthcare.

"They [immigrants] don't pay taxes," Eddie said angrily. "They're working under a certain [false] name. You go to a King Taco [a Mexican restaurant], you got everybody in there that don't even speak English. How you think they got their job? They can't even pass the US citizenship [test]. So, you know, behind all that is some type of illegal documents that they got. It should be a reverse discrimination [case]. Somebody [a citizen] could go over there, try to apply for a job, and not get hired because they speak English."

"They [immigrants] don't take pride in their community or being from East LA or living in East LA," John added. "Chicanos [Mexican Americans], we're the minority now. You better speak Spanish or they'll look at you like something's wrong with you."

"Yeah, they get mad if you don't speak Spanish," Alberto said. "I'm like, 'What the hell? You're in my country! You speak my language!' They're always like, 'Your blood is from over there. Why don't you speak Spanish?' I say, 'I'm not over there. I'm here.'"

On another day I hung out with Chico and Jacob, who was another Maravilla old-timer. He sometimes stopped by on weekends to catch up with the homies. I told them my worries about the rising anti-immigrant sentiment in this country. Chico argued that immigrants acted disrespectfully and refused to assimilate.

"You have to be proud to be American. You know, you can keep your [Mexican] cultura, your culture. But just know that you're

American and be proud to be American. At least work on your citizenship. One time there was a bunch of Mexicans in the park, and they were just throwing their trash on the ground even though the trash can was right there near them. I go, 'Qué está pasando? [What is happening?]' One of them said, 'Well, that's why the county workers have jobs to pick up this trash.' 'Cause they look at me like I'm one of them. They don't even know that I'm assimilated, that I speak English, but that I still keep my cultura, that I keep my [Spanish] language. They look at me like I'm strange when they hear me talk English."

"They don't understand that you're in a different place than them," Jacob said. "You're something different than what these guys are already because of your history in East LA. That's when you realize that you're different. That's when you realize that you're different to the guy throwing the trash on the ground. People have different histories. They come from different places."

"They have to assimilate, that's what it is," Chico said. "They have to learn to speak English. They have to become American. Take pride in being American."

Disturbed, I countered their anti-immigrant rhetoric. "The thing is that when you look at it historically, there's always a first immigrant generation that everyone always complains about," I explained. "Everything you're saying about Mexican immigrants was said about the first generation of almost every immigrant group in this country, like Italians and Jews and other groups. Assimilation is happening. It's just not happening as fast as you want. It never happens as fast as Americans want. They want it to happen instantly [I snap my fingers]. Think about it. Why do you think that historically there's been all these different ethnic communities in Los Angeles and New York City? They have Little Italy, Chinatown, Koreatown, and other places like that because they [immigrants] established a community where they could speak their language and stick to their culture to deal with racism and discrimination. But the second generation, the children born here, they're the ones that start assimilating the most, especially once they start going to school. And it's always been like that throughout the history of this country. I just don't understand how you expect someone who lived their entire life in another country to come here and instantly start speaking English or instantly give up their culture. Especially when they see how so many people here hate them. People yell at them on the street, people threaten to call immigration [authorities] on them. People rob them, beat them up . . ."

I thought I made a great case against immigrant bashing, but Chico responded by blaming Mexican immigrants for their terrible treatment. He denied their victimhood. "I get what you're saying. I could agree with that. But how about this: the reason people don't like them [Mexican immigrants] is because they don't value being American. They get here and they don't love this country. They don't want to learn the American culture. I think that's also part of it. You can't forget that part. Once they start showing respect to this country, then everybody will give them respect."

Chico had made up his mind. He often wore American flag lapel pins on his shirts and offered them to the homies whenever we attended events. I still remember his surprised look when I refused his gift. He probably thought I was a crazy liberal anti-American. I found it hard to explain to him how I loved my country but could not accept a lapel pin that, in the moment, symbolized his anti-immigrant position.

"I'm just gonna say this to you, Randy," Chico told me more than once, "we gotta build that border wall to stop all these immigrants from coming in. Immigrants are getting out of control. Just look all around you right here in East LA. This place is becoming a little Mexico. They're bringing all their bad habits here with them. They gotta remember that they're in our country now. We do things different here. They gotta learn our culture. They gotta learn to be respectful, to be clean."

Pentecostals against Immigration

Surprisingly, Pentecostal Maravillas seemed to despise Mexican immigrants the most. I had thought their religious identity intersected with their Chicano identity, which politically would translate into protecting Mexicans from white racism. However, for them, the political part of "Chicano" had disappeared. Their Chicano identity just meant that they were Mexican American, or born and raised in the US. If anything, mainstream white evangelicals influenced their anti-immigrant sentiments.

As historian Ulrike Stockhausen notes, right after World War II white evangelicals advocated for Cuban and South Asian immigrants and refugees who fled communism.[9] Evangelicals then touted biblical injunctions to love strangers and treat foreigners as their own. "You shall not wrong a stranger or oppress him, for you were strangers in the land of Egypt," reminded Exodus 22:21. "The stranger who sojourns with you shall be to you as the native among you, and you shall love him as yourself; for you were strangers in the land of Egypt; I am the Lord your God," commanded Leviticus 19:34.

When the Cold War ended in the 1980s, white evangelicals changed their politics.[10] Capitalism now reigned globally, and the United States had less need to squash communists. Muslims also replaced Russians as the enemy, and white evangelicals did not welcome them—or any immigrants for that matter. During the 1990s, some conservative politicians cast immigrants as the criminals of all criminals simply for entering the United States without documents. They also courted white evangelicals, encouraging an anti-immigrant stance. The new politics changed their religious views toward immigrants.[11] The theology of hospitality, or loving the stranger, disappeared. God's love could no longer extend to those disrespecting national boundaries. They now quoted Bible verses that reflected a yielding to government authorities, such as "Render therefore to Caesar the things that are Caesar's, and to God the things that are God's" (Matthew 22:21).

They also ignored the popular Bible parable of the Good Samaritan.[12] Though belonging to an ethnic group considered vile and unclean, the Samaritan is only one of three individuals who stopped to aid an injured robbery victim lying on a road. The lesson: even those we consider outsiders can be our best neighbors. Such Bible lessons no longer mattered. Republican politics mattered more.

Not all evangelicals criminalized immigrants.[13] The Mennonites and some Latino evangelical leaders, including Pentecostal leaders, fought for compassion. They urged white evangelicals to return to the theology of hospitality and act according to Bible verses that commanded kindness and inclusion. To this day, however, the compassionate evangelicals have been ignored.

I did, however, have wonderful, respectful debates about immigration with Raúl, an ultrareligious Maravilla. He once did heavy drugs and crime, and then, in his midtwenties, he used religion to redirect his life. Now nearing sixty years old, he retired from a state job early because of health issues. Though not a pastor, he often spoke like one, and he held a high position in his church. But he always created moral distinctions between Mexican Americans and Mexican immigrants. For instance, he criminalized Mexican immigrants who wore rural dress and drove new pickup trucks.

"Why does it seem that Mexican Americans don't like Mexicans from Mexico," I asked him one day.

"It's not that we don't like them," he responded. "I personally don't have any animosity toward them, any hatred toward them, or anything like that. They come here to work. At least the good ones come here to work. The ones that are, you know, in the cartels are bringing over the drugs. The ones with the big trucks, with the big hats, with the big belt buckles—you can tell that those are the moneymakers. So they come over here and they could buy property.

They can do whatever they can, but they're not doing it right [lawfully]."

He also framed working immigrants as dirty, disrespectful drunkards. "They throw the trash out their door," he said. "They open up their car and throw dirty Pampers out. It's like, there's no respect for this country. That's the way they're used to living. They are not real respectful for the laws that are here. They drive drunk. They speed. Even the hard workers. You got the hard workers working hard and drinking beer while they're working."

I remembered how Raúl once described his crimes and those of his American-born homeboys. He downplayed their unlawful behavior, and sometimes excused it. He made no such excuses for immigrants.

"Whenever I take photos all over East LA," I said, "and Chico sees me with the camera around my neck, he says, 'You're lucky you weren't around here back in the seventies because someone would have taken your camera. Hell, I would have taken your camera from you!' So, he makes it seem like it was difficult to walk around here without being victimized. But today I feel like I can walk around almost anywhere in East LA and nothing would happen to me. And there's more immigrants here today than when you and Chico were growing up."

"To me, he's being a little bit exaggerated," he answered. "I mean, back then people didn't really do that during the day. I mean, you might get purse snatchers. I mean, there were times when I seen my brother take the flower guy's flowers and rip him off. Not to sell them, but to give them away to people. We're doing things like that. But as far as you leave your camera down somewhere and you weren't looking, someone would take it. But they just wouldn't rip it off your neck or take it from your hands. I mean, back in the day a lot of the guys were burglars because back then Chico was a heroin addict. All the heroin addicts needed to get their fix. So they did a lot of burglaries, a lot of robberies. But it was mainly minor stuff so that they can get a fix for the day. You know, break in your car and take your stereo. Your car battery."

Then he unleashed his Republican and evangelical talking points: he was not against legal immigration, but only *illegal* immigration. "Now I always have this debate with people. When they say, 'Why do you always complain [about immigrants]? This used to be Mexico. Why are you so against people coming over here illegally? This place belongs to Mexico.' I go, 'There's a way for people to come into this country, and they need to come in the right way. And you don't know who you're letting in unless you're letting them in the right way. As long as they're not selling all those drugs and they're not criminals. If we just let everyone come from Mexico, we're going to have this place looking like Tijuana. It's going to be smelling like Tijuana. Do you want to live in Tijuana?' Tijuana is only 150 miles from here and it's a horrible city. They don't even have sewage. All their sewage runs into the ocean, into the US."

Although his views are not supported by data, Raúl turned to the issue of immigrant drunk driving, which conservative media sources use to vilify immigrants.[14] He used his brother-in-law to make his case, adding that immigrants could commit crimes and then escape punishment by fleeing to Mexico. "He [his brother-in-law] was here in California and was my friend on Facebook," Raúl explained. "He would be posting up himself driving in his van. And he was a worker, a painter. He was well talented. But he has a problem with alcohol. So he would go to work, and he would get drunk, and he would video-tape himself driving drunk on the freeway and everybody would be like, 'Oh my God.' And he went to North Carolina, where my wife's family is working, and he's there illegally. They're all working illegally in North Carolina. He went over there, and he got popped for drunk driving. And they deported him."

"But from what you told me before, in terms of your wife's family, all of them are working hard and not doing illegal things. They aren't criminals."

"They're not at all," Raúl agreed. "But what they have is what's called carte blanche. They have that get out of jail free card. And what that means is that they can kill you here and then go back to Mexico and never be found. Only if you're a high-profile individual who has status in your community, then they'll go looking for you in Mexico and bring you back. But if a Mexican kills another Mexican over here, the Mexicans don't care about it. So the Mexicans over here can do anything they want and head back over there [Mexico] and live their lives again."

"But most of them are following the laws here," I said.

"Yeah, they are," Raúl agreed. "Most of them are. The thing is that they're here. They're working. Why couldn't they come in the right way and be accountable? Even if it's just 1 percent or even 0.5 percent of the immigrants doing illegal things and committing crime, they get to go back [to Mexico and avoid prosecution]. We're talking about one person's life and one person's life is worth more than anything you can say. There has to be some type of tracking responsibility to know who these people are and where they're coming from. A person who comes here illegally, we don't know their names. They could make something up. . . . It's just that when a situation arises where a drunk driver might kill a whole family and boom, they're gone. We don't know where to find them. They have more likelihood of getting away with committing a crime than Americans do."

As I listened to him, my mind was on Jesus. Chico had gifted me a Bible, which I sometimes read to understand the Bible verses that he and others referenced. I read about how Jesus was angered by social injustice, communicated love, and became a champion for the marginal, from sex workers to lepers to the poor. So how could the Pentecostal Maravillas speak so ill of Mexican immigrants, a stigmatized and powerless group?

"But you know that the immigration detention centers have separated parents and children," I said. "Some children have gotten lost in the system and it seems like they'll never be reunited with their parents. How do you reconcile that with your Christian identity?"

"I'll tell you this much," he explained. "They were coming here illegally, which is against the law. And they were coming in here with their children. And what happens here in the United States is like, for instance, if I were to get pulled over while driving drunk with my son in the back seat, they don't take him to jail with me because they don't want him to be in danger with other criminals. People don't understand, and this is just common sense. If you're doing something criminal, you're a criminal. So if you're doing something illegally, you're committing a crime. You can't take a criminal and put them together even with their child. That's why we have social services, because we have to remove children from a home where they're experiencing abuse and neglect. So these kids are being brought over here with their family and they get caught. And they can't put them together in the same place with other criminals because their lives could be in danger."

"As far as my Christian thoughts on that, I mean, of course I have compassion for them. Of course I don't want to see anyone separated from their family. But like I said, they brought that upon themselves. I mean, I'm blessed to be born on this side. Nobody has a choice of where they're going to be born. And that was just the hand that was dealt to them. I'm not saying it in a cold way. I'm just saying that we all have to think for ourselves out here. I mean, that's why in this country everybody has a wall—everyone has a lock to not let strangers into their homes. They're talking about, 'Let them come in. Let's feed them.' Well, let them into your house. You're going to let a stranger into your house? You going to let a stranger into your yard at night? You know, you're going to call the cops. I mean, I don't care. I don't think my personal belief has anything to do with the way I feel about that because if I see someone out there hungry, of course I'm going to feed them. If I see someone out there that's cold, I'm going to give him a blanket. Even if I wasn't a Christian. But as a Christian, I should do those things."

So Raúl focused on how immigrants were foremost criminals because they entered the country without documents. When it came to family separation during detention, he blamed the victims—the immigrant parents and their children who crossed the border for a better life. He seemed not to know that seeking asylum is legal under US law, and that immigrants must be in the US or at a port of entry to apply. He then lumped undocumented immigrants together with murderers, robbers, rapists, and child abusers who endanger children, and likened them to criminals violating private property.

Raúl soon alluded to the verses in the book of Romans in which the apostle Paul told followers to respect government authorities: "This is also why you pay taxes, for the authorities are God's servants, who give their full time to governing. Give to everyone what you owe them: If you owe taxes, pay taxes; if revenue, then revenue; if respect, then respect; if honor, then honor" (Romans 13: 6–7). Here he appealed to a higher loyalty—to God—to rationalize his harsh stance toward immigrants. He claimed that, unlike immigrants (as he portrayed them), he respected the government that he believed God had put in place. He said, "As a Christian, I have to respect authority. We all have to be accountable to something. We all pay rent. We all got to pay bills. We all go to work. At the end of the day, whoever is running this country as long as I'm okay, everything else is going to be alright. Take care of your own. Take care of your family. Help out those that need help. I'm not cruel. I've never been raised to be cruel."

I never once believed that Raúl was cruel. He was a victim of the latest evangelical teachings that shunned undocumented immigrants. He was also a victim of the conservative media, which often led with isolated cases of immigrants who caused drunk driving deaths. Rather than discussing the issue of widespread drunk driving in America, the media turned it into an issue about immigration.[15]

In the end I realized that Raúl and other Pentecostal Maravillas could be kind to some people while being insensitive to others. As much as they complained about immigrants, they had lots of US-born homeboys who were burglars, robbers, dopefiends, drug dealers, and murderers. As Pentecostals, they showed them compassion, never shouting for their detention or expulsion from the country. It was a double standard. Citizenship status determined *how* they showed Christian love.

Trump

In late October 2016 I called Chico from Toronto. After we caught up, I asked if his prison record blocked him from voting in the upcoming presidential election. He answered that he was unsure and would find out. Then I said, *It would be crazy if Trump won!* He paused and chuckled, which led to an awkward silence. I then said goodbye because I had to teach a class. A few days later, on the day before the US election, he texted me to let me know that he had received a money order I sent him. He also included the following in the text message: "I got bad new[s] and good news. I can't vote[,] never got my record expunged, now the good news[,] Trump will win the election 😜 but forgot about the bad news again. When he wins Obama is gonna decree marshal [*sic*] law because of all the chaos & rioting. Hope I'm wrong about [the] marshal [*sic*] law."

It was fascinating. Chico believed that if Trump won, President Obama would institute a temporary military government to control angry Hillary Clinton voters. I texted him back, saying that I was glad he received the money. But since he always asked me if I would ever return to live in California, I also texted, "If Trump wins, I'm staying in Canada! But it's gonna be a tight race. I don't know what's gonna happen."

He then responded, "If Hilary [*sic*] win[s] stay away from U.S. of A."

I responded, "Chale, it's Trump who won't let me back in! A lot of hate and fear—that's what Trump is doing to get votes. But let's see what happens."

The day after the election results shocked the world, I texted him, "A lot of my friends are telling me that they now want to move to Canada now that Trump is Prez. It's going to be a long four years."

He responded, "If [you're] up to no G 😬 😬 D you got something to worry about with him as President. Or better yet if you know to[o] much about how the Clintons do things you should worry, a lot [of] those guys are winding up mysteriously dead."

I texted, "Imagine with Trump! But we'll definitely talk when I get back in early December. I want to see what the larger MV [Maravilla] community thinks."

He responded, "They're hating, fearful, talking as if they know something about politics and just thinking Oh!! No!! It also depends on who you talking to."

I was surprised by Chico's support of Trump. I was surprised when other Pentecostal Maravillas supported him too. Trump was what Frankfurt School scholars Leo Löwenthal and Norbert Guterman referred to as a prophet of deceit, or, more exactly, an American agitator.[16] They wrote their classic work because of the horrors, such as the Holocaust, that occurred in Europe between the 1920s and 1940s. Fascist leaders such as Hitler and Mussolini had secured one-party rule through violence and deceived the masses into believing that intense nationalism could restore their nation's greatness. They also targeted groups, such as Jews in Germany, claiming that they caused their nation's economic woes. After the defeat of Italy and Germany in World War II, Löwenthal and Guterman wondered whether the same atrocities could happen in America. The existence of American agitators, especially from the Christian right, suggested that they could. Below are some of the traits they found in American agitators:

1. They intensify their audiences' irrational fears, xenophobia, and racism by likening foreigners (code for Jews) to swarms of rodents and insects.
2. They blur the lines between democracy and fascism, providing wild justifications for the immoral treatment of foreigners (Jews).
3. They call for extreme nationalism, or self-preservation, so that the nation can return to a former glory.
4. They claim to be persecuted because of their inside knowledge of secret conspiracies to strip the masses of resources.
5. They entertain audiences through dramatic performances in which they are blunt and offensive and brag about their toughness and smarts.
6. They claim to be the only ones that can lead the fight against sinister foreigners, liberals, and government institutions.

Donald J. Trump had all these traits.[17] Led by political advisors Stephen Miller and Steve Bannon, Trump kicked off his political campaign espousing division and hate, which succeeded in rallying people behind him.[18]

He falsely claimed to have evidence that President Barack Obama was a Muslim born in Africa.[19] Without evidence, he created conspiracy theories that tried to delegitimize the government.[20] He claimed that Mexican and Central American immigrants entered the country illegally to victimize Americans, calling them rapists, murderers, and animals.[21] He also repeated anti-immigrant and anti-free-press messages that encouraged violence and blurred the lines of morality.

Critical scholar Panayota Gounari found that even Trump's tweets expressed the classic strategies of the American agitator.[22] Trump tweeted "Make America Great Again," a nationalist message that harkened to a time when America was supposed to have been fantastic, even though it had been terrible for women, Native

Americans, African Americans, Asians, Latinos, Jews, and Catholics. He presented himself as a savior, often ending his tweets with, "Only I can fix . . . ," "I am the only one that can fix it," or "I WILL FIX IT!" He tweeted about doom at every turn: Islamic terrorism, a flood of immigrants, a border with no wall.

Trump also claimed to be persecuted by the media for uncovering the truth. As he told it, the media was the real foe: "The FAKE NEWS media (failing @nytimes, @NBCNews, @ABC, @CBS, @CNN) is not my enemy, it is the enemy of the American People!" And he entertained crowds by insulting liberals and government, leading his followers to believe that his bluntness reflected his honesty.[23] He was their champion.

But he was the champion of a particular set of people. As sociologist Arlie Hochschild has found, many conservative white Americans, especially white men, applauded Trump as their savior.[24] They saw themselves as hardworking Americans who could not attain economic stability despite playing by the rules. They believed that the federal government overtaxed them; that elites ridiculed them; and that liberals unfairly supported immigrants and minorities rather than them. Trump declared that he would fight for them, evoking imagery of whites regaining dominance (though they had never lost power) in the United States.

So I wondered why Pentecostal Maravillas supported him. First, they were not Trump's conservative white base, which could easily be primed to fall for his American agitator techniques. The Maravillas also quoted Bible verses describing Jesus's love and compassion, and they criticized homeboys who were loud, disrespectful braggarts. In fact, when I first started my research, many Maravillas went out of their way to introduce me to homeboys who they thought carried themselves respectfully and had "a good head on their shoulders." They appreciated coolness and tact—the opposite of the qualities that Trump demonstrated.

Yet Trump's divisiveness emotionally moved the Pentecostal Maravillas. They condemned the condemners, rationalizing their support of Trump by asking, "What about Hillary [Clinton] and her emails?" "What about the Clintons and all they're doing?" And then later, "What about Hunter Biden?" What about, what about, what about: an affliction of whataboutism gave them an excuse to support someone who contradicted much of what Christians claimed to stand for.[25]

I soon learned that Trump's anti-immigrant stance resonated with them. The Pentecostal Maravillas wanted to establish a moral boundary between themselves and Mexican immigrants.[26] Trump provided the hateful rhetoric that they used to ethnically rise and become sub-oppressors. For instance, on one unusually cold and windy day I met with some shivering Maravillas in East LA. After some small talk, I asked Chico and Antonio, both born-again Christians, about Trump's executive order banning immigration from Muslim-dominated countries. Their responses showed their support for President Trump.

"Part of the danger," explained Antonio," "is that the way he did it [the immigration order], you can't really see the good. There's some good things there. What do you think?"

"Me, I'm super-progressive," I answered. "All the way to the left. So you can already imagine what I think."

"Oh, I see," Antonio said, with a smirk. "You're all the way to the left. So you would have issues with him."

"I mean, Trump is just always lying," I said.

"Well, he's not a good liar," Antonio said in Trump's defense. "Other guys [politicians], they lie a lot, but they know how to cover it up. Trump is like more ghetto. He just says whatever comes to his mind. He's not that smart when he lies. I don't like everything he has to say, but he says things some people are afraid to say, you know what I mean?"

"Well," I responded, "he said that all immigrants are criminals, rapists—"

"All?" Antonio asked, cutting me off. "Are you sure he said, 'all'?"

"Well, he said that maybe a few aren't, but that most of them are," I clarified, remembering that Trump always used language that gave him plausible deniability for any offensive statements.[27]

"Uh-huh, alright," Antonio said skeptically. "It's just that to me, you have to have the ear, not to say that you're wrong. But when I hear him, to me, there's a little emphasis where he does talk about gang-bangers and drug dealers."

I then explained how research shows that immigrants commit the least amount of crime in the United States—even less than native-born whites.[28] In fact, although immigration increased during the last twenty years, crime has decreased dramatically.[29] Trump outright lied when he said that immigrants were dangerous.

"Wo-o-o-w," Antonio answered in a patronizing way. "When I was a kid—first of all, my mom and dad came from Mexico—but now when I was a kid, the immigrants were coming over illegally. But they came here to work, and they knew that it was a great opportunity to be here. But now immigrants are arrogant. They're starting to come here and do scams, take advantage of the system, doing stuff they're not supposed to do. It wasn't like that before. In one sense, you know, that's human nature. You start off right, but then as time goes on you start getting too comfortable."

I stayed quiet since we were in Antonio's neighborhood, and I sensed his annoyance with me (he could banish me). Instead, I let him and Chico argue that previous Mexican immigrants, like their parents and grandparents, were moral and respectful. That Mexican immigrants in the past kept their cultural traditions but still took steps to become American citizens. That earlier Mexican immigrants never burned the US flag, which they claimed lots of immigrants do today.

"Do you think immigrants should assimilate?" I asked, knowing that it was a safe question.

"Big-time!" answered Chico. "That term you just said [assimilate], I just heard that word this year from a gabacha, a white lady. She said that we wouldn't have all these problems if immigrants just assimilate. So assimilate, yeah, big-time! I say yeah, sure, keep your cultura, keep your Mexican roots, or Guatemala roots, or Honduran roots, or whatever. But if you're in America learn the culture, learn the language, learn the history, learn about it. Assimilate. Learn to respect the country. That's what all of the other immigrants had to do. The Italians, the Irish—they all came to America and they had to assimilate. They had to become Americans. So immigrants [today] should want to become Americans."

"So [do] you think that because Italians and Irish were whiter in terms of skin color—do you think it was easier for them to assimilate than it is now for immigrants of color?" I asked, which was another safe question.

Chico looked confused as he searched for an answer. He ended up saying nothing and we moved on to other topics about Trump, until Antonio addressed me in a stern tone.

"We been here all this time talking about politics—and everything you said is negative about him [Trump]," he said.

Now I knew that I had angered him. Worse, I did so in his neighborhood. I changed my tune a bit, saying that I also criticized Democrats (which was true). We then changed the topic to matters of everyday life. Later that day, as Chico and I drove around East LA to take photos, I asked him what Antonio had meant when he said that immigrants today acted too comfortable.

"What he meant by 'comfortable' is that they [immigrants] are not proud," Chico explained. "They want to keep their ways, the Mexicano ways, and almost like taking over. [He pretends to be an immigrant speaking] 'We don't have to assimilate. We're taking over, this is us. This is what we're gonna do.' In other words, when he said 'comfortable,' meaning that when they [immigrants in the past] were here, they were a little more humble. They were grateful to be in America and have jobs and raise a family and have a great life. Make a life here. Immigrants now don't feel that way."

They also loved Trump because he supported evangelical Christians, his voting base. After the police murder of George Floyd and the remobilization of the Black Lives Matter movement, there was a peaceful protest and sit-in in Lafayette Square, near the White House. Trump had law enforcement violently clear the space using tear gas, rubber bullets, flash grenades, and batons, a shattering of First Amendment rights. Once the smoke cleared, Trump went with senior officials for a photo opportunity in front of St. John's Episcopal Church. He solemnly held up a Bible to show support for evangelicals.[30] He seemed to link evangelical goals to the squashing of liberal America. The Pentecostal Maravillas loved it.

"Man, Trump probably never attended a church in his life and probably never opened the Bible to read it," I once told Chico. "And then he disrupted a peaceful protest through violence just for a photo op? To hold a Bible up that he doesn't believe in?"

"You see, the way I take it is that he respects Christians," Chico answered. "He showed that he believes in Jesus and wants to do the right thing by God. He showed us a lot of respect."

"But he seemed to not even know how to hold the Bible up naturally," I said, joking. "I'm surprised that the Bible didn't start burning in his hands, hahaha."

"No, Randy," Chico said seriously. "That was the ultimate respect he showed Christians. He wants this country to follow the faith of Christ. He wants the country to follow the Christian path. This country is a Christian nation, and he was just representing that. He stands by Christians."

Other Pentecostal Maravillas admitted that Trump sometimes said terrible things, but they felt that his heart was in the right place. It was his love for America, they reasoned, that made him crazy. For instance, Raúl sometimes wore a red MAGA (Make America Great Again) hat and attended local Trump rallies. Though he admitted that Trump had character flaws, he backed him because of his stance toward religion and immigration. He also used a conservative talking point that I heard from other Pentecostal Maravillas: *Look beyond Trump's faults and just focus on his policies.* This excused their support of Trump by appealing to higher loyalties: to the US and God.

"I don't like President Trump's character," Raúl said. "I don't like his attitude. I don't like his demeanor. I don't like none of that. But I do like some of his policies. I do agree with some of his issues. I agree with a lot of things, and some are biblical, and some are legislative. As a person, I think he's arrogant, but I support what he's doing for the country. I know there's a lot of division in the country right now. There's a lot of haters in the country. I've been called everything from a coconut, to a . . . whatever. Whatever they want to call you. But I'm awake."

"If Jesus were alive today, would he support Trump?" I asked.

"He would," answered Raúl. "He would teach you to render unto Caesar what belongs to Caesar. So the same thing for Trump. You respect Trump because he's over you and he's in charge. That's what Jesus would do. That's what he said."

Raúl was evoking the right-wing evangelical stance on government, derived from Jesus's statement that one should pay taxes to the Romans. Of course, taking this stance depended on the context. I never heard Pentecostal Maravillas support liberal leadership. In fact, a few of them questioned the legitimacy of President Obama's birth certificate and believed that he had wanted to transform America into a country that followed Sharia law. Still, they conveniently used biblical quotes to justify their support of a wild, xenophobic, narcissistic leader who was the antithesis of the Jesus that they claimed to follow.

Conflicts with Anti-Trumpers

Not all Maravillas supported Trump. In fact, some of them rejected him outright. They hated his misogyny, the way he talked about women, and his anti-Mexican stance. They criticized Chico, Raúl, and others for supporting the hate-mongering president. For instance, I once sat with Emilio outdoors at a fast-food place, where he ate while we talked. I asked him about Trump's presidential victory. Through his usual methadone-induced slur, he said:

"I'm not really a political person, but I think having Trump in there is a big mistake. He doesn't have a political background. And to me, he's supporting the KKK [Ku Klux Klan] themselves. He's talking about deporting people and building that great wall, that big ol' wall, talking about how society is in jeopardy right now. But I'm not too worried too much. I don't think he can follow through on all those things. He doesn't [politically] understand them."

"I know that there's a lot of hysteria over here amongst the Hispanic community. They're afraid. They're under the impression that he's gonna take their visas away and deport everybody [immigrants] back. . . . I kind of feel that our servicemen [the US military] are gonna see a lot more action than they anticipated. I think now with the way he talks about ISIS, you know what I mean, I think he's the kind of man that will go into a country and just destroy them, bomb 'em out. He's very temperamental."

"What do you mean by 'temperamental'?" I asked.

"He just projects . . . he just . . . he's a very outspoken man and he's really out there," he answered. "He says some things that you would never hear another politician saying, you know? Like grab a girl by the cooch [vagina] and still want a . . . I don't know. He's out there."

Chico and Raúl, though, interpreted such remarks as reflecting a liberal bias and divisiveness. They portrayed themselves as victims for supporting a president who, they claimed, loved America and believed in Christianity.

"Let's get back to being a civilization under God," Raúl told me. "Just one nation. We don't need this divisiveness. I got friends that say that their parents are going to disown them if they vote for Trump [in 2020]. I got a friend in Denver that said his dad wants him out the house in the cold if he votes for Trump because he's afraid of his future. I'm like, man, there's so much fearmongering going on, so much hatred going on. You know what? Just keep your vote to yourself. Vote for whoever you want to vote for. I support Trump. I can't put a sign in my front yard that supports Trump. I can't put a flag out there. Yet I see a lot of Biden and Harris flags all over the place. If I put a Trump flag out there, my car would get burned. My house would get rocked. I would have to sit in my car if I put a sign out on the front. I can't sit in my car for the rest of my life because somebody would try to come and burn my house down because I like Trump."

Indeed, it is their right to support or criticize whomever they want. We live in America. But some Maravillas considered anyone who disliked Trump as someone who believed in fake news. Trump was truth. As Chico once told me, "You got these hateful liberals believing all this fake news about Trump. They should get better informed before they talk all that nonsense. Trump loves America and he has the greatest message that will bring peace and prosperity to this country."

Yet Chico got his news from right-wing news outlets that peddled conspiracy theories. For instance, when Trump got COVID-19, Chico claimed that Democrats had secretly let the virus loose during a Trump rally to assassinate the president. When Trump supporters stormed the Capitol building to halt the certification of the election on January 6, 2021, Chico claimed that the FBI planted agitators in the crowd to work it up into a violent mob (and he claimed that Antifa was in on it too). When I told him that more than sixty court cases across the country determined that Trump had no evidence to support his election fraud claims,[31] Chico responded, "That goes to show you how corrupt the justice system is in this country. Everybody's against Trump. They got it in for him. I know there's a lot more than what we know. A ton more than what we see. A lot more behind the scenes that's taking place."

Tensions grew between Trumpists and anti-Trumpists. When a journalist from a small media organization interviewed Chico about his support for Trump, the clip went viral within the Maravilla community. In fact, Chico was approached by an anti-Trump Maravilla who saw the interview. They got into a heated political debate about whether Trump helped or hurt the country. The anti-Trumpist became visibly angry. A bit frustrated himself, Chico finally said, "Sabes qué [You know what]? I think this conversation needs to stop right now because none of us are going anywhere. It's just getting heated. You're getting more heated than I am."

"Let me say one last thing," continued the anti-Trumpist, which then led to a repeat of some of the points he had already mentioned.

A few days later, Chico told me that one of his neighborhood homies called to give him a heads-up: the anti-Trumpist had told people that Chico better not show up in his neighborhood.

"Man, that's going too far," I said.

"Yeah, but that's the mentality," Chico said. "And for the most part, that's how the opposite party [Democrats] thinks. That's their mentality. So my homie told me, 'I just want you to be aware that that's what this guy is saying.' And then I say, 'Okay, thanks for the heads-up.'"

Chico eventually hung out peacefully again in that neighborhood, but it was clear that Chico saw anti-Trumpists as hotheaded and violent. And hotheaded and violent anti-Trumpists did exist in Maravilla. For example, one time some Maravillas hung out in their favorite Saturday spot. One Maravilla, Luis, who was not a regular, stopped by to chat as he ran an errand. Suddenly, a parade of Trump supporters in cars appeared. They honked their horns and waved both American and Trump flags. Luis, an anti-Trumpist, lost it. He walked into the street and yelled, "Fuck Trump! Fuck Trump! Fuck Trump!" He then stuck up his middle finger and added, "Fuck you, motherfuckers! Fuck you!" The Trumpists jeered back. Luis then spit on some of cars, saying, "Get the fuck out of here!" After the cars left, he announced to everyone, "They're lucky. If I would'a had a cuete [gun], I would'a let them have it."

"You see, Randy," Chico told me later, "that's what I'm talking about. You have a lot of Trump haters and they're just so divisive. They don't know how to act civilized."

I told Chico that regardless of political party, no one should act disrespectful since it just deepens division. Yet I also tried to explain to him—as I did in other conversations—that Trump rarely gave speeches or sent tweets that focused on unity. It was always "us" versus "them" or he insulted people about their looks rather than coming up with reasoned arguments. It was always about creating conspiracy theories with no evidence, which increased distrust of anything but him.

Chico would never see Trump's attempt to divide the country. *What about Hillary?* Chico always asked me. *What about Hunter Biden?* For him, Trump was a patriot: "Trump is the only president that I know of that fulfilled his promise. Everything that he said he was going to do before his election, he did it all within the first year of taking office. Trump loves this country and wants to make America great. People just need to stop hating on him so much."

Over the years Emilio grew tired of Chico's support for Trump. Clearly, he loved Chico, who had done a lot for him. In fact, Emilio often reflected fondly on Chico's support. However, he hated how Chico went to Trump rallies and debated with anti-Trumpists, and how Chico supported a president who disrespected women and minorities. He then claimed that Chico supported Trump because he liked going against the political grain (most of LA votes Democrat). He also argued that Chico desperately wanted approval from whites at Trump rallies.

"You know why I think he's into the whole going to Trump rallies thing?" Emilio asked me one day. "It's because he loves the way white people at those places react to him. They see a Mexican and they get all happy that they found a Mexican that thinks like them. He told me that the gabachos [white people] always compliment him on his clothes, the way he dresses, his style, you know. They like being around him, they're all friendly with him. I really do believe that he gets off on all of that. That's the only way I could explain why he likes Trump. Because I don't believe that Trump acts like a good Christian brother should act. The way he talks down on people, it's disgusting. The way he disrespects women—oh my God! I would never talk to a woman like that. I respect women. He [Trump] has a foul mouth. In my mind, he's not a good person. What do you think?"

"You already know how I feel about Trump," I said. "He's a horrible human being."

"Exactly," Emilio said. "He's a horrible, horrible person. He just wants to lock up Mexican immigrants for no reason. He takes children away from their families. That's not Christian brotherly love in my book. Like I said, Chico's all into that so that he could be around gabachos when he goes to Trump rallies. That's my theory about him."

Emilio's fascinating folk analysis supported the research on conservative Latinos. Scholars have shown that some Latinos try to reduce the status gap between themselves and whites by taking on white conservative worldviews.[32] In doing so, they adopt a color-blind ideology that denies the existence of racism, and they adopt conservative white culture to gain acceptance by whites.[33] In the process, they display anti-immigrant attitudes to distinguish themselves from undocumented immigrants. Voting for Trump sealed the deal, signaling that they were full-blooded Americans.

I often heard Chico dismiss racism when discussing poverty in East LA: "You can't put the blame on anything but yourself. 'Oh, I grew up in the barrio and my parents were no good . . . I grew up in a bad environment,' and all that, those shouldn't be excuses." He also sympathized with police officers accused of police brutality: "You have these knuckleheads today that for every little thing when they're getting arrested, they're crying police brutality. 'Oh, he hit me! He did this and that to me!' Of course, you're gonna get roughed up if you're resisting arrest. Don't resist arrest. If you resist arrest, you should expect to get smacked a couple of times in the head." When we add in his evangelicalism, anti-immigrant stance, support of Trump, and consumption of extreme right-wing media, Chico was the poster boy of current-day conservatism.

Except that he was Chicano to his core. Perhaps he did love being accepted by whites at Trump rallies. Perhaps he felt special when he stood out in a white crowd that shared his political views. But I cannot say with confidence that he supported Trump for white approval. He developed his anti-immigrant sentiments during the early 1980s, before he had even heard of Trump or assumed a political identity. And I cannot imagine him giving up Mexican food, R&B oldies, and Chicano culture to align himself with whites. I can say that his anti-immigrant attitude reflected a desire to create moral distance between himself and those born in Mexico. He wanted to be closer to whites in ethnic rank.

MELAGA—Make East LA Great Again!

I once invited Chico to two of my Zoom classes to speak to students. He spoke about his support of Trump and which right-wing media had influenced him politically (including the hyper-conspiratorial *Real America's Voice*). Then he mentioned how once Trump took office, East LA had changed for the better. He now saw fewer Mexican immigrants around because they were scared to walk outside. For him, this was a good thing. He wanted East LA to return to its Chicano heyday of the 1970s to 1980s, a time, he claimed, when its residents loved America and did not resist assimilation. He was tired of going to stores where cashiers spoke only Spanish. Tired of immigrants waving Mexican flags. Tired of immigrants telling him to keep his Mexican roots.

I then mentioned how he had both the American flag and the Mexican flag next to each other on the wall behind him. He threw a curveball: he loved America, he said, but also believed in keeping some of his Mexican roots. He still spoke Spanish, but he always mixed it with English. He just hated how today's immigrants reject America. He was happy that Trump became president, which made East LA Chicano again.

Chico had made it clear: East LA was a space that rightfully belonged to Mexican Americans. He was not alone. Even Nato, a Maravilla who was anti-Trump, shared those feelings.

"Do you want to know what I see now?" Nato said. "A lot of different races. This used to be nothing but Raza before. Mexican Americans. And now it's all mixed."

"So when you say that there's different races here, what do you mean?" I asked.

"Salvadorian, Guatemalans . . . everything," Nato answered. "Everything is here now."

"You know what you have along with that?" Chico asked. "You have the American ways, the cultura, leaving us. You don't hear the music anymore, the R&B, the oldies but goodies. Now the culture has changed. And the paisas [Mexican immigrants] that are here—this is what I experienced—they expect you to speak Spanish. And when you talk to them in English, and not speak to them in Spanish, they kind of look at us like—"

"Like Martians!" Nato said, laughing.

"Like we're sold out," Chico continued. "Like we're not a hundred percent. Like they demand for us to speak Spanish. And I speak Spanish. I'm fluent in Spanish. Pero hablo de los dos. I speak English and Spanish."

"So let's say more Salvadorians move in. How does that change East LA?" I asked.

"I don't think that they will overpower the Mexicans," Nato said, using the language of invasion. "But there's a lot of them. And the bad part is that if something happens with them, then they'll blame it on us Mexicans. Like if someone from one of them does something [criminal], right away they'll say it was a Mexican."

"Does that bother you?" I asked, noting his criminalization of Central Americans.

"It don't bother me, but it's the way they act," Nato said. "The way they carry themselves."

"So when you say 'the way they carry themselves,' what do they do?" I asked.

Nato stayed silent, struggling to explain.

"Okay, let's go back to the respect part," Chico said, jumping in to help. "They don't have that same code. They don't have that same respeto [respect]. In fact, if they see us, they would say, 'Mira, son cholos [Look, they're gangsters]. Don't pay attention to them.'"

"Yeah," Nato agreed.

"Back in the day," Chico explained, "the guys like us, vatos locos, they saw us, they get out of the way. Because they knew. They had that respect mixed with fear. And they didn't have to be fearful.

They don't have to be intimidated. But just to the respect part. And today, they can't get that right picture of us. Like, when we were in the barrio, and we were in front of a house, there would be ten, twenty, fifteen of us right there, and one of the older ladies would be walking by and the older homies would say, 'Hey, make a hole. Ahí vienes una señora [Here comes a lady].' And then the lady would come by and say, 'Buenos días, muchachos. Cómo están? [Good day, boys. How are you?]' We would go, 'Bien, señora [Good, ma'am].' She would walk by and then we were back to normal again. That level of respect was huge."

"One change I have noticed since I first started coming here years ago," I said, "is that there's more Black people walking around. And I see more of them sitting at bus stops."

"It's the immigrants that are letting this happen," Chico said, turning my positive observation into a negative one. "They don't care about the neighborhood. They don't patrol the neighborhood like the way we did [in the past]. If we saw Black people walking around, we would check [do violence against] them. But now you're starting to see them everywhere. Randy, Maravilla isn't what it used to be. They [immigrants] don't appreciate the work we did [to protect East LA]. They don't even know who we [the Maravillas] are."

Like Chico and Nato, most Maravillas resented how East LA was no longer dominated by Mexican Americans, the ones who mostly spoke English, who worshipped the classic oldies and R&B songs, and who took pride in pachuco and Chicano culture. East LA had become an immigrant space where *corrido* music, or Mexican country music, drowned out all the historic sounds. And while immigrants perhaps feared the neighborhood gang, they (in the eyes of Nato and Chico) did not respect them. This made them appear arrogant rather than vulnerable. The Maravillas did not want them empowered. Chale!

Their criminalization of immigrants was ironic. Most Maravillas were Americans who had led lives of crime—who beat up people, killed people, used drugs, sold drugs, robbed Chicanos, burglarized Chicano homes, and spent years—sometimes decades—in jail and prison. Still, they vilified immigrants whose crime was unlawfully entering the country; who worked long hours for low pay; and who led lawful lives when compared to native-born Americans. But the Maravillas did boundary work to morally uplift themselves through the oppression of others.

In all, a sense of loss and low status drove some Maravillas to champion Trump. The irony was that the former president's messages catered to white nationalists, a group that criminalized people of color like the Maravillas. And Chico still believed in flying two flags, a Mexican one and American one; in speaking two languages, Spanish and English; in keeping parts of Mexican culture as a Chicano—all outrages to white Trump supporters. But these Maravillas covered their ears when I explained that they hurt themselves by supporting white nationalist policy. They held on to the falsehood that immigrants were criminal and invading East LA. As Chicanos, they wanted to matter.

MELAGA—*Make East LA Great Again!*

III *Dealing with Change*

7 *Negotiating Race, Aging, and Fatherhood*

Most participants disliked not only Mexican immigrants but also Black people. I heard them call Black people loud, uncivilized, and unclean. They also claimed that Black people raised children to be selfish, deceitful, and disrespectful. The Maravillas, however, spent almost no time in the Black community, and only a handful had a Black acquaintance. Their ideas about Black people came from racist stereotypes and their combative relationships with Black inmates in jail and prison.

There was a historical reason for their racism as well. As law scholar Tanya Katerí Hernández shows, Latinos have a history of oppressing Black people, even the Afro-Latinos in their communities.[1] The racism comes from their colonial past, when European colonizers created racial classifications that placed whites on top and Black people at the bottom. Even after European colonizers were overthrown, the new Latin American nations reinforced white supremacy.[2]

For instance, early Mexican leaders and intellectuals adopted the *mestizaje* identity that was prevalent in Latin America.[3] This race identity captured the mix between white and indigenous people, with the idea that the white race improved the nation's biological and cultural traits (the whiter the better).[4] Yet it denied the Blackness of Mexicans who descended from more than two hundred thousand

African slaves.[5] Whiteness became the desired racial trait since Mexicans felt that it diluted—for the better—the biology of indigenous people.

As Mexicans migrated to California at the turn of the twentieth century, they joined the descendants of California's first Mexican settlers, the Californios. During the late 1800s, whites had racially demoted Californios to the Mexican category, putting them alongside the despised Chinese, Native Americans, and Black people of the time.[6] Even as Mexicans experienced white hatred into the next century, they perceived a racial bond with their white oppressors. As law scholar Ian Haney López documents, Mexicans hoped to assimilate into the white community, with many of them arguing that they were also white.[7] They also refused to align themselves with the Black community, which they saw as beneath them.

During the 1960s, the younger generation of Mexican activists recognized the plight of Black people. In fact, they based their social justice work on the Black Power Movement.[8] After 1968, they identified as Chicanos to both distinguish themselves from whites and stress their indigenous past. And they sometimes joined forces with Black activists in community building and protests. Mainstream Mexicans criticized them for using "Black" political tactics.[9] They preferred to create a moral boundary between Mexican and Black people, portraying the latter as disorderly and violent, and portraying themselves as sharing values with whites. Nevertheless, the young activists inspired a whole generation of Mexicans to identify as Chicano and fight for Brown justice.

Anti-Blackness

The Brown militants, though, could only inspire the Maravillas to identify as Chicano and proclaim their love for La Raza. Rejecting racism in all its forms—that part never sunk in. Like mainstream

Mexicans, they created racialized moral boundaries by making racially insensitive comments. In fact, they enforced what anthropologists Philippe Bourgois and Jeff Schonberg refer to as *intimate apartheid*, or intimate racial segregation.[10] This practice mostly occurred in jail or prison since East LA had few Black residents.

For instance, Marcos remembered how Mexican inmates refused to befriend Black inmates, and physically punished those who did. But they felt fine hanging out with white inmates. It seemed as if they found common ground with racist whites.

"You were allowed to talk to Blacks, like if you worked with them. You just couldn't hang out with them. But when shit hit the fan, you know, like in a [race] riot, that's why you never got too close. Stuff happens and you gotta hit the Black guy you were just hanging out with. So you could talk to them if you have to, but you can't hang out. No [sharing] food, no smokes, no nothing. You got jigged [stabbed] for that. Your own homeboys got you. First, they'll tell you that you're fucking up. 'Don't do that no more.' If you keep it up, they'll hit [stab] you. It didn't matter if it was Maravilla or not. But on their [Black] side, they could smoke and drink with almost anybody and nothing would happen to them. We had different rules. We didn't have no problems hanging out with the Peckerwoods or the Aryan Brotherhood. They're some hardcore guys in them. Some of them wouldn't even talk to a Mexican. I mean, to each his own. They were alright. They never caused problems. In fact, I had a lot of buddies that were white. In fact, there were a couple of Black guys that I got along with also, but I couldn't hang out with them."

Diego also explained how race informed inmate violence. His comments showed how prison life was not a life in which individuals interacted as balls of energy, with no race, no face, no skin, no color. Instead, it was rich with social constructions that justified racial oppression. He even remembered race politics trickling down to juvenile institutions.

"I remember one time in YTS, a youth training school, we were watching this movie and it was called *Women in Chains*. So this Black broad in the movie tells on this other broad. So somebody [Mexican in the audience] says, 'What do you expect out of a nigger?' So one of them [Black youth] throws a bag of potato chips and it hits one of us. It was on. All the seats were getting thrown. Back then, the movie machine used to get thrown. We had one big giant riot. Doom-doom-doom-doom-doom! So there was tension for about the next month or so. So when they let us out of the lockdown, we got into another riot, hahahaha!"

Rarely, a few African Americans who grew up in East LA joined Maravilla gangs (though I never met them). According to participants, they could outdo their Mexican peers in dress and talk. As Chico often said, "The Black Maravillas were more Mexican than Mexicans. Those vatos dressed sharper and spoke better Spanish than their own Mexican homeboys. I would trip out whenever I saw them and heard them do gritos [Mexican celebratory shouts]. They tried to be more Mexicano than Mexicanos. They probably felt like they had to prove themselves more because they were Black."

Yet their adoption of Mexican culture did not satisfy everyone. Diego, for example, seemed ashamed to have Black homeboys in his neighborhood.

"'Cause back in the day, some Maravilla neighborhoods had Blacks," Emilio explained one day as we hung out.

"We never had Blacks," countered Diego.

"Your neighborhood had two of them," Emilio said.

"Puerto Ricans," Diego said, correcting him.

"Oh, they're Puerto Ricans?"

"They're Puerto Ricans."

"But they were Black," Emilio countered. "But they had heart. Oh my God."

"I remember we were in the county jail," Diego said. "There were a bunch of us in the same tier. So one of those Puerto Rican guys comes in, and they're like, 'Aye, who's that nigger right there?' Those are all the youngsters saying that, right. I look up and it's him, hahahaha! I started [joking], 'Aye, what's up Blood [a Black gang greeting]?' Then I had to tell them, 'He's a homeboy, dog. He's a homeboy.' Hahahahaha! It was funny!"

I also had heard stories about imprisoned Maravillas refusing to acknowledge Black members. I then asked Diego about whether Mexican gangs recruited Black people. His response showed that he saw them as outsiders even if they identified as Chicanos.

"I told this one Black dude [in a Mexican gang]—'cause he was running with our car [a group in prison]—I said, 'Hey brother, let me ask you a question. What are you gonna do when a [race] riot kicks off? What are you gonna do? You say you're running with the Mexicans, but you're a Black dude. Where do you stand?' He goes, 'I'ma go with the Mexicans, homes.' I go, 'But you ain't a Mexican. In reality, you're not.' He goes, 'But that's who I run with.' I go, 'You know what? I hate to be in your shoes. 'Cause you're in the streets running with the Mexicans, kicking back, you're partying, doing whatever it is you're doing, and then you come to jail and the ballgame changes. 'Cause ethnically-wise, you're Black and they [prison authorities] mark you down as a Black. They don't mark you down as Mexican because that's what you not. You guys put yourself in a bad situation, I tell you that much, hahahahaha!'"[11]

Over the years a few Maravillas softened their criticism of Black people. If they made a racist remark, sometimes they admitted that it was wrong. A few even got romantically involved with Black women as they ran the streets. For instance, Giant, who always mentioned the importance of La Raza, once had a Black girlfriend. She was a heroin addict with whom he fathered two children. At that point he let go of some of his racism, which his friends criticized.

"My friends, they would clown me," Giant explained one day. "But the thing is, at the same time they got to know her. And it was alright. They saw that I loved her and that she treated me right. Mexican girls are the one[s] that gave me more hell. The Chicanas. They said, 'Aw, you can't find beauty in your race,' and all that shit. 'It's just because she got a big ol' fuckin' ass,' and all that shit. And on top of that, some of my family ain't care for her too much. I had an auntie once say, 'Don't be bringing that girl over here' and all this stuff. I say, 'I'm sorry, but this is my girlfriend.' I wasn't gonna leave her 'cause she was Black. She was my old lady, you know what I'm saying? I had two kids with her."

Other Maravillas confronted interracial relationships involving their children. They had daughters in relationships with Black men, which they spoke about with awkwardness or embarrassment. Since their time in juvenile detention centers, they had laid brick upon brick of racial hatred toward Black people. Now, they had to consider their daughters' happiness and the potential for biracial grandchildren. Marcos's daughter, for example, had a boyfriend with an African American mother and Salvadorian father. For Marcos, this meant that the boyfriend was Black.

"They kept it [the relationship] secret from me for three years. They knew I don't like it. Even my son, my twenty-year-old son, asked me, 'Dad, so what you think about Black people?' I remember the very first time he asked me that question a couple of years ago. I said, 'You know what? I ain't got nothing against Black people. You know what it is? I just don't believe in that interracial stuff. Blacks should stay with the Black people and Mexicans should stay with the Mexicans.' He asked me the same question again [later]. I said [to myself], 'Why am I being interrogated? There's a reason for this. He's hopefully learning something.' Later on, I found out that it was because my daughter was with a Black guy."

"So how do you feel now?" I asked.

"Aw man, we're getting along pretty good," he said, upbeat. "He's a good guy. He ain't a Mexican, but he's my . . . I want to say my son-in-law [laughing]. I feel funny, though. They been together four years now, going on five. The guy works, man. He takes care of my daughter. Now they're talking about having kids. He's like, 'What do you think about that?' I tell him, 'Hey, she's happy, I'm happy. That's what I want.' Once in a while, I think back [to] how I used to talk about Black people. But now I know there's a handful of good Black people. Then you still got them loud ones that are just are annoying. I don't even want to talk about it [laughing uncomfortably]. Out here [outside of prison] I can deal with it. You grow accustomed to it. They're all the same. There's only a handful of good ones."

It was sad that Marcos's family felt that they had to hide his daughter's interracial relationship from him. It was inspiring, though, that his children had resisted his racism. And when he found out about the relationship, there was nothing he could say. The boyfriend loved his daughter and had a strong work ethic. The last part of Marcos's remark, however, showed how he struggled to reconcile the Black boyfriend's decency with his stereotypes of Black people. In fact, he acted as if he were a racial authority that could decide which Black individuals were acceptable or not. Racial acceptance was made on his own terms.

That said, Marcos made slow strides. He told me occasionally about how he had a great time at the movies or dinner with his daughter's boyfriend. Even Chico had a few talks with him to help him see Blackness through a positive lens. "I told Marcos that he should just be happy that his daughter is in a good relationship," Chico explained. "Her boyfriend is a good guy. He works. He takes her out. He really loves her. It doesn't matter that he's Black. What matters is that he provides for her the right way. That's all you ever want for your daughter."

Then Chico revealed that one of his daughters had a Black Belizean boyfriend. "My daughter's boyfriend is Black and she's happy with him. So, for me, that's what matters. As long as he doesn't mistreat her or do anything crazy, I don't care what he is, Black, Chinese, White, Mexican, or whatnot. At first I was surprised that she had a Black boyfriend, and it was strange. It was something that I wasn't used to. Back in the day, when a Chicana went [out] with a Black guy, it was frowned upon in the neighborhood. You grew up hearing that it's bad, that Chicanas should only be with Chicanos, all of that stuff. But she seems really happy and, like I said, that's what matters. He's a good guy. So I got nothing against him. I remember this guy I know was like, 'Chico, how can you let your daughter go out with a Black dude?' And I told him, 'First of all, he's not Black. He's from Belize even though he looks like an African. Secondly, he could be whoever as long as he's taking care of her and he likes her, he's treating her right. That's all that matters to me. I don't care what he is.' I was going to say, 'Thirdly, you better back off before I knock you out for coming at me like that.' I was getting ready to slap him around a little bit."

Clearly, some Maravillas refused to accept Blackness. In fact, they criticized Mexicans in South Central who sometimes acted "Black." I once hung out with Juano and Tito, who, without prompting, distinguished themselves from Mexican gangs outside East LA.

"The other [Mexican gang] neighborhoods," Juano explained, "you go to South Central and shit, you see Mexicans say [using an urban Black accent], 'Hey cuz . . . Ay, whattup nigga?' Fuck no! You try to talk like that around the older [Maravilla] homies and we'll be like, 'Hey, what the fuck? What the fuck you doing, homie? You talkin' like a chango [monkey]!' I don't want to disrespect the Black [people] or nothing, but that's the way it is."

"I never seen a Black wanna be a Mexican," Tito added.

"We're fuckin' Mexicans," Juano emphasized. "Somos Mexicanos orgullosos [We're proud Mexicans]. Why the fuck you tryin' to talk Black for?"

"Around here before, you wouldn't see no Blacks," Tito continued. "Now it's changing. A lot of homies [gang members] ain't around no more. Like the projects there. Now you got your Blacks here and there."

"There's a few," Juano said, "but not that we don't let them in. It's just that they know [not to come]. There was an incident that happened a while back. Not that we don't want them here, it's just that they were so fuckin' . . . we're so used to them putting us down and fuckin' . . . I was saying, 'Fuck that.' And a [Black] family came in here and shit, and some incident happened, whatever, and fuckin', aye, got rid of them."

Since I was recording the conversation, they never mentioned exactly what happened to the Black family, According to other Maravillas, the local Maravilla gang had harassed them until they moved out. This account showed how some Maravillas encouraged Mexicans to enforce racist territorial and cultural boundaries. They did this despite their own admissions of criminality and violence. For example, Chico and I once had the following conversation:

"Those *negros* [Black people in Spanish] can't be trusted, Randy," Chico said. "They always have something up their sleeve. You just can't count on them . . . they're always trying to get over on you. Mexicans—we're proud and we have honor. We hold ourselves up to a higher standard, especially in Maravilla. You won't see any Maravillas acting like the *negros*."

"But you told me lots of stories where you hustled people on the streets," I countered. "When you were addicted to heroin, didn't you lie and cheat people? Isn't that what you told me? So how is that different than a Black person lying and cheating?"

"That's true," Chico responded after a pause. "But it's just that Black people are different. Mexican dopefiends lie and cheat and whatnot, but they don't lie and cheat like Black people. They take it to a whole other level. It's hard to explain."

I continued to challenge Chico, but like the other Maravillas, he brought up his prison experiences to support his argument. Yet there were moments when Chico experienced emotional turmoil because of his racism. He knew it was horrible and wanted to act righteously, but his racist demons sometimes overpowered his Christian love. For instance, Chico once recounted a moment when his violent masculine identity battled with his Christian identity because of race.

"I had an incident with a Black bus driver," he explained, "and I got crazy. Some of the old Maravilla might have come out of me. And the bus was full of people."

"What happened?" I asked.

"I rang the bell when I was supposed to stop and apparently it didn't go off," he said. "I was thinking he [the Black bus driver] was going to pull over and I was standing by the exit, and I said, 'Right here! Right here! I want this bus stop right here!' And he said, 'Well, you didn't ring the bell.' And he went on and on. 'You're supposed to ring the bell,' and he emphasized it over and over and over. He said, 'You're supposed to know. You people don't pay attention.' And he went on and on. And I said, 'Alright, you made your point already. Keep driving, you stupid. I'm going to get off at the next stop, man.' And he said, 'It's my bus. I can do what I want to and I can talk what I want.' I was this close to saying this, but I didn't, 'Hey, man, why are you acting like a nigger? You talk more than it's necessary. You're in East LA.' I would have really went on and on and on because I was right here in Maravilla, on Ford. I was going to tell him, 'I don't care if this is your bus, I'll tie you to the bumper of this bus, you stupid.' But what I said and what I was thinking was wrong. It was not Christian-like. I'm looking forward to seeing him again so that I could apologize. I was wrong in so many ways."

Chico was not all talk. He tried to create positive interactions with Black people. For instance, when he first moved into his subsidized SRO in downtown LA, he was concerned about the formerly incarcerated Black people in the building. They had probably experienced the race riots between Mexican and Black inmates in prison. Fortunately, a Black resident introduced himself to Chico, explaining that he had grown up in a Black and Mexican neighborhood in South Central.

"He told me that he grew up with a lot of Mexican homies," Chico explained, "And that the Black families and Mexican families all got along in his neighborhood. He said that he would eat dinner with Mexican families and loved Mexican food. He even said that his best friend was Mexican and how his friend's mom was like a mom to him. In other words, he was trying to let me know that he wasn't with all that racial prison politics, and that this place was different. . . . He was trying to keep things from getting heated. So, before you know it, I was greeting and talking to the Black people in there. Even now when I cook my chili beans, I offer it to them with neighborly Christian love. At first I could tell that they were hesitant, like they didn't trust me. But once they got to know me, and I got to know them, we started to trust each other. Say 'Hi' to each other. Talk to each other."

Whenever I dropped Chico off in front of his building, he greeted the Black residents standing outside with a wide smile. It appeared that, in keeping with his Christian identity, he started leaning away from the racism that he had learned on the streets and in prison. But as the bus driver incident showed, when he was involved in a confrontation with a Black person, ugly racist terms immediately came to his mind. Overcoming racism was a slow process; just like in his drug recovery, he had to deal with his racism one day at a time, always at risk of falling backwards.

I was heartened, though, when a few years later he revealed in a giggly, adolescent manner that he had started a relationship with a Black woman.

"I met this girl, a morena [Black woman]," Chico said. "She's an intellectual girl. You know, she's a college girl, a college graduate."

"How did you meet her?" I asked.

"Here in the complex," he answered. "I would see her around and I would say, 'Good morning. How you doing?' Things like that. Just greetings now and then. And she hates Trump, hahaha. That's kind of our little pet peeve. She doesn't have any issue with me liking him. She says, 'I'm a conservative too, but I don't like Trump.' And I understand that. I mean, we don't let politics interfere with our . . . our friendship. She's kind of like you. You're civil [about my support for Trump]. So, like I said, I met her here and she wanted something put in her closet. The rack in her closet was falling apart and the maintenance man wasn't fixing it. So I stepped in and repaired it for her. She wanted to pay me, but I was like, 'No, no, it's okay.' So she gave me a case of some special waters and we just hit it off."

"So, it's a romantic relationship?" I asked.

"Yeah, it's getting like that," he said. "Yeah, we're keeping it simple. We're just getting to know each other. I'm liking her and she tells me that she likes me. But yeah, she's good people."

"That's good to hear," I said.

"I know the homies are going to trip when they see me with a little morenita [Black girl]," Chico said. "They're going to say, 'Chico is with a *negra* [Black woman]. We always knew that he had a little bit of *negro* in him.' Haha. I'm going to say, 'Hey, don't get it twisted. I'm mulatto. I'm more on the mulatto side.' Haha."

"I mean, it goes to show you, man, that people could get along regardless of race," I said. "If people click, they click."

"Yeah, man," Chico said. "She goes, 'I'm with a man from Mata-villa.' I say, 'Baby, it's not Mata-villa, it's *Maravilla*.' Hahaha! She trying to sound like a Chicana. It's funny, huh?"

Other Maravillas also started to shift their anti-Black attitudes. Several years before, Antonio had seemed open to friendships with Black people. He even spoke to one Black person who sometimes stopped by his house for a chat. But that was it. When I asked him why, he answered that if he allowed more Black people in his front yard, then he would break the neighborhood "rule." A gathering of Black people would make it seem like they had taken over the neighborhood.

Three years later, though, Antonio welcomed Black people on his block. For instance, I once hung out with him outside to catch up after the COVID-19 lockdowns. As we spoke, I saw a Black teen walking toward us. Antonio noticed him too. I waited for a negative reaction since most old-timers complained about Black people in East LA. Antonio, though, simply nodded and said, "How's it going?" The young Black man responded with a smile and said, "Hi."

We continued our conversation as if it were normal for Black people to stroll down an East LA street. I said nothing since I did not want to turn a positive interaction into a negative discussion. We kept talking about politics, a conversation in which Antonio calmly tried to prove that I was a close-minded liberal not open to conservative policies that helped the poor. His was a truer Christian approach, he argued, that differed from the mainstream Republican evangelicalism that started in the late 1980s. I then told him that after reading the books of Matthew, Mark, Luke, and John in the Bible, I was surprised at how some Pentecostal Maravillas disliked non-Chicano groups, especially African Americans.

Did you ever call them out on it? Antonio asked.

No, I didn't, I responded.

Well, you should have, he said. *You should've said, "How does that match up with the teachings of Christ? How does feeling that way make you a good Christian?"*

I nodded.

You see, you have to call them out on it to remind them of what it means to be a Christian, he continued.

Yeah, I said, *I read about the Good Samaritan and how the story means that even someone who is considered vile could actually be your friend and help you when no one else will.*

That's right! he said, excited to talk about the Gospels. *You see, the Bible tells us to love our neighbor. We're supposed to love and get along with people who are different than us. The Bible even speaks about racism, and we could use its teachings to help us get through everything that's going on with racism today. There's something called a Black theology. I don't know if you ever heard of that. You have Black Bible scholars that show that there was racism against people from Galilee. . . . If you lived in Galilee, you were considered to be what we call "ghetto." It was a real poor part of the country. It would be like South Central or like East LA. But that's where Jesus lived and preached, and he helped the Gentiles even if everybody hated them. He was showing us that we all have to come together even if we come from different races.*

Like the Black kid that passed by earlier. You don't see a lot of Black people around here. But now you got more Black people moving in here 'cause they got housing vouchers and there's less and less places to live in South Central. So where are they gonna go? They're coming here. There's not a lot of them, but there's more now. The first time I seen that Black kid walking by, I just followed my Christian faith and I said, "Hey, how's it going?" You know, real friendly. He looked at me like, "What?" Hahaha, like real surprised. He wasn't expecting that from me. Look at the way I dress. I look like an old-school cholo, hahaha. [He was wearing a pair of Nike Cortez shoes, baggy shorts, and white socks pulled up to his knees] *But I made it my business to be friendly. There's another Black family that moved around the block. They got like a ten- or eleven-year-old kid. He walked by to go to the grocery store one day, and when he came back, I said, "Hi, how are you?" His face got all lit up and he said, 'Hi,' with a big ol' smile. But I think he told his mother and she must've told him something. Maybe not to trust Mexicans or not to trust strangers or something like that. Because the next time he came around and I said,*

"Hi," he just ignored me and kept a serious face. [Antonio took a few steps with hunched shoulders and a surly face] *Hahahaha. But I get it. I'm not mad or surprised. I get it, hahaha.*

Antonio then described his new Black neighbors, who lived about four houses from him. He said that he spoke to them often and even got to know a few of the family members who visited them. He just hoped that none of them sold drugs or were in gangs. If so, the local Maravillas would see it as a challenge to their drug business and a disrespect to their turf. Antonio said all this with no ill will toward the new Black residents. He seemed concerned about potential racial conflict.

I've come a long way, he admitted. *I probably wouldn't have thought like this ten years ago. You see, me and all the homies were institutionalized. We feel a certain way about Black people because of everything we learned in the penitentiary. But I'm breaking away from that with my Christian faith. I'm still taking baby steps, but I'm getting there.*

Mattering as Aging Men

The aging Maravillas often expressed nostalgia and viewed the past through a romantic lens. They recalled their earlier lives as idyllic, even though heroin use, gang violence, and overall crime rose in East LA back then. This nostalgia had a purpose: it assured them that they lived a meaningful life.[12] And, as the sociologist Fred Davis notes, nostalgia goes beyond the personal; it can also represent a collective identity.[13] For example, people who have experienced a particular past might share a longing for it, claiming that life at the time was authentic and simple. This allows them to construct an ideal self by omitting their most shameful and terrible experiences. It also strengthens their bonds with significant others, which constructs a positive collective identity.[14]

The Maravillas' nostalgia romanticized the 1970s and early 1980s, when they wore pressed slacks, dress shoes, and the classic *tando* hat as everyday wear. For special events, they were required to wear pressed suits, pachuco style: suit jackets with wide shoulders; baggy dress pants with wide legs; sometimes a vest under the jacket; and always the pointy, shiny Stacy Adams shoes. And their hair: it was full and combed back with grease. For them, it was a marvelous period when gangsters earned respect through pachuco clothes—and men were men. They experienced what cultural theorist Svetlana Boym calls *restorative nostalgia*, as they wished for the old gangster dress to return.[15] It seemed as if highlighting their past elegance erased or diminished their drug use, violence, and crime.

Marcos, for example, remembered how he and his homies went to school dressed as if they were going to a major social event. "'Cause in junior high, ninth grade, tenth grade, we were already wearing pleated pants, you know, Stacy Adams [shoes] to school. The dressing with khakis, the Pendletons, pleated pants with the shirts, and stuff like that. That's what I liked. That's what I wished we got back to. All of the homeboys getting all slicked up and the girls dressing nice. Everybody always dressing to the T. All clean-cut. Your haircut always on point."

Most of their nostalgia focused on mattering as authentic gangsters, or as the last generation of Maravillas that had *estilo*, or style. They often disparaged younger Maravillas, claiming that the youngsters insulted Maravilla talk, dress, and demeanor.

"I don't want to fucking brag about Maravilla," Juano told me one day, "But we got class. When you go to a wedding, you got to go sharp. You wanna look like a man. You walk into a party and its 'Aye, man, who's that vato there?' The fuckin' '90s generation, the 2000 generation—all the youngsters of that generation, if they could hear me, I'll say it to their face, 'You fuckin' dress ugly.' They have their big pants covering their shoes. If they're walkin' down the street, they're like . . . [he pretends to plod through mud]. The youngsters don't really get what it means to be from Maravilla. They talk just like

Black guys now, 'Nigga this, nigga that.' They call each other 'dog'—
'Whattup dog?' . . . This new generation don't understand the Maravilla culture, our nuestra cultura, entiendes [our culture, under-
stand]? They don't know what it means to dress with class. These
days you'll see the youngsters going to a wedding in sneakers—
wearing Air Jordans [basketball sneakers]! Chale, homes!"

The older Maravillas also conjured up a golden era, a time when
they claimed to have schooled youngsters with their wisdom. According to them, they had grown up witnessing older homies scold or
beat up younger Maravillas for wrongdoing. The youngsters never retaliated or held a grudge. Today's youngsters, they claimed, resisted
the older homies in deadly ways. For example, one day Chico told me
about an incident that occurred a few days before. A youngster had
gotten into a heated argument with another youngster and threatened to shoot him. An old-timer confronted that youngster and told
him that neighborhood conflicts were only handled through fistfights. The youngster got angry at the old-timer's parental tone and,
after they exchanged words, the youngster shot him. Fortunately, the
old-timer lived. But for Chico, this just reinforced how Maravilla
youngsters were wilder and more disrespectful than in the past.

"Most of these youngsters got no respect," he explained. "They
don't hold up the Maravilla traditions. If you're from the same barrio
[gang/neighborhood], you don't try to kill each other. Back in my
day, if you had a problem with a homeboy, it was okay if you fought it
out with your hands. Shooting your own homeboy, that was a no-no.
I mean, unless he crossed the line, like he raped your sister, or something like that. Now the youngsters shoot anybody for any little reason, even [if it's] an older homie trying to school him."

Since I did not observe the participants when they were young,
I could not determine if youth attitudes had changed. It seemed,
however, that they felt that the youngsters had no need for them. But
I understood why youngsters sometimes dismissed them. Many

old-timers struggled with drug addiction and wandered around untidy, pushing shopping carts filled with recyclable items and their belongings. Some of them even hung out on corners under a sleepy heroin nod or drunk off cheap liquor and beer.

Emilio, for instance, dealt with many medical conditions, including obesity and hepatitis C. He was undergoing methadone treatment, but he constantly relapsed, using heroin and liquor. One time we visited his neighborhood and hung out with some homies around his age. I also met some youngsters in their mid to late twenties who were just hanging out. Drunk, Emilio bragged about how he was one of the originators of his neighborhood. The youngsters seemed bothered by his drunkenness. When we returned a few days later, Emilio was even drunker. The youngsters weakly shook his hand when he greeted them. Then, in slurred speech, he demanded that they speak with me about their gang experiences. The youngsters said that they were busy and departed. His inebriation seemed to annoy them again. A drunken Emilio interpreted the situation differently.

"You see how they [the youngsters] respect the older homies?" Emilio asked. "You saw that when I told them talk to you, they were like, "'Órale, we could do this another day.' They know that I'm a[n] older homie. If I say they gotta talk to you, they gotta talk to you no questions asked. I'm an older homie." *An older homie who could get shot for being disrespectful,* I thought to myself. For me, the youngsters tolerated Emilio rather than respected him. I even drove around one day, looking for them to apologize for Emilio's rudeness (I never found them). I did not want Emilio killed.

Despite their complaints, a few Maravillas found ways to matter to the youngsters. Mostly, they tried to get them off drugs. One day some youngsters approached Chico, Giant, and me as we walked through the streets, and Chico later stayed in contact with one of them, whom I will call Juno. Afterward, Chico and Marcos contacted Juno's father (an old homie), who told them that Juno had a crystal meth addiction.

The old-timers met with Juno several times (I also met Juno a few times and found him to be deferential to his elders) and started slowly. They simply asked him to think about the hard times that lay ahead of him, playing down their Christianity to keep him tuned in. They invited him to church, but they were not pushy about it. Juno always agreed to go but never showed up when they drove by to pick him up. After some time, Chico shared his reflections with me.

"He isn't ready [to get off of drugs]," he explained. "He's very respectful, though. [He's] very open to us, welcoming us. He heard us out. But we didn't force him to do anything. I'm lenient and understanding because I know what it's like. When you're in the mix [drug use and gang life], you can't just hang up the towel on the rack and walk away. It takes a lot of work."

Several weeks later, Juno got shot in the leg. Most of the old-timers speculated that it was not gang-related since no gang war followed. They figured that he owed a drug dealer money and never paid it back. Chico and Marcos visited Juno in his home after his release from the hospital and offered to get him into a drug treatment program. Juno seemed open to the suggestion, but after he healed, he returned to the streets. Juno was soon arrested and convicted of drug possession, then sentenced to a drug treatment program. Chico thought the drug treatment program was no help.

"I saw on Facebook that Juno is posting stuff up. He isn't posting about, 'I'm in [drug] recovery.' He isn't posting the Serenity Prayer or nothing like that, hahaha. He's posting neighborhood stuff, like, 'Maravilla' and all that. That tells me that he's just playing games while he's in there. 'Cause I'm almost sure that he isn't supposed to have that cell phone, not that quick. He's probably going against the program's rules. These kinds of things don't help. But I'm here for him. And that's what I do, Randy. I reach out. I understand that it takes time to change."

Chico, Marcos, and some other Maravillas addressed the generational divide through patience and care. But they still expressed nostalgia, a longing for the years when they came of age. This reflected their perceived—and sometimes real—fall from neighborhood grace. They criticized the younger Maravillas, claiming that they were more violent, disrespectful, and rude than in the past. And they said all of this because they felt invisible. They then created a collective identity based on their pasts, another way to matter in the world, which they felt was leaving them behind.

Mattering as Fathers

Apart from being gangsters and Christians, Trumpists and liberals, the Maravillas were also fathers. Most of them had spent more than a decade in prison for various offenses, which meant that they started their parental duties late in their children's lives. Worse, they had trouble letting go of their violent masculinities, a masculinity that they began constructing as teenagers, then cemented as inmates, then reinforced when they retold tales of their greenlight past. Violence sometimes emerged as they settled in as parents and supported their children.

When I first met Juano, for example, he was nearing his fifties, and he sometimes brought his stocky twelve-year old son to the handball court. They lived together, and despite his criminal background, Juano tried to impart proper guidance to him. He told him to take school seriously; he told him to avoid gangs. However, he could not help it: he did violence in front of his son. Juano once described how his son witnessed him fight in a mall parking lot. They had just parked their car, and as his son opened the door to get out, a guy in the car next to them became angry.

"My son starts to get out of the car," Juano recounted, "And this guy wants to open his door first. My son's a kid, and I'm getting out and I hear him say, 'Oh, sorry.' And I look up [and the guy says], 'Aye, watch it, man.' My son right away closed the door. So my son's like looking at the [car] hood and this big ol' fat boy lookin' at him. I say, 'Fuck you say?' The guy goes, 'What, ese?' So my son's like, 'Dad, come on, let's go.' I said, 'Nah, nah, look.' I told the guy, 'Aye, man, why are there always cholos [gangsters] like you starting shit? We're just coming to the fuckin' mall to buy something and you gotta act stupid with my son? He's a little kid.'

"So, I'm walking away and he says, 'That's right, walk away, ese. I'll fuck you up.' I turn around again, and I say, 'That's what you fuckin' want? You're with your wife and I don't know who else is in that shit [car]. What do you gotta prove?' He's like, 'What ese?' He shut the door and starts talking about, 'You better get the fuck outta here, ese, or I'll fuck you up.' I said, 'That's what you want to do, man? Fuck me up? You want to do that? What, ese?' So I'm already like this [motioning how he's getting closer to the guy and feigning having trouble hearing him but positioning his body to throw a punch]. I'm left-handed. He's like, 'What, fucker? I'll kick your ass.' And he gets to about right here, and I'm telling, you, man, I went—boom! [He throws a solid punch] He fell like deadwood, like I dropped a tree. Bam! She's [his wife] like, 'Honey! Honey!' I said, 'That's what you fuckin' got? A dumb motherfucker like this? Tell'em next time to know who the fuck he's dealing with. I'm a real motherfucker. I'm from Maravilla.' Later, my son's like, 'Dad, how did you do that?' I told him, 'You gotta let them think you're retarded. Let 'em think he's over you. That's when you make 'em drop their guard. And then you—bam! [He punches his fist against his palm.]'"

Over the years Juano struggled to contain his violent masculinity. When problems arose, his street reflexes kicked in and violence became his solution. He also reasoned that being a caring parent meant that he had to do violence to protect his children, whether the situation seemed to merit it or not. For instance, he once described how a teacher allegedly mistreated his daughter in the classroom.

"My daughter that's in elementary, bro, a fuckin' teacher pulled her hair. She was in the fuckin' kindergarten. I get home from work, my wife says, 'You won't believe that this fuckin' Black bitch' [her teacher]—I know it's wrong to say it, but that's how she said it—'Black bitch pulled her hair!' And when I picked her up and asked her [his daughter] what happened, she goes, 'Oh, I don't know. She pulled my hair.' I said, 'What? I'll be back.' My wife said, 'Where you going?' I said, 'I'll be back.'"

Juano then recounted how he rounded up some of his homeboys and homegirls and they drove to the school. His brother walked in the school with him. "So I walk in and I'm next to the [assistant] principal," Juano recalled. "And they said, 'I'm the assistant principal.' I said, 'I didn't ask for you, man. I want the fuckin' principal and I want this teacher here and I want her fuckin' now.' One of the people that volunteered for the cafeteria, they were one of my homeboy's older sisters. She recognized me, she was like, 'Juano, what's going on?' I tell her what happened and go, 'I want the fuckin' teacher and I want her here fuckin' now. And if not, you know me, and you know my brother. You know your brothers and how we run. Look outside the fuckin' window. Fourteen people, girls and guys.' 'What are they doing here?' 'I just want to talk to the teacher.' The principal comes out and he says, 'Sir, we're gonna call the cops.' [I say,] 'But before the cops get here, what do you think'll happen if I call in the fuckers [friends] outside the school? They're gonna fuckin' beat you down before the cops get here. Think about it: you call the cops, it'll take them about five or six minutes [to get here]. I want that fuckin' teacher here and I want her fuckin' now.' So he says, 'We're sorry. She didn't mean to do that. She said that she wasn't trying to pull her hair. She was trying to get her from the shoulders.'

"I said, 'Don't give me that fuckin' bullshit. I'ma wait for you and I'ma wait for you outside. Bitch touched my daughter. I don't even hit my daughter. So expect the worst from me. And anybody else that gots a problem with it, we're outside.' The cops got there and everything. But my brother and them, they were just leaving. I'm like, 'Aye, these guys ain't even from around here. It's just me.' I then told the cops what happened. They went in, pulled the teacher out. They made a big fuss."

High on the emotional energy that came from reliving that event, Juano then immediately described an incident in which his son was disrespected at school. His son, who was being punished for not submitting his homework, was told to get at the end of the line on the way to lunch. He misunderstood the instructions and stayed behind in the classroom, hungry and alone. When Juano found out, he stormed off to the school. The principal stopped him from confronting the teacher.

"I told them," Juano remembered, "'Look, I'll tell you people right now, before I fuckin' leave, I'ma get that motherfucker [the teacher] over there. I'ma beat his ass. Or if anybody's gonna do something, you better fuckin' do it now, 'cause I'm ready.' And that fuckin' teacher is scared as fuck. He got lucky that day. But I'll tell you what, Randy, for my son and daughters, I'll kill a motherfucker. Straight out. I won't fuckin' hesitate a bit."

Juano then calmed down as he reflected on his children. Despite not being able to untangle his parenting from his violent masculinity—a masculinity that did not match the middle-class environment of the teachers and school—he hoped that his children appreciated him as father. He was doing everything he could to raise and care for them, especially his son, whom he was now raising on his own. He soon learned that he mattered to them, and that the outside world saw that he mattered as a father too.

"I go to this parents' conference and meet his teacher," he remembered. "She goes, 'Mr. Juano, I must say I'm grateful to meet you. Your son talks so highly about you. He says you're his hero.' I said, 'Wow, he said that about me? I don't even know math and I try to help him.' She goes, 'Let me tell you something, Mr. Juano. Today when we were coming from recess, I told him that he was holding up the line. So we waited to get into class and I asked him, "Why didn't you hurry up so that we don't have to wait for you and come to class?" This was his answer . . .' And she started getting a fuckin' napkin and she has tears in her eyes, 'and he answered me, "Teacher, it's because I went up to the gardeners [who were working on the grounds] and asked them, 'Is there any work for my dad? Could you give him a job?'"'

"That right there fuckin' touches my heart. And I tell her, 'Is that what he said?' And she's cleaning her eyes. And she says, 'Those wonderful words came out of him and I didn't know how to react. I told him that he could sit down.' I also spoke with the principal and [he said,] 'I didn't know you were a single father.' I go, 'Well, I've been with him for the last four or five years.' He says, 'I'm glad to say, you're doing a good job.' And with that I got home and I go, 'Come here you knucklehead! Come here. Give me a hug.' He goes, 'Dad, you said we don't hug man to man.' 'Give me a fuckin' hug, cabrón [bastard]! Don't you ever stop hugging your dad.' He goes, 'Okay, I love you, Dad.' I say, 'Thank you for asking the gardeners for a job for your dad.' He goes, 'Yeah, Dad, but they say there's no work.' That touched me right there."

Other Maravillas fathered several children as heroin addicts. Marcos was lucky to get off drugs and establish bonds with his sons and daughters. He visited them on holidays and birthdays and went out with them to eat. He rarely discussed negative interactions with them, only describing his fatherly advice. Giant, though, rarely mentioned his children. Heroin and street life were first on his mind. Most Maravillas straddled a fatherhood status in between that of Marcos and Giant. They tried to connect with their adult children, who were still bitter about their parents' neglect.

Chico desperately tried to bond with his two middle-aged daughters, whom he fathered in different relationships. He often contacted them on their birthdays or just to catch up. They mostly rejected him, rarely answering or returning his text messages or calls. In his first marriage, for instance, Chico fathered two children, a daughter and then a son. The older one, Jenny, seemed angry at his drunken violence that had terrorized her mother. She remained distant from him close to forty years later.

"I think she wants me to feel the pain," Chico reflected. "I think she wants me to feel uncomfortable. Like keeping me in the dark. I did some stuff when I was with her mom that she held against me for a long time. I beat her mom down one time. Real bad. I just lost it and I took off on her [beat her up]. I beat her down like a dude. I know she knows about that. She watched it. She [his wife] was following me around the house, cursing at me, accusing me of this and that. 'Why don't you just leave then? You're no good.' And that day I was drunk. I was probably high on heroin and alcohol. And that's when I assaulted her."

A few years ago, Jenny had seemed open to a relationship with Chico. Every now and then he happily discussed speaking with her and potentially visiting her. Then talk of her ended. I later found out that after she and her Belizean boyfriend had a falling out, Chico said negative things about him to show that he was on her side. She did not appreciate his input.

"Jenny doesn't call me for nothing now," he told me, hurt. "She's upset because I got involved in the relationship that she was having. I said some things and she decided that it wasn't my place. I haven't earned my right to act like a dad. That's one thing that pissed her off as far as having a relationship with me or returning my calls or anything. After so many years of not being there for her, she feels that I just can't walk in the door and act like her dad. . . . I reached out to her the last time it was her birthday in June, and I didn't get a response from her at all. But it's funny because she's in touch with my mom. Not a lot, but she keeps in touch with my mom and my sister. But I think she's letting me know that I'm out of the picture. The last time I checked, she was in Tucson, Arizona. That's all I know."

Chico also fathered a daughter and then a son with his second wife, the white heroin user from Orange County. As dopefiends, they were up and running in front of the children. Chico temporarily secured a low-wage job for a stable income, but he and his wife kept using heroin in the seedy motel room that was their home. His daughter, Valerie, saw it all.

"After work," Chico explained, "I would go to the [drug] connection and then go home and get right [high]. And one day I came home, and I rushed to the restroom like the way I would always do. Go to the restroom to fix before I had dinner and did anything. And I was in the restroom cooking up my stuff, and I felt that the door was open to the restroom. And I turn around and I saw my daughter, Valerie, standing there. She was about five or six years old. Maybe four. She was holding my belt to tie my arm off. She had it out, handing it to me. That messed me up. Of course, I was hooked. What could I do? It [heroin] had a chokehold on me. Seeing her left an impression in my head, like, 'Look what you're doing! Your daughter already knows your routine. She's accepted it.'"

He often recounted to me what happened later. His wife's mother often picked the children up to go eat, buy them toys and clothes, and spend a night at her Orange County home. One day she offered to keep them for a week. Chico and his wife agreed, seeing no harm. The grandmother never returned the children. Instead, she drove them to her son's house in Las Vegas. The children's uncle eventually won guardianship over them, and then let Valerie live with her grandmother in Orange County while he raised the boy. Chico was angry. But after getting off drugs, he deeply regretted raising them in an unhealthy environment.

Now in her thirties, Valerie resented Chico for exposing her to drugs as a child. She also seemed angry because she wanted her own daughter to have a grandfather in her life. "She's still holding something against me," Chico explained. "But I also think it's because she has a child. And I'm always forgetting her daughter's birthday. My ex-wife calls me up every year to scold me about not remembering that it's my granddaughter's birthday. I'm not being the grandpa that I'm supposed to be. I got caught up in my own little world. When I got clean, I had a routine and had things going on. And I didn't really include my daughter the way I should have. So I think that's one of the reasons why she's still pissed off at me. We're not that close anymore. She doesn't return my calls. She doesn't return birthday greetings or anything like that anymore."

On the other hand, he had strong relationships with two of his sons. His son Frank, from his first marriage (Jenny's brother), moved to Oregon in his early twenties. He eventually became a firefighter, got married, and had children. Once Chico got off drugs, he tried to bond with Frank.

"I tried to make up with Frank, to reconcile and get close to him when I got clean," Chico recalled. "He saw that I was making a lot of effort. But he was kind of beyond that point and he said, 'Don't make up what you can't make up. Just forget about it. It's too late for me. I'm already twenty-four. You could never catch up. Too much time and too much stuff has gone on.'"

Despite the rough start, he made up with Frank, and they called and texted each other often. In fact, Chico visited him once for Christmas, taking an Amtrak train all the way to Oregon. When I called him there, he was so excited because he had played with his grandchildren in the snow. I heard the children in the background calling out to him. Chico cut the call short to spend more time with them. It was a highlight of his life.

His second son, Michael (Valerie's brother), who was taken away to live in Las Vegas, rarely returned Chico's messages. I was surprised since early in my research, Chico had visited him a couple of times. Now they went a year without communicating. It seemed like Michael could not forgive him for being a neglectful parent. Chico no longer mattered to him.

"My son Michael is the one that stood up there in [Las] Vegas. We're not that close. I reach out quite a bit and I even went to Vegas to visit him. He stood there after he left his aunt and uncle's house because he was raised there. He got a job up there. And I took a few trips up there to visit with him. We had a fallout because I reached out a couple of times and he never got back to me. It could take months before he gets back to me. I haven't heard from him for about a year."

Chico, though, played a strong role in the life of his third son, Tomás. He fathered him with his third wife, who had a stable job and did not do drugs. When she was at work, Chico stayed home with him. He felt a bond with his child. But Chico was in a volatile marriage because of his drinking and drug use. During one argument, his wife called the police on a drunken Chico.

"When he was about one," Chico explained, "His mom called the cops on me. And that's when we broke up. And I said, 'That's one thing you don't do. You don't call the cops for nothing.' I mean, I could see if I was beating her or stealing or doing all kinds of crazy stuff, robberies or whatever. Anyhow, she called the cops and I said, 'That's it.' It was the straw that broke the camel's back as far as our relationship was concerned even though I was in the wrong. I did [jail] time for that. It was a misdemeanor. It was an 'under the influence' charge. Because I had a bad record, they gave me like four months [of jail time]."

He then described how the remaining marital resentment sometimes interfered with his relationship with his son. The feud sometimes caused him to consider using heroin again to relieve the hurt:

"I was already committed to being in my son's, Tomás's, life. We had bonded and he was still little. Even though his mom gave me an extremely hard time. I mean, I could tell you some stories that would piss you off and you don't even know her. Like I would travel long distances to see him because of the agreement we had to see him on a certain day and certain time. And I would get there after traveling three hours on the bus and train. I would get there and she would slam the door in my face and say, 'Not today.' There was one time when I went to her house. She was going to go to work and I was going to watch him. And she slammed the door in my face. I didn't make a scene about it, but I was so hurt and had all these emotions. I walked away kind of like shaking almost. I'm shaking like angry. And I walked back to the train station that was about a mile from her house. I was thinking, 'If that train comes and it's going to LA, I'm going to LA to score some heroin.' That's how hurt and pissed off I was. I just wanted to kill that pain. I had already been clean for about a year or two already. And then I said, 'If it's the train that's going to San Bernardino, then I'm safe. I'll go back and I won't use.' So it was just like a toss-up. And I sat at that train station and I heard the train, 'beep beep!' And I looked up and it was coming from LA and going to San Bernardino. And then I kept my word. I took the train back to San Bernardino. I just put my head back and I said, 'Thank you God. You rescued me again from myself.'"

According to Chico, once he committed to drug recovery and kept picking up Tomás, his ex-wife softened. She began dropping him off at Chico's mother's home, where Chico celebrated holidays and birthdays with his son. She was so proud of Chico for mattering as a father.

"There was one time when I was dropping him off at her house," he remembered. "Her brother was there and they were going to have like a dinner or something. And she turns around and she tells her brother, 'Chico's doing so great. He's the best dad.' And she's bragging about me. And I'm listening to her and I'm like, wow, that's such a big change from when she threw me out of the house and called the cops on me, hahaha. But it was because I was clean [off drugs] and I was doing the right thing."

When I met Tomás, he was an undergraduate at a university about thirty miles from East LA. He was taller than Chico, smiled easily, and made easy conversation. Chico often took the train from downtown LA to visit him twice per week. While his son was in class, Chico walked his dog, did his laundry, washed his dishes, and cooked dinner. He was keeping a promise to his ex-wife and himself that he would support Tomás to the end.

"His mom passed away," Chico explained. "She died of cancer. I gave her my word that I was going to stay in his life. No matter what, I was going to put him first. And she thanked me and told me that would be good. I actually helped him move from his house where he lived with his mom after she passed away. We rented a U-Haul and we're moving and packing everything up to a room he was going to rent by the university. He was driving the truck, and he just stopped and he broke down. He said, 'I miss my house. I miss my mom.' It broke my heart, Randy. I just hugged him and said, 'Don't worry about it. I'm with you until the hubcaps fall off. You're not alone. I'm with you on this one.'"

As Chico told me this, he choked up and tears welled in his eyes. "And that's been my . . . that's been my . . . that's been my . . . That's been one of my missions in life. You know what, Randy? Now it's not about staying clean anymore. I think I got way past that station re-garding relapsing and all that. At this point right now, it's more about being there for him. [He cleared his throat] I'm continuing my journey. Staying focused. Try to be there for somebody else. That's just one of my assignments in life. To stay close to him."

His son mattered to him. He mattered to his son.

8   *Mattering No More*

Some Maravillas found a rhythm to life that provided steady emotional highs. Chico and Marcos stayed energized by doing volunteer work and attending church and Bible study groups. Giant and Nando stayed energized by mentoring street youth on crime, by doing crime, and by consuming heroin for dreamy escapes. Both groups had meaning, purpose, and structure, or activities that kept them busy and feeling good. They also mattered to their peers.

Some Maravillas, however, fell emotionally flat. They searched for meaning yet never found it. They had little structure in their lives, so they had nothing to do. They wanted to matter to friends and family, but no one cared. They experienced what Durkheim famously called anomie.[1] Anomie refers to an anguished human condition caused by a social or personal crisis that weakens society's moral grip. People feel disoriented by a sudden loss of moral order, which can lead them to lose control and live in unrestrained ecstasy or bouts of despair. They must morally readjust to their change in fortune, whether it is adjusting to a windfall of money (*Now, I can do and buy whatever I want—drugs, cars, sex, yachts, and homes*) or adjusting to an economic depression (*I lost my job, my house . . . I am a failure . . . what I am going to do?*) At anomie's worse, an individual can spiral out of control emotionally and develop a suicidal state of mind.

Emilio often experienced anomie. His entire life was an emotional roller coaster. He was down when he grew up in a heroin-using household. He lifted himself up as a gang member. He fell back down as a drug addict and inmate. He got back up through Maravilla-based inmate solidarity. He fell back down when unemployed after prison. He raised himself up by getting a trucking job, getting married, and forming a family. He fell back down when his and his wife's drug use escalated. He fell further when his wife left him and he lost his job. He fell even more when his daughters no longer respected him and he lived out of his car. Then he found hope in church. Then he relapsed and began using heroin again. Then he renewed contact with his daughters. Then he binged on liquor and beer. Then he attended church again. Then he lost respect on the streets, feuded with his daughters, and turned to alcohol and heroin again.

Emilio occupied an anomic limbo. Since he was not committed to civilian life, he did not experience sustained emotional highs from its activities and relationships. Since he was not committed to *tecato* life, he did not experience sustained emotional highs from crime and solidarity with other dopefiends. I became concerned. One Maravilla told me not to worry: "Imagine, his mother and father were dopefiends and he grew up in a crazy family. So he learned to be dramatic. Don't you notice that he's always getting into some type of mess? He's just one of those people that always gets into something and then wants everybody to help him get out of it. You gotta remember that he's a dopefiend. He knows how to manipulate people."

True, Emilio showed hustling skills. For instance, he often told me how if he only had three thousand dollars, he could get his trucking license back. Then he immediately followed up with nonchalant questions about my income. I suspected that he wanted the money from me. Still, Emilio had experienced so many losses of moral order that I thought that he was close to the point of no return. But then he got an emotional boost. I worried less.

♪
Ooh-ooh child,
Things are gonna get easier,
Ooh-ooh child,
Things'll get brighter.
♪

After about two years of living in his car, Emilio finally got accepted into an assisted-living facility. I often visited him there and saw many of the other residents. A few of them always sat out front smoking cigarettes, greeting me when I arrived. Most of them spent time in a recreation room, where they played cards and board games or watched television. If it was mealtime, they went to the cafeteria, a large space with tables and chairs. A lot of them seemed to have been homeless, looking unhealthy and rough. Some of them seemed to have mental illness, like the resident who always wore a sorcerer's cap. A good number walked around like zombies, heavily medicated, staring past everyone.

Emilio was happy to have safer lodgings. His room had its own bathroom and was furnished with two single beds, a small sofa chair, a medium-size television, and a large recliner. He shared the room with another resident, who often lay so quietly in his bed that I sometimes forgot that he was there. Sometimes we talked and watched football games, but I would also drive him to a fast-food joint or the local park to talk freely. He looked healthier, peppier, and had gotten off heroin. He even showed discipline by weening himself off methadone and selling the leftover amounts for cash.

Big Emilio was back!

But he struggled to remain drug free. He started consuming methadone for its high again and smoked weed to fall asleep. It helped little that he still took the bus into East LA about three or four times a week. There, he hung with homeboys committed to the streets. After about a year, his life spiraled downward. He drank cheap beer again, and Chico and I suspected that he was back on heroin. I needed to do an intervention.

I always thought about the first conversation we had, when I told him that I was from New York City.

"Are you a native from New York?" Emilio asked.

"Yeah, born in the Bronx," I said proudly.

"I tell you, I've been wanting to go to New York so bad, man," he said, smiling. "I want to go to Harlem, Spanish Harlem, all those places."

I had already taken Chico to a conference in Newark, New Jersey. During my free time, we ventured into Manhattan and the South Bronx twice. I wanted to do the same for Emilio. He had helped me so much. I contacted my colleague, Michaela Soyer (Michi), who taught a class on prisons at Hunter College. I asked her if I could visit the class with Chico and Emilio so that they could discuss their prison experiences. She agreed! I booked the plane tickets and lodging, then met with both Emilio and Chico to tell them that in a few months we would be walking the streets of my hometown. Emilio yelled out, "Woo-hoo!" He could not stop smiling, an authentic smile that made him look boyish. To prepare for the trip he stopped drinking alcohol and using heroin and started the methadone program all over again.

We were in New York City for three days. We stayed at a hotel in the South Bronx, which was surprisingly nice and close to the subway. Chico was so energized that he got up before everyone—at 5 a.m.—every day to walk the Bronx streets alone. We also visited my mother to eat her home-cooked Dominican food. *Señora, esta comida está sabrosa* (Ma'am, this food is so tasty), Emilio complimented my mother's cooking. *Este arroz con habichuela está tan rico!* (This rice and beans is so delicious!) Chico even brought flowers to charm my mother. And he kept saying that my sister, who dropped in for a visit, was "pretty" and later asked me if she had "an old man."

Chico could not help it. He tried to start relationships with most women he met.

We took the subway everywhere. We got on and off trains often, an elaborate transportation system that amazed them. (Chico gleefully remarked that the subway's darkness, barred gates, and echo reminded him of LA County Jail.) We visited Washington Square Park in Greenwich Village to see all walks of life in one space. We went to the southern tip of Manhattan, where we could see the Statue of Liberty in the distance. We walked on the High Line, the elevated park and trail on Manhattan's west side. We visited the classroom at Hunter College, where Chico started off with *Just so that you know, I'm a Trump supporter. I know how most people feel about Trump, so I prefer that you don't ask me any questions about him.* Then he and Emilio did a marvelous job—they were so calm and charismatic—discussing their prison experiences with students. We then had dinner in a somewhat fancy nearby restaurant with some Hunter College colleagues. ("You let me see a different side of the world," Emilio later said. "I never been around people so intellectual"—which made me feel bad, because he sounded insecure.) We walked through East Harlem and marveled at its beautiful murals. We were guided by my colleague Amy Andrea Martinez, who lived there and later attained her PhD (and about whom Chico later asked, "Does she have an old man?").

All the walking, however, hurt Emilio. Though he was off alcohol and hard drugs, he still weighed about three hundred pounds. He often trailed behind us, huffing and puffing, sometimes stopping completely. We had to slow down for him, especially when he tired while going up subway stairs. It was a reminder that his health was still poor. Still, he fought through the foot and knee pain and apologized often as he perspired and grimaced his way around. He did not want to let us down. In all, he and Chico had a blast.

Back in LA, we took an Uber, which dropped them off at Chico's place before heading to mine. *You made my dream come true, brother,*

Emilio told me before getting out. He had a huge smile and sincere eyes. Later, Chico sent me text messages asking if I could help him move to New York City. He wanted to live in Spanish Harlem so that he could help Mexican youths learn the Maravilla culture and style. Wow! The trip had a tremendous impact on him too.

A week later I visited Emilio to catch up. "So, how do you feel after being away from New York for one week?" I asked.

"You know, I miss it," he said. "I miss the hustle and the bustle. It was quite an adventure that I'd love to do again. Like I told you before, you made my dream come true. I've always dreamt about going to New York out of all the places in the world. And you made that happen. And I'm forever grateful for you."

Then he said something that concerned me. "One thing I loved was the difference from city to city [neighborhood to neighborhood] that we went to," Emilio explained. "I mean, when we got to Spanish Harlem, it's like, 'Whoa!' It was like being back at home. But like I said, everything was high over there. And it seems like everyone's *high* over there, hahaha."

"So when you say that you felt like it was back home, what do you mean?" I asked.

"I mean, when I went to [Spanish] Harlem and I seen all the drug addicts," he said, "that reminds me of East LA, right here on Atlantic [Avenue] and Whittier [Boulevard]. That's what you see there is dope-fiends, and that's all I seen in Spanish Harlem. I didn't see too much in the Bronx where we were at. It was a little bit more mellow over there."

I could have asked him several sociological questions on this topic, but I stopped being a sociologist right then. I did not want him to focus on heroin. I wanted him to feel energized about positive things. I changed the subject.

"What did you think about Hunter College?" I asked.

"Hunter College was a big difference," Emilio answered. "You go over there and you see nothing but people who are going to school.

The intelligent people. Hunter, it seemed more like on the educated side. It was nice being in the classroom, being able to address the questions that came from the classmates."

"So how did you feel in the classroom?" I asked.

"To tell you the truth, I felt kind of nervous," he admitted. "I've never been in that kind of situation before, addressing certain questions. I have a hard time hearing as it is. But I did the best that I could do. I hope it was good enough. . . . I mean, I couldn't ask for a better classroom. They were all attentive and they all seemed to have a question. It was a great experience all around. It's hard to say in words, Randy. Because that trip meant a lot to me. And like I said, man, it fulfilled one of my longtime dreams. And that was more than I could ever ask for. And I have you to thank for that. So, thank you from the bottom of my heart. This is something that's going to go with me for the rest of my life. The memories that I have. The pictures I have."

Later, he walked me to my car. "Randy, man, again, thanks for everything you've done for me," he said. "I love you, man."

"Thanks, man," I said, surprised at the kindness of his words. I then drove off as he waved.

A few days later I met with Chico. I asked him about his most memorable experience in New York City. "You know, when I seen all the dopefiends," Chico answered, "Me and Emilio were saying to each other, 'Watchalo! Watchalo!' Watchalo means to watch with your eyes. In other words, 'Check out that dopefiend. Look at that one.' In fact, Emilio's nose opened up. We were souvenir shopping in one of the areas of the Bronx when you went to visit your mom again. There was a hype [heroin user] panhandling. I gave him some change. He looked like he was on it [heroin]. Emilio was like, 'Man, he's on that stuff. It must be good.' I said, 'You want to go ask him? Go ask him where he got it from.' I was just kidding around with him. Emilio was like, 'Don't start. I'm already thinking about it. It's already getting to me, man.' And I said, "Well, let's keep walking then.'"

I was not surprised that they were fascinated with New York City's heroin scene. I was more concerned, though, about Emilio than about Chico. Chico was solid. He used his Christian faith, networks, and activities to rebuke heroin. Emilio still solved problems by embracing heroin. As he often told me, if he had a physical problem, heroin reduced the pain. If he had a family problem, heroin reduced the anxiety. If he had a financial problem, heroin helped him forget.

About six months later Emilio was a mess. The emotional high from NYC had worn off. It was back to hopelessness. When I spent time with him now, he always spoke about his failures as a father and man. He felt worthless to his children. In a vulnerable moment, he told me, "I tell you, in spite of my mom being a drug addict, the way she was, she tried to give me all the things that I needed. She really tried. But I still can't help but having this anger toward them [his parents]. Because I'm a father now and I didn't break the cycle. You know, my kids are good kids, don't get me wrong. One of them went to college for a little bit. Economically, she couldn't do it since she had to go to work. She didn't have the money to keep on going to college and have a part-time job. So she just ended up working. I couldn't help her."

Then he reasoned that it was too late for him to have a meaningful existence. His body was broken, his money had been misspent, the sand in the hourglass had run out. "That's what I wanted to tell you," he continued. "A lot of people tell you that it's not too late. And I disagree with that. Because I wake up and I look at my life. I suffer from rheumatoid arthritis. I have hepatitis C. There comes a point when you open your eyes and you realize that it's too late. I couldn't dedicate my time to go to school because who would support me? I couldn't then go back to work because of my physical condition. But people say that it's never too late. I hate to say that it is too late. You wake up one day and you realize . . ."

His voice cracked as he teared up. Then he said it: he was facing an existential crisis. Where was the meaning in his life?

"I wake up here and say to myself, 'Is this what my life is? Is this what it come to be? This room, sharing it with somebody that I don't really know?' I'm here because they classified me as 5150. That's a mental condition. A mental disability. That's how I got here. I get depressed a lot. I don't know if it's because I think a lot more than these people [other residents] do. These people are content with what they have. I'm . . ."

More tears dropped from his eyes. He struggled to speak.

"I'm just happy I have it [this place]. Because I was living in a car for almost two years."

A staff person walked in to let Emilio know that it was almost lunchtime. He nodded. After she left to alert others, Emilio gathered himself. He seemed to want to tell me about the huge disappointment he felt in himself. It wounded him to think that there was no more time left to make him special. "I really do a lot of soul-searching and I look at my life," he said. "Sometimes it makes me want to cry because it's like, 'Is this what your life came to? Is this it?' There's people that are living their life, enjoying their life, enjoying what it has to offer. But I was never really exposed to that, you know what I mean? Now that I'm older, I see it . . . I'm gonna . . . gonna be sixty in March . . ."

He was about to cry but stopped himself. I stayed quiet, seeing his pain. I tried to comfort him. "You could get satisfaction from being there for your children, by seeing them a lot," I said.

Emilio no longer looked at me. He peered into space, seeming to be recovering from the effects of his own words: *Is this it?* He then got up and I followed him out of the room so that he could eat lunch. I departed with sadness. I wanted to help.

♪
Someday, yeah, we'll put it together and we'll get it all done,
Someday, when your head is much lighter.
Someday, yeah, we'll walk in the rays of a beautiful sun,
Someday, when the world is much brighter.
♪

A few months later I was scheduled to speak to students at the Borough of Manhattan Community College in lower Manhattan. Since I would present on my Maravilla project, I asked if I could bring two Maravilla participants to share their views. No problem, I was told. I gave Emilio and Chico the good news: *Back to New York City!* They were excited again: *Woo-hoo!* I wanted them to share their stories with students. Especially Emilio. He had so much to say about marginality.

As the date neared, we got bad news. The COVID-19 pandemic had reached the US and was spreading rapidly. Our trip was canceled for safety reasons. Chico, the risk-taker, still insisted on going even if the virus had shut down New York City. Given my health condition, I told him that he would have to sneak into the city alone. Emilio was upset, but he was also concerned about his own health. He just hoped that COVID-19 would be controlled quickly so that we could re-schedule the trip.

That would not happen. Most of the nation was on lockdown for the next two years. For my safety, I mainly stayed home, going only to grocery stores. But the lockdown was helpful: it stopped me from doing more fieldwork. This allowed me to focus on writing and tran-scribing my recordings, which I had fallen behind on. Since Chico had access to Zoom, I still invited him to my speak to my classes. Emilio, though, had no Zoom access, so I only spoke to him by phone.

Emilio, who was vaccinated, was cautious. He often criticized the unvaccinated Chico, who believed in vaccine-related conspiracy theories and moved about as though no pandemic existed. Eventually, both caught COVID-19. Over the phone, they described it as being almost worse than heroin withdrawal. They experienced terrible bone aches, fevers, chills, congestion, coughs, breathing problems, and more. After Emilio's first week of having COVID-19, I followed up with him.

"To prepare for COVID, they [the facility] warned you about hurting and aches," he said. "They tell you that it's supposed to be expected. I had a lot of soreness yesterday. I felt really bad. Chico's like in a whole different world than me. He's out and about. He tested positive for COVID, you know that, right?"

"Yeah, but he got over it, right?" I asked.

"Well, apparently," Emilio answered. "He still sounds messed up, but he's still getting all around. So my advice to you is to stay away [from him]. I'm only telling you that because I care for you. I know that he's your friend. He came around looking for me. But he's a [virus] carrier. We don't know for how long the carrier carries it for."

"He told me that he doesn't really see anyone except for Pastor Nito," I said.

"Yeah, that's right," Emilio said, "but I still keep my distance. Because he came here last week to give me my Christmas gifts. We were about to exchange gifts and I just did my distance. I stayed more than seven feet away from him. I had my two masks on. I'm not taking no chances with nobody. I'm just telling you so you know. Just a warning. You should try to avoid any confrontations [contact] with him, you know what I mean? I don't know, just be careful."

Emilio cared about me—I mattered to him!

I then asked if he was in contact with others.

"Ever since I lost my homeboy [to COVID-19], I don't go out of my door," he said. "I don't have no association with anybody. There are some people that still do. They go walk around. Not me. It's just me and my freaking TV. All I do is that if I have an appointment, I just go downstairs. I call them and let them know that I have an appointment on this day. And then I go meet them outside and they take me. And if I go outside and I do see somebody without a mask, I yell at them and say, 'Go put your fucking mask on, man!' I got into an argument with my roommate because he was going outside and I told him, 'You know what, man? I'm not going to lose my life for you or for nobody else, man. You know, I got three kids.' But Randy, anytime you wanna come by and pick up the Christmas present I got you, feel free to meet me outside. I'll take a lot of precautions. I'll be all covered up [with masks]. Whenever you can make it down here, come and pick up your present. It's here for you."

I felt honored that Emilio had gotten me a Christmas gift, but it was still early in the pandemic, and there were many unknowns about COVID's aftereffects. So I put it off. I did stop by once a few months before to help him out with money. But I had opened my car window only about half an inch and passed him the money in an envelope. Later he texted me, playfully addressing me as "B," which is short for "brother," since he had heard guys using it in New York City. "My brother B, I don't know what to say but thanks. You always seem to come through when least expected. If I could ever be there for you, big B, all you have to do is ask. Your friend for always and [have] a [good] day."

Afterward, I did not communicate with Emilio for months as I caught up with my work. He sometimes called to check in and remind me that he still had my gift. I always told him that I was still taking health precautions against COVID-19, but that I would pick it up soon. After being out of touch for about three months in late 2021, he texted me, "Hey Mr. B I hope and pray that you and the family are doing well. When the time allows please let me know how everyone is. Love you, Mr. B."

I called him the next day. As I expected, he was lonely. Like many sick, elderly, and vulnerable people across the country, the COVID-19 stay-at-home orders forced Emilio to remain in his room. This increased his sense of loneliness since he lost access to desired social connections, like his church friends and homies on the street.[2] Unlike Chico, he had no access to Zoom and did not know how to use other virtual technologies to meet with friends and family. His lack of integration into a social group—another dangerous condition that Durkheim called "egoism"—seemed to increase his anxiety and depression.[3] His desperation for human connection led him back to heroin. Chico had already told me about this about a month before.

"You really have to go see Emilio," Chico said. "His health is not really that good. He's struggling big-time. I was really disappointed with him. I had to put him in check a few times because he was talking all kinds of stupidity. He stopped by and he was talking way too much. Because there was a guy there talking with him. And you know, he used a few curse words. He was saying, 'Oh, that guy's no good. He's a child molester. And I hope he gets it.' And there were people right there listening. I had to tell him, 'Hey Emilio, córtatela [cut it out].' He goes, 'Oh, oh, I'm sorry.' He said he wasn't loaded [with heroin]. But I'm a dopefiend. I know behavior. I know speech. He's using again, between me and you."

I wanted to uplift Emilio's spirit so badly.

♪
Ooh-ooh child,
Things are gonna get easier,
Ooh-ooh child,
Things'll get brighter.
♪

When I called Emilio, he focused on his failures as a parent since his daughters were mad at him again. They thought he was an unreliable father. "They're just mad in general," he explained, "because the last six or seven years of their lives haven't been . . . there has been no stability. They were just like lost in the woods. They didn't know where to turn. And that's what I was supposed to be there for. I mean, I'm being a little hard on myself, but I feel it. And these kids don't think I feel it. And I do have a lot of regrets."

His voice cracked. He then cried softly.

"But I just look at the cycle, Randy," he said, sobbing. "It's a vicious cycle. Like, I tell you, my mom and dad were drug addicts. So I wasn't taught anything really, you know? And I didn't have the strength to learn. [He clears his throat] They made it easy for me not to go to school and all that shit."

"If it makes you feel better," I said, "whenever I speak with your daughter, she says that everything was cool before you and your wife broke up. It was one big, happy family. And she sees you as this father who was always happy, always joking. So she has fond memories of you before the breakup."

"The other day," he said slowly, "my oldest daughter told me, 'What you should have done when my mother was in the condition that she was in, you should've left her and got us, and took care of us.' But it didn't play out that way. So I just got to deal with my pain and my suffering. And I have just been asking God for strength and to help me get through this monster that I've created. Not really a monster . . . but I've been getting down too hard on myself."

I felt bad. The COVID-19 pandemic had shut him down. He no longer volunteered to feed Skid Row's homeless. He feared attending Bible study and church services. He had no one needing or wanting him. Heroin waited for him at every turn. He used the drug to self-medicate and fill the moral and social void. Sadly, he stopped using heroin just to admit himself to a hospital with severe withdrawal symptoms. There he had human interaction with a caring community of doctors and nurses. After a while, though, even they seemed not to care.

"I have nowhere to go," Emilio said. "Everywhere I go, there's always dope [heroin]. So it's hard. And I'm just stuck in here and I'm afraid to go into the streets. Because I know what I'm going to find in the streets. . . . When we went to New York, everything was good. You see, what I had substituted heroin with was methadone. So right now what I'm trying to do is try to take the methadone, the heroin, and everything. So it's been really rough, brother, believe me. I went to the hospital on Sunday through Wednesday because I was kicking. I had a lot of pain in my abdomen, and I was sweating. I went to the hospital and they kept me there for three days. And they finally said, 'Get out of here.' So these last couple of days haven't been too easy on me."

Then he explained how his isolation made him feel stuck. He badly needed structure, even if it was only medical appointments that organized his life. "But for the last year, we began the COVID and all that. I've been locked up in this room. And when I went to the doctor, he said they weren't doing surgeries right now because of the COVID. But he sent the paperwork and then I didn't get no response. And then we got hit with the COVID here [at the facility]. Even I got it. I was one of the fortunate ones. You know, God still has his eyes on me. You know what I mean? I'm still here. So we were on lockdown for what seems like an eternity, bro. They were keeping us in our rooms. You know what I mean? So I couldn't go to the doctor. I couldn't do anything. Everything came to a standstill. This whole world is in a mess right now, brother."

He then asked questions about current politics, which I answered. "Please keep in touch," he said suddenly. "Don't forget me. Please keep in touch with me."

"I didn't forget that you have that gift for me," I said. "I'll be picking it up soon."

"Yeah, it's here. It's been waiting for you brother. You know, whenever you can, just let me know and I'll be super careful. I'll double mask if you want me to."

"Yeah, I'll definitely go pick it up in a few days," I said.

"Like I said, I've been getting down on myself," Emilio said, "but then I try to like flip the switch. You know what I mean? Because I used to get up and call the girls [his daughters] and I stopped. But that's life in the barrio, hahaha. How do you like that, Mr. B?"

"That's right, I'm Mr. B from New York City," I said loudly, glad that his mood had shifted. "That's me."

"Yeah, you're my bro, that's why I call you Mister B," Emilio said. "You've earned that right to be called 'mister.' And I really admire you. From what you tell me, your life wasn't always pretty. You made the best out of your situation. How did I ever let my life get out of control? Pussy-whipped. I was pussy-whipped. And I just wanted to have a family."

"You did the best that you could," I said, noting his self-emasculation. "From what your daughter told me, you tried to make a family life."

"It was a family when it was good," he said. "Then when the blanket of night covered us, it was a different story. That's when the demons came out, bro. But anyway, I'm going to get busy and watch this football game. Just do me a favor. Don't forget me. Keep in touch with me."

"I will," I said, making a note on my calendar to pick up the gift on the weekend.

♪
(Right now) and you just wait and see how things are gonna be,
(Right now) if you just wait and see how things are gonna be,
(Right now) if you just wait and wait and see . . .
♪

Two days later I got a call from one of his daughters. Emilio was dead.

The staff had found him slumped on the floor of his bathroom, lifeless. When I asked for the cause of death, his daughter said that it was still unknown. She added that it was not suicide since her father was "no pussy" and would never go out like that. In the end, no one learned how Emilio died. Chico suspected that he had passed away from a heroin overdose, which might be too embarrassing for his daughters to admit. I stopped following up since I respected his family's wish to keep the details secret.

Later, when Chico announced Emilio's death on Facebook, only one Maravilla remembered him vaguely. It seemed like Emilio no longer mattered in the Maravilla community—the community that he loved so dearly and gave him his only meaning. And I had never picked up his gift, an act that would have made him feel valued. So whenever I spoke about or thought of him, I got a huge lump in my throat and felt the heaviness in the chest that comes before really grieving. A few times, I even silently cried away from everyone. Emilio, with all his ups and downs, mattered to me. If he had only waited to see, just waited, waited, waited, I was sure that . . . nothing. That was so easy for me to believe.

Close to a year later, I was speaking with Chico.

"Oh man, the other day I was thinking about Emilio," he said. "I had told him once that I was seeing somebody. He looked at me with a smile, with that smirk on his face, and he goes, 'It's hammer time!' Hahaha. He's a fool, man. Emilio is a fool, hahaha. I miss that fat head, man. He goes, 'It's hammer time!' Hahahahahaha . . . hahaha . . . Man, he got that . . . hahaha . . . that corrupt Maravilla mentality . . . hahaha. I miss that fat head. Memories are good though. When someone's not around anymore, it keeps your memory alive. You know, advice, experiences."

"It's hard for me," I said. "I think it's hard for me because I listen to his voice over and over again because of the recordings I took of him. And then it just sort of brings me back to when he was alive, you understand? I have actual documentation of his voice. It's just weird listening to him and he's not here. It's a weird feeling because sometimes it makes me feel like he's still here."

"I get it," Chico said. "Well, all I have is a memory of him. A voice in my head. I have a few pictures. You got more than I got."

"I think this is it," I said, choking up. "Once I'm done with the book. I can't listen to those recordings anymore. That's it. I'm writing the last chapter now."

"If you want something to add to it or you want more information on something, don't hesitate to call me," Chico said reassuringly.

"I mean, it's just sad for me," I said. "It's just sad that when you put it out on Facebook that he died, not many people knew him, you understand? Maybe like one person knew him. Man, Emilio died alone. One of the last things he told me was, 'Don't forget me.' But except for his daughters, he's been forgotten by everyone. So I want people, like readers, to remember him through my book. But like I said, once I'm done with this chapter, I'm not listening to the recordings anymore because it just brings me down."

"Yeah, well, don't stay down," Chico said. "Enjoy life and keep doing what you got to do. You gotta live your legacy."

"Yeah, I'll try."

"Well, do that, alright?"

"Alright."

"I love you, man."

"I love you too, man."

To Emilio, Chico, and all the Maravillas: You matter so much.

Final Thought

I do not want to write anymore.

I still grieve Emilio's death. Recently I was virtually discussing my ethnographic approach with a graduate methods class in Northern California. When I was asked about my bonds with study participants, I answered by describing my relationship with Emilio. When I mentioned his death, a sadness overwhelmed me. My eyes watered. My voice trembled. I lowered my head and, with one hand, I covered my eyes. I cried. I was so embarrassed. But I missed Emilio.

Perhaps this brief final thought can give me closure. I think about how Emilio and the other Maravillas experienced intense traumas and interpret their suffering through a masculinity that celebrates pain and violence. Though this could be a psychological survival mechanism, I fear that their masculine interpretations have kept them focused on individual or private orbits, such as their run-ins with rival gangs on the street and struggles to manage heroin addictions. Unfortunately, such foci mask the social forces that shaped their lives. If you ask them, they are simply the original LA Mexican gangsters who embrace violence. If you ask me, they are so much more.

The Maravillas come from generations of Mexicans who faced extreme racism as they settled in the United States. They come from poorly resourced East LA, which has had to mobilize and protest to meet its most elemental needs. They were once bright, independent, and resistant youths who sought creative outlets under disadvantaged conditions. If born under more privileged circumstances, they might have excelled at conventional pursuits: school, work, business, family, activism, and so forth. But they were not, so they realized their creative potential as gang members, drug addicts, and inmates, all making them matter as daring and violent men.

I am thankful that some of them have left gang life to become redeemed. The most successful ones, like Chico, have used religion to matter as men. I know that Pentecostalism locks them into an individualistic framework that solely blames the individual for criminality. I also know that it has given them belonging and love. The daily rituals and events also bring them joy and help them fulfill their potential. As best they can, they help those in need: the homeboy still chasing dope; the homeboy wanting to give up the streets; the youth going down the wrong path; the professor wanting to understand the community.

It still bothers me that in becoming conventional, some Maravillas now embody this nation's most horrible traits. Racism and xenophobia rear their ugly heads through their anti-Black and anti-immigrant sentiments. Such hatred reflects a traditional America, where racist whites vilify groups that they see as challenging their power. The Maravillas have internalized this white supremacy, relieving racist whites of some of their dirty work: now the Maravillas call Black people and immigrants culturally backward and criminal; now they claim that Black people and immigrants ruin the United States. "Lock them up, send them back"—such sentiments have become their rallying cry. Yet they do not see the contradiction, that the conservative movements they join work against them. Making America Great Again is all about keeping them—people of color—low on the racial totem pole.

I am happy about how the redeemed Maravillas have come a long way. Chico recently secured Section 8 housing in a trendy area and has a beautiful, spacious one-bedroom apartment with wonderful views. I was so happy for him as he gave me a tour of his home (it was a far cry from the tiny, cramped SRO apartment he had occupied in Skid Row). It was a bit messy. Grooming aides, such as shaving tools, hair gel, and bottles of cologne, cluttered his large bathroom counter, and his ironing board was out, with the iron on it, next to a few items of clothing. This was Chico's back stage, where he prepared himself to look so neat and sharp in the world. *Old-school, ese.*

I also think of the Maravillas still on the streets. On a recent walk in East LA, Chico and I came across Giant. We happily greeted each other and made some small talk. A young man, who appeared to be in his late twenties, stayed several yards away. Giant, who was under a light heroin high, informed us that the youngster was his "protégé." He was teaching him how to survive on the streets. As always, Giant had stepped into the old-head role to school others on street matters. After a few minutes Giant abruptly said that he had to go and gave me a big hug. The duo then went off to get something done. I was convinced more than ever that Giant would never leave the streets. Not only had he been a heroin addict for the last forty years, but he also shone brightly in this world. Here he mattered precisely because was a wise and violent dopefiend.

But I think back to Emilio. I think about his heroin-addicted family and the criminal mentorship he received at home. I think about his gang days, his drug use, his experience with violence in jail and prison. I think about how he tried to raise a family and live the American dream. I think about how his drug addiction dragged him back to the streets. I think about how he was a beautiful person when not drunk. He laughed easily. He told jokes. He always had a gleam in his eyes. I think about how he asked lots of questions with an unending curiosity about the world. I think about how he—a romantic—believed in love and loved his ex-wife unconditionally. He also loved his children and cared about what they thought of him. I think about how he was always tormented and could not overcome the tragedy that was his life. I think about his death. *I am so sorry, Emilio.*

I am getting emotional again. I must stop writing. I hope that readers now understand how people come to live and die for a neighborhood. How people fall into and struggle to free themselves from drug addiction. How the most marginal and forgotten members of society try to matter in the world. Most of all, I hope that this book reaches readers who have family members and friends with similar lives. To them, I say the following: Tragically, this is often how they become who they are. This is how they attain meaning in their lives. This is how they sometimes die.

Notes

Introduction

1. Chris Blatchford, *The Black Hand: The Bloody Rise and Redemption of "Boxer" Enriquez, A Mexican Mob Killer* (New York: HarperCollins, 2008).

2. Gang studies have been extremely popular since the early twentieth century, making the literature on gangs extremely vast. To save space, I will refrain from providing honorific citations and only list the following literature: Scott Decker and Barrik Van Winkle, *Life in the Gang* (New York: Cambridge University Press, 1996); Robert Garot, "Gang Banging as Edgework," *Kriminologisches Journal* 44, no. 3 (2012): 167–81; Robert Garot, *Who You Claim: Performing Gang Identity in School and on the Streets* (New York: New York University Press, 2010); Robert Garot, "Where You From!," *Journal of Contemporary Ethnography* 36, no. 1 (2007): 50–84; David Harding, *Living the Drama* (Chicago: University of Chicago Press, 2010); Jack Katz, *Seductions of Crime: Moral and Sensual Attractions of Doing Evil* (New York: Perseus, 1988); Timothy Lauger, *Real Gangstas: Legitimacy, Reputation, and Violence in the Intergang Environment* (New Brunswick, NJ: Rutgers University Press, 2013); Felix Padilla, *The Gang as American Enterprise* (New Brunswick, NJ: Rutgers University Press, 1992); William Sanders, *Gangbangs and Drive-bys* (New York: Aldine de Gruyter, 1994).

3. C. Wright Mills, *The Sociological Imagination* (New York: Oxford University Press, 1959).

4. David Brotherton, *Youth Street Gangs* (New York: Routledge, 2015).

5. The following gang scholars were some of the first to provide historical backdrops to their research: Joan Moore, *Going Down to the Barrio: Homeboys and Homegirls in Change* (Philadelphia: Temple University Press, 1991); John

Hagedorn, *People and Folks: Gangs, Crime, and the Underclass in a Rustbelt City* (Chicago: Lakeview Press, 1998); James D. Vigil, *Barrio Gangs: Street Life and Identity in Southern California* (Austin: University of Texas Press, 1988); James D. Vigil, *The Projects: Gang and Non-Gang Families in East Los Angeles* (Austin: University of Texas Press, 2007).

6. Sudhir Venkatesh and Steven D. Levitt, "Are We a Family or a Business? History and Disjuncture in the Urban American Street Gang," *Theory and Society* 29, no. 4 (2000): 427–62.

7. Dennis Rodgers, "Living in the Shadow of Death," *Journal of Latin American Studies* 38, no. 2 (2006): 267–92.

8. Deborah Levenson, *Adios Niño: The Gangs of Guatemala City and the Politics of Death* (Durham, NC: Duke University Press, 2013).

9. Luke Billingham and Keir Irwin-Rogers, *Against Youth Violence: A Social Harm Perspective* (Bristol, UK: Bristol University Press, 2022); Luke Billingham and Keir Irwin-Rogers, "The Terrifying Abyss of Insignificance: Marginalisation, Mattering and Violence Between Young People," *Oñati Socio-Legal Series* 11, no. 5 (2021): 1222–49.

10. Psychiatrist Francis Broucek used this term to describe the troubled feelings of infants who have unresponsive parents. Cited in Billingham and Irwin-Rogers, *Against Youth Violence*, 59.

11. Critical criminologist Anthony Ellis used this phrase to describe the terrible feeling of not mattering. Cited in Billingham and Irwin-Rogers, *Against Youth Violence*, 59.

12. R.W. Connell, *Masculinities* (Berkeley: University of California Press, [1995] 2005); R.W. Connell and James W. Messerschmidt, "Hegemonic Masculinity: Rethinking the Concept," *Gender & Society* 19, no. 6 (2005): 829–59; James W. Messerschmidt, *Masculinities and Crime: Critique and Reconceptualization of Theory* (Lanham, MD: Rowman and Littlefield, 1993).

13. Randol Contreras, "The Broken Ethnography: Lessons from an Almost Hero," *Qualitative Sociology* 42, no. 2 (2019): 161–79.

14. Contreras, "The Broken Ethnography."

15. Mitchell Duneier, *Sidewalk* (New York: Farrar, Straus, and Giroux, 1999).

16. For instance, the film *American Me* describes the origins and rise of La Eme, or the Mexican Mafia. Edward James Olmos, who created and acted in the film, took great liberties, using fictitious accounts to enhance the storyline. Some parts of the film depicted acts that never occurred, such as a rape in a juvenile

detention center and the way a gang leader was killed. It is rumored that La Eme became angry at the inaccurate depictions and killed several of the film's gang consultants. The word on the street is that Olmos also had a bounty put on his head, which made him flee to Toronto for safety. The bounty was removed after he paid an extraordinary sum of money. Whether or not this occurred, the lesson remains: be accurate or leave it alone. This is why Mexican gang members in Southern California often hesitate to give prison accounts. They refuse to be quoted giving false or criminalizing information.

17. Randol Contreras, "Transparency and Unmasking Issues in Ethnographic Research: Methodological Considerations," *Sociological Forum* 34, no. 2 (2019): 293–312.

18. Contreras, "Transparency and Unmasking Issues in Ethnographic Research."

19. Randol Contreras, *The Stickup Kids: Race, Drugs, Violence, and the American Dream* (Berkeley: University of California Press, 2013).

20. Rebecca Hanson and Patricia Richards, *Harassed: Gender, Bodies, and Ethnographic Research* (Berkeley: University of California Press, 2019).

21. Matthew Desmond, *Evicted* (New York: Crown, 2016).

22. Nancy Scheper-Hughes, *Death without Weeping: The Violence of Everyday Life in Brazil* (Berkeley: University of California Press, 1992); Philippe Bourgois, *In Search of Respect: Selling Crack in El Barrio* (Cambridge: Cambridge University Press, [1995] 2003); Ranita Ray, *The Making of a Teenage Service Class: Poverty and Mobility in an American City* (Berkeley: University of California Press, 2018); Teresa Gowan, *Hobos, Hustlers, and Backsliders: Homeless in San Francisco* (Minneapolis: University of Minnesota Press, 2010).

23. Tanya K. Hernandez, *Racial Innocence: Unmaking Latino Anti-Black Bias and the Struggle for Equality* (Boston: Beacon Press, 2022).

24. Contreras, *The Stickup Kids.*

Chapter One

1. United States Census Bureau, 2022, www.census.gov/quickfacts /eastlosangelescdpcalifornia.

2. Gold first spurred large-scale Mexican immigration in the mid-1800s to the land up north, which had become part of United States after the Mexican-American War (1846–48). Miners were needed to help enterprising whites strike it rich, and Mexicans responded to the labor demands. They settled mostly in

Arizona and New Mexico, close to their homelands. Agriculture also attracted more Mexicans after improved irrigation allowed farming on unfertile land. Now Mexicans filled the labor demands of California, which would soon become the largest producer of fruits and vegetables in the Southwest. Richard Romo, *History of a Barrio: East Los Angeles* (Austin: University of Texas Press, 1983); David Torres-Rouff, *Before L.A.: Race, Space, and Municipal Power in Los Angeles, 1781–1894* (New Haven, CT: Yale University Press, 2013); George Sanchez, *Becoming Mexican American: Ethnicity, Culture, and Identity in Chicano Los Angeles, 1900–1945* (New York: Oxford University Press, 1993).

3. The end of the Mexican Revolution was comprised of a whirlwind of events: the resignation and exile of President Díaz and the landslide presidential win of Francisco Madero; the forced resignation and then assassination of Madero; the counterrevolutionary and murderous regime of General Victoriano Huerta and his ousting by revolutionaries after a year; the one-year civil war, which was fought between the once united revolutionary factions; and the final victory of the US-backed future president, Venustiano Carranza, and then the assassination of Zapata and exile of Pancho Villa. See Sanchez, *Becoming Mexican American*.

4. Torres-Rouff, *Before L.A.*

5. Romo, *History of a Barrio*.

6. Mike Davis, *City of Quartz: Excavating the Future in Los Angeles* (New York: Verso, 1990).

7. Sanchez, *Becoming Mexican American*; Romo, *History of a Barrio*.

8. Sanchez, *Becoming Mexican American*; Romo, *History of a Barrio*.

9. The Roosevelt administration later prohibited discrimination in the distribution of welfare relief based on legal status. Nevertheless, LA officials resisted such efforts, trying to deport or repatriate Mexican immigrants to Mexico rather than provide welfare support. Sanchez, *Becoming Mexican American*.

10. MaryEllen Garcia, "Pachucos, Chicano Homeboys, and Gypsy Caló: Transmission of a Speech Style," *Ethnic Studies Review* 32, no. 2 (2009): 24–51.

11. Eduardo Pagan, *Murder at the Sleepy Lagoon: Zoot Suits, Race, and Riot in Wartime Los Angeles* (Chapel Hill: University of North California Press, 2009); Catherine S. Ramirez, *The Woman in the Zoot Suit: Gender, Nationalism, and the Cultural Politics of Memory* (Durham, NC: Duke University Press, 2009).

12. Luis Alvarez, *The Power of the Zoot Suit: Youth Culture and Resistance During World War II* (Berkeley: University of California Press, 2008).

13. Edward Escobar, *Race, Police, and the Making of a Political Identity: Mexican Americans and the Los Angeles Police Department, 1900–1945* (Berkeley: University of California Press, 1999); Alvarez, *The Power of the Zoot Suit*.

14. Kathy Peiss, *Zoot Suit: The Enigmatic Career of an Extreme Style* (Philadelphia: University of Pennsylvania Press, 2011); Pagan, *Murder at the Sleepy Lagoon*.

15. Pagan, *Murder at the Sleepy Lagoon*.

16. Ramirez, *The Woman in the Zoot Suit*; Elizabeth R. Escobedo, "The Pachuca Panic: Sexual and Cultural Battlegrounds in World War II Los Angeles," *Western Historical Quarterly* 38, no. 2 (2007): 133–56.

17. Pagan, *Murder at the Sleepy Lagoon*.

18. Pagan, *Murder at the Sleepy Lagoon*; Peiss, *Zoot Suit*.

19. Ramirez, *The Woman in the Zoot Suit*; Peiss, *Zoot Suit*; Alvarez, *The Power of the Zoot Suit*.

20. Peiss, *Zoot Suit*.

21. Peiss, *Zoot Suit*.

22. Alvarez, *The Power of the Zoot Suit*.

23. It also appears that Mexican Americans had more combat honors than any other ethnic group in proportion to their enlistment. See Raul Morín, *Among the Valiant: Mexican Americans in WW II and Korea* (Los Angeles: Borden, 1963).

24. Alvarez, *The Power of the Zoot Suit*.

25. Alvarez, *The Power of the Zoot Suit*; Pagan, *Murder at the Sleepy Lagoon*.

26. The attacks on minority civilians by military men were not unique to Los Angeles. Reports show that military men in San Diego and Oakland, California, committed violence against minority civilians and tore off the zoot suits of young minority men. Similar incidents occurred in Baltimore, Philadelphia, and Detroit, but mostly by white civilians, who even went after white zoot-suiters. See Alvarez, *The Power of the Zoot Suit*.

27. Pagan, *Murder at the Sleepy Lagoon*; Alvarez, *The Power of the Zoot Suit*.

28. Ramirez, *The Woman in the Zoot Suit*.

29. Torres-Rouff, *Before L.A.*

30. Romo, *History of a Barrio*.

31. Sanchez, *Becoming Mexican American*.

32. Davis, *City of Quartz*; Sanchez, *Becoming Mexican American*; Romo, *History of a Barrio*; Jorge García, "Forjando Ciudad: The Development of a Chicano Political Community in East Los Angeles" (PhD diss., University of California Riverside, 1986).

33. As electric trolleys expanded and automobiles became popular, Jewish, Italian, and Russian residents of Boyle Heights began moving to the outer suburbs, which later created spaces for Mexicans to settle in Boyle Heights in high numbers too. Romo, *History of a Barrio*. See also George Sanchez, "What's Good

for Boyle Heights Is Good for the Jews: Creating Multiculturalism on the Eastside during the 1950s," *American Quarterly* 56, no. 3 (2004): 633–61.

34. See García, "Forjando Ciudad." Mexican families also settled in southern Los Angeles, becoming a sizable proportion of the Watts community. Railroad companies created this initially squalid community in 1902 to house their laborers. Romo, *History of a Barrio.*

35. García, "Forjando Ciudad."

36. According to Rodolfo Acuña, by 1951 the areas east of Indiana Street had started to become officially known as East Los Angeles. Rodolfo F. Acuña, *A Community under Siege: A Chronicle of Chicanos East of the Los Angeles River, 1945–1975*, Chicano Studies Research Center, Monograph 11 (Los Angeles: University of California, 1984).

37. Reynaldo Macías et al., *A Study of Unincorporated East Los Angeles* (Los Angeles: Aztlán Publications, 1973).

38. García, "Forjando Ciudad"; Macías et al., *Unincorporated East Los Angeles.*

39. García, "Forjando Ciudad."

40. Macías et al., *Unincorporated East Los Angeles.*

41. García, "Forjando Ciudad"; Macías et al., *Unincorporated East Los Angeles.*

42. Mike Davis and Jon Wiener, *Set the Night on Fire: L.A. in the Sixties* (New York: Verso, 2020); Dolores D. Bernal, "Chicana School Resistance and Grassroots Leadership: Providing an Alternative History of the 1968 East Los Angeles Blowouts" (PhD diss., University of California, Los Angeles, 1997).

43. Mario T. Garcia and Sal Castro, *Blowout! Sal Castro and the Chicano Struggle for Educational Justice* (Chapel Hill: University of North Carolina Press, 2014); Davis and Wiener, *Set the Night on Fire.*

44. Though they were not as extensive, a few student walkouts also occurred in predominantly African American schools in South Central. See Davis and Wiener, *Set the Night on Fire.*

45. Louis Sahagun, "A Day of Rage in East L.A.," *Los Angeles Times*, August 23, 2020. For a documentary on the protest march and its aftermath, see Thomas Myrdahl, dir., *Chicano Moratorium: A Question of Freedom*, produced by Nikolai Sherbin and Thomas Myrdahl.

46. Acuña, *A Community under Siege*; Edward J. Escobar, "The Dialectics of Repression: The Los Angeles Police Department and the Chicano Movement, 1968–1971," *Journal of American History* 79, no. 4 (1993): 1483–1514; Charles T. Powers and Jeff Perlman, "One Dead, 40 Hurt in East LA Riot," *Los Angeles Times*, August 30, 1970.

47. Acuña, *A Community under Siege*; García, "Forjando Ciudad."

48. Acuña, *A Community under Siege*; García, "Forjando Ciudad."

49. Joan Moore, *Going Down to the Barrio: Homeboys and Homegirls in Change* (Philadelphia: Temple University Press, 1991). See also Joan Moore, *Homeboys: Gangs, Drugs, and Prisons in the Barrios of Los Angeles* (Philadelphia: Temple University Press, 1978).

50. Acuña, *A Community under Siege*.

51. Moore, *Going Down to the Barrio*, 31.

52. Acuña, *A Community under Siege*.

53. Josh Sides, "Straight into Compton: American Dreams, Urban Nightmares, and the Metamorphosis of a Black Suburb," *American Quarterly* 56, no. 3 (2004): 583–605.

54. Acuña, *A Community under Siege*; Michael A. Urquhart and Marillyn A. Hewson, "Unemployment Continued to Rise in 1982 as Recession Deepened," *Monthly Labor Review* 106, no. 2 (1983): 3–12; U.S. Bureau of Labor Statistics https://data.bls.gov/pdq/SurveyOutputServlet (accessed December 31, 2022).

55. Acuña, *A Community under Siege*.

56. Jonathan S. Jones, "Opium Slavery: Civil War Veterans and Opiate Addiction," *Journal of the Civil War Era* 10, no. 2 (2020): 185–212.

57. David T. Courtwright, *Dark Paradise: A History of Opiate Addiction in America* (Boston: Harvard University Press, 2001).

58. Courtwright, *Dark Paradise*.

59. Courtwright, *Dark Paradise*.

60. African Americans increased their heroin use after they migrated to northern cities, such as New York, Philadelphia, and Chicago. See Courtwright, *Dark Paradise*.

61. Courtwright, *Dark Paradise*.

62. Alfred McCoy, *The Politics of Heroin: CIA Complicity in the Drug Trade* (New York: HarperCollins, [1972] 2003).

63. Eric C. Schneider, *Smack: Heroin and the American City* (Philadelphia: University of Pennsylvania Press, 2008).

64. Schneider, *Smack*.

65. Schneider, *Smack*. For a recent discussion of heroin "source" and injecting practices, see Sarah G. Mars et al., "The Textures of Heroin: User Perspectives on 'Black Tar' and Powder Heroin in Two U.S. Cities," *Journal of Psychoactive Drugs* 48, no. 4 (2016): 270–78.

66. Schneider, *Smack*.

67. Schneider, *Smack*.

68. Schneider, *Smack*.

69. Schneider, *Smack.*

70. Moore, *Homeboys.*

71. Moore, *Going Down to the Barrio.*

Chapter Two

1. James Diego Vigil, *The Projects: Gang and Non-Gang Families in East Los Angeles* (Austin: University of Texas Press, 2007); Martín Sánchez Jankowski, *Island in the Street: Gangs and American Urban Society* (Berkeley: University of California Press, 1991).

2. See Philippe Bourgois, "Overachievement in the Underground Economy: The Life Story of a Puerto Rican Stick-up Artist in East Harlem," *Free Inquiry for Creative Sociology* 251 (1997): 23–32; Randol Contreras, *The Stickup Kids: Race, Drugs, Violence, and the American Dream* (Berkeley: University of California Press, 2013).

3. Here Reich builds on Bourdieu's concept of field. In a field, or social arena, people compete with their resources to gain dominance, often using high-value resources in one field to gain dominance in another. Adam Reich, *Hidden Truth: Young Men Navigating Lives In and Out of Juvenile Prison* (New York: Oxford University Press, 2010).

4. As Baird showed in his research on Colombian gangs, marginalized boys often join gangs to emulate role models demonstrating daring, violence, womanizing, and conspicuous consumption. Adam Baird, "Becoming the 'Baddest': Masculine Trajectories of Gang Violence in Medellín," *Journal of Latin American Studies* 50, no. 1 (2017): 183–210.

5. Deborah Levenson, *Adios Niño: The Gangs of Guatemala City and the Politics of Death* (Durham, NC: Duke University Press, 2013).

6. In fact, one of the Sleepy Lagoon defendants, José "Chepe" Ruíz, who had frequent run-ins with the law, had attended the school. See Mitchell R. Stone, *Historic Resources Technical Report for the Proposed Central Middle School No. 9 on the Site of Sunrise Elementary School,* 2821 E. 7th Street Los Angeles, CA (San Buenaventura Research Associates, 2007).

7. For a similar attitude from someone who eventually became a South Central "ghetto star," read Sanyika Shakur, *Monster: The Autobiography of an L.A. Gang Member* (New York: Grove, 1993).

8. Philippe Bourgois and Jeff Schonberg, *Righteous Dopefiend* (Berkeley: University of California Press, 2009).

9. Jack Katz, *The Seductions of Crime: Moral and Sensual Attractions of Doing Evil* (New York: Perseus, 1988); Contreras, *The Stickup Kids*; Richard T. Wright and Scott H. Decker, *Armed Robbers in Action: Stickups and Street Culture* (Boston, MA: Northeastern University Press, 1997).

10. R.W. Connell, *Masculinities* (Berkeley: University of California Press, [1995] 2005).

11. Jeffrey J. Arnett, "Emerging Adulthood: A Theory of Development for the Late Teens through the Twenties," *American Psychologist* 55, no. 5 (2000): 469–80. Sociologist Megan Comfort applies the concept of "emerging adulthood" to the mass incarceration of young minority men that began in the 1990s. Megan Comfort, "It was Basically College to US: Poverty, Prison, and Emerging Adulthood," *Journal of Poverty* 16, no. 3 (2012): 308–22.

12. Hans Toch, "Hypermasculinity and Prison Violence," in *Masculinities and Violence*, ed. Lee H. Bowker (Thousand Oaks, CA: Sage, 1998), 168–78; Marie R. Lindegaard and Sasha Gear, "Violence Makes Safe in South African Prisons: Prison Gangs, Violent Acts, and Victimization among Inmates," *Focaal—Journal of Global and Historical Anthropology* 68 (2014): 35–54; Sasha Gear, "Rules of Engagement: Structuring Sex and Damage in Men's Prisons and Beyond," *Culture, Health, and Sexuality* 7, no. 3 (2005): 195–208; Sasha Gear, "Behind the Bars of Masculinity: Male Rape and Homophobia in and about South African Men's Prisons," *Sexualities* 10, no. 2 (2007): 209–27; Yvonne Jewkes, "Men behind Bars: 'Doing' Masculinity as an Adaptation to Imprisonment," *Men and Masculinities* 8, no. 1 (2005): 44–63.

13. Craig Haney, "The Perversions of Prison: On the Origins of Hypermasculinity and Sexual Violence in Confinement," *American Criminal Law Review* 48 (2011): 121–41.

14. Randall Collins, *Violence: A Micro-Sociological Theory* (Princeton, NJ: Princeton University Press, 2008). For analysis of prisoners that put up a masculine front to avoid victimization, see Nick de Viggiani, "'Don't Mess with Me!' Enacting Masculinities under a Compulsory Prison Regime," in *New Perspectives on Prison Masculinities*, ed. Matthew Maycock and Kate Hunt (New York: Palgrave, 2018), 91–121.

15. Rosemary Ricciardelli. "Unpacking Harm: Correctional Officer Framing of Sex Offenders and Protective Custody," *Howard Journal* 59, no. 4 (2020): 465–83; Rosemary Ricciardelli and Mackenzie Moir, "Stigmatized among the Stigmatized: Sex Offenders in Canadian Penitentiaries," *Canadian Journal of Criminology and Criminal Justice* 5, no. 3 (2013): 353–86.

Chapter Three

1. George M. Camp and Camile G. Camp, *Prison Gangs: Their Extent, Nature, and Impact on Prisons* (Washington, DC: US Department of Justice, Federal Justice Research Program, 1985); Rene Enriquez and Ramon Mendoza, *The Mexican Mafia Encyclopedia* (Spartanburg, SC: Police and Fire Publishing, 2021); Geoffrey Hunt et al., "Changes in Prison Culture: Prison Gangs and the Case of the 'Pepsi Generation,'" *Social Problems* 40, no. 3 (1993): 398–409; David Skarbek, *The Social Order of the Underworld: How Prison Gangs Govern the American Penal System* (New York: Oxford University Press, 2014).

2. Enriquez and Mendoza, *The Mexican Mafia Encyclopedia*.

3. Robert Weide, "The Invisible Hand of the State: A Critical Historical Analysis of Prison Gangs in California," *Prison Journal* 100, no. 3 (2020): 312–31.

4. Chris Blatchford, *The Black Hand: The Bloody Rise and Redemption of "Boxer" Enriquez, A Mexican Mob Killer* (New York: HarperCollins, 2008).

5. Ramon A. Mendoza, *Mexican Mafia: The Gang of Gangs—From Altar Boy to Hitman* (Spartanburg, SC: Police and Fire Publishing, 2005); Robert Morrill, *The Mexican Mafia: The Story* (San Antonio, TX: Munguia Printers, 2005); Weide, "The Invisible Hand of the State."

6. Enriquez and Mendoza, *The Mexican Mafia Encyclopedia*.

7. Blatchford, *The Black Hand*.

8. Barbara Ransby, *Ella Baker and the Black Freedom Movement: A Democratic Vision* (Durham: University of North Carolina Press, 2005); David J. Garrow, *Bearing the Cross: Martin Luther King, Jr., and the Southern Christian Leadership Conference* (New York: HarperCollins, 1986).

9. Peniel E. Joseph, ed., *The Black Power Movement: Rethinking the Civil Rights–Black Power Era* (New York: Routledge, 2006); Peniel E. Joseph, *Waiting 'til the Midnight Hour: A Narrative History of Black Power in America* (New York: Holt, 2007).

10. Ian Haney López, *Racism on Trial: The Chicano Fight for Justice* (Cambridge, MA: Harvard University Press, 2003); Yolanda Alaniz and Megan Cornish, *Viva La Raza: A History of Chicano Identity and Resistance* (Seattle, WA: Red Letter Press, 2008).

11. Robert Weide, *Divide and Conquer: Race, Gangs, Identity, and Conflict* (Philadelphia: Temple University Press, 2022).

12. Azadeh Zohrabi, "Resistance and Repression: The Black Guerrilla Family in Context," *Hastings Race and Poverty Law Journal* 9, no. 1 (2012): 167–90.

13. Weide, *Divide and Conquer*.

14. Skarbek, *The Social Order of the Underworld*; Rebecca Trammell, *Enforcing the Convict Code: Violence and Prison Culture* (Boulder, CO: Lynne Reiner, 2012).

15. Hunt et al., "Changes in Prison Culture."

16. Skarbek, *The Social Order of the Underworld*.

17. Weide, "The Invisible Hand of the State."

18. Weide, "The Invisible Hand of the State."

19. Robert Weide, "Structural Disorganization: Can Prison Gangs Mitigate Serious Violence in Carceral Institutions?," *Critical Criminology* 30, no. 1 (2022): 1–20.

20. Patrick Lopez-Aguado, *Stick Together and Come Back Home: Racial Sorting and the Spillover of Carceral Identity* (Berkeley: University of California Press, 2018).

21. Julia Reynolds, *Blood in the Fields: Ten Years Inside California's Nuestra Familia Gang* (Chicago: Chicago Review Press, 2014).

22. Reynolds, *Blood in the Fields*.

23. Reynolds, *Blood in the Fields*.

24. Reynolds, *Blood in the Fields*.

25. Reynolds, *Blood in the Fields*; Enriquez and Mendoza, *The Mexican Mafia Encyclopedia*.

26. Enriquez and Mendoza, *The Mexican Mafia Encyclopedia*; Reynolds, *Blood in the Fields*.

27. Max Felker-Kantor, *Policing Los Angeles: Race, Resistance, and the Rise of the LAPD* (Durham: University of North Carolina Press, 2018).

28. *New York Times*, "The 1990 Census: California," February 26, 1991, www.nytimes.com/1991/02/26/us/the-1990-census-california.html; Amanda Bailey and Joseph M. Hayes, "California Counts: Population Trends and Profile," *Public Policy Institute of California* 8, no. 1 (2006): 1–27.

29. Weide, "The Invisible Hand of the State."

30. Blatchford, *The Black Hand*; Enriquez and Mendoza, *The Mexican Mafia Encyclopedia*.

31. Blatchford, *The Black Hand*; Enriquez and Mendoza, *The Mexican Mafia Encyclopedia*.

32. Weide, "Structural Disorganization."

33. Weide, "Structural Disorganization"; Weide, "The Invisible Hand of the State."

34. Hannah Arendt, *The Origins of Totalitarianism* (New York: Harcourt, [1951] 1973); Raymond Aron, *Democracy and Totalitarianism* (New York: Praeger, 1968).

35. StreetTV, "Lowell Street Gets Put on the Greenlight," YouTube video, www.youtube.com/watch?v=U11iWleNbDE&list=PLQwhRJvmotyF1njuco1H1r mzAFgVXYMXM&index=4.

36. Enriquez and Mendoza, *The Mexican Mafia Encyclopedia*.

37. Jesse Katz and Robert J. Lopez, "Mexican Mafia's Impact on Gangs Questioned," *Los Angeles Times*, September 28, 1993; Kathryn Wexler, "East L.A. Gangs' Uneasy Peace Hangs on a Wish and Prayer," *Washington Post*, March 29, 1995.

38. Randall Collins, *Violence: A Micro-Sociological Theory* (Princeton, NJ: Princeton University Press, 2008).

39. Collins, *Violence*.

40. Randall Collins, *Interaction Ritual Chains* (Princeton, NJ: Princeton University Press, 2005); Émile Durkheim, *The Elementary Forms of Religious Life* (New York: Oxford University Press, [1912] 2001).

41. Donald Liebenson, "Robin Leach Defined the Wealth-Obsessed 80s, and We Never Got Over It," *Vanity Fair* August 28, 2018.

Chapter Four

1. Gastón Espinosa, *Latino Pentecostals in America: Faith and Politics in Action* (Cambridge, MA: Harvard University Press, 2014).

2. Joel Robbins, "The Obvious Aspects of Pentecostalism: Ritual and Pentecostal Globalization," in *Practicing the Faith: The Ritual Life of Pentecostal-Charismatic Christians*, ed. Martin Lindhardt (New York: Berghahn Books, 2011).

3. Robbins, "The Obvious Aspects of Pentecostalism."

4. Émile Durkheim, *The Elementary Forms of Religious Life* (New York: Oxford University Press, [1912] 2001).

5. Durkheim, *The Elementary Forms of Religious Life*, 162–63.

6. Randall Collins, *Interaction Ritual Chains* (Princeton, NJ: Princeton University Press, 2005).

7. Joel Robbins uses Randall Collins's theory of interaction rituals to explain the quick global expansion of Pentecostalism. He argues that the attractiveness of Pentecostalism comes from its requirement of many meetings, services, and activities. This then increases the number rituals in which participants feel emotional entrainment in the presence of others. See Robbins, "The Obvious Aspects of Pentecostalism."

8. Robert Brenneman, *Homies and Hermanos: God and Gangs in Central America* (New York: Oxford University Press, 2012).

9. In his research on evangelical former gang members, Edward Flores also found that pastors often played music and made statements to raise enthusiasm among congregants, sometimes making them cry. See Edward Flores, *God's Gangs: Barrio Ministry, Masculinity, and Gang Recovery* (New York: New York University Press, 2014). Martin Lindhardt also found that a preacher's tone of voice and sudden interruptions to praise God during several parts of a sermon raised the emotion of congregants. See Martin Lindhardt, "When God Interferes: Ritual, Empowerment, and Divine Presence in Chilean Pentecostalism," in *Practicing the Faith: The Ritual Life of Pentecostal-Charismatic Christians*, ed. Martin Lindhardt (New York: Berghahn Books, 2011).

10. Flores, *God's Gang*; Edward Flores, "I Am Somebody: Barrio Pentecostalism and Gendered Acculturation among Chicano Ex-Gang Members," *Ethnic and Racial Studies* 32, no. 6 (2009): 996–1016.

11. Jessie Gutgsell, "The Gift of Tears: Weeping in the Religious Imagination of Western Medieval Christianity," *Anglican Theological Review* 97, no. 2 (2015): 239–53.

12. Gutgsell, "The Gift of Tears."

13. Kevin L. O'Neill, *Secure the Soul: Christian Piety and Gang Prevention in Guatemala* (Berkeley: University of California Press, 2015); Kevin L. O'Neill, "Delinquent Realities: Christianity, Formality, and Security in the Americas," *American Quarterly* 63, no. 2 (2011): 337–65; Kevin L. O'Neill, *Hunted: Predation and Pentecostalism in Guatemala* (Chicago: University of Chicago Press, 2019).

Chapter Five

1. For an analysis of a similar restroom phenomenon, see Mitchell Duneier, *Sidewalk* (New York: Farrar, Straus and Giroux, 1999).

2. Ronald F. Levant and Shana Pryor, *The Tough Standard: The Hard Truths about Masculinity and Violence* (New York: Oxford University Press, 2020).

3. The Southeast Area Social Services Funding Authority was created in 1979 to provide senior services, and then, later, workforce services. See www.sassfa.org/about-us/.

4. Tatiana Flores, "Latinidad Is Cancelled: Confronting an Anti-Black Construct," *Latin America and Latinx Visual Culture* 3, no. 3 (2021): 58–79; José F. Buscaglia-Salgado, "Race and the Constitutive Inequality of Modern/Colonial Condition," in *Critical Terms in Caribbean and Latin American Thought: Historical and Institutional Trajectories*, ed. Yolanda Martínez-San Miguel, Ben Sifuentes-Jáuregui, and Marisa Belausteguigoitia (New York: Palgrave Macmillan, 2016);

Christina A. Sue, *Land of the Cosmic Race: Race Mixture, Racism, and Blackness in Mexico* (New York: Oxford University Press, 2013).

5. Randall Collins, *Violence: A Micro-Sociological Theory* (Princeton, NJ: Princeton University Press, 2008).

6. See Elijah Anderson, *Code of the Street: Decency, Violence, and the Moral Life of the Inner City* (New York: W. W. Norton, 1999).

7. Collins, *Violence*.

8. Mike Davis, *City of Quartz: Excavating the Future in Los Angeles* (New York: Verso, 1990).

9. Alex Alonso, "Out of the Void: Street Gangs in Black Los Angeles," in *Black Los Angeles: American Dreams and Racial Realities*, ed. Darnell Hunt and Ana-Christina Ramón (New York: New York University Press, 2010).

10. Paul Robinson, "Race, Space and the Evolution of Black Los Angeles," in *Black Los Angeles: American Dreams and Racial Realities*, ed. Darnell Hunt and Ana-Christina Ramón (New York: New York University Press, 2010); Josh Sides, "Straight into Compton: American Dreams, Urban Nightmares, and the Metamorphosis of a Black Suburb," *American Quarterly* 56, no. 3 (2004): 583–605.

11. Alonso, "Out of the Void."

12. Joan Moore, *Going Down to the Barrio: Homeboys and Homegirls in Change* (Philadelphia: Temple University Press, 1991).

13. Robert Garot, "Gang Banging as Edgework," *Kriminologisches Journal* 44, no. 3 (2012): 167–81; Robert Garot, *Who You Claim: Performing Gang Identity in School and on the Streets* (New York: New York University Press, 2010); Robert Garot, "Where You From!," *Journal of Contemporary Ethnography* 36, no. 1 (2007): 50–84.

14. Like Garot, I found in my previous research in South Central and Compton that this response stripped gang members of a spatial identity based on race. See Randol Contreras, "From Nowhere: Space, Race, and Time in How Young Minority Men Understand Encounters with Gangs," *Qualitative Sociology* 41, no. 2 (2018): 263–80.

15. For a thorough discussion of gang-related spatial identities, see Patrick Lopez-Aguado and Michael Walker, "'I Don't Bang: I'm Just a Blood': Situating Gang Identities in Their Proper Place," *Theoretical Criminology* 25, no. 1 (2021): 107–26.

16. Michael Walker, *Indefinite: Doing Time in Jail* (New York: Oxford University Press, 2022).

17. Pierre Bourdieu, *The Field of Cultural Production* (New York: Columbia University Press, 1993); Pierre Bourdieu and Jean Claude Passerson, *Reproduc-*

tion in Education, Society, and Culture (London: Sage, 1990); Pierre Bourdieu, *Distinction: A Social Critique of the Judgment of Taste* (Cambridge, MA: Harvard University Press, 1984).

18. Philippe Bourgois and Jeff Schonberg, *Righteous Dopefiend* (Berkeley: University of California Press, 2009).

19. There appears to be a relationship between high opioid intake and sugar cravings. See David J. Mysels and Maria A. Sullivan, "The Relationship Between Opioid and Sugar Intake: Review of Evidence and Clinical Applications," *Journal of Opioid Management* 6, no. 6 (2010): 445–52.

20. For similar phenomena, see Stuart Forest and Reuben J. Miller, "The Prisonized Old Head: Intergenerational Socialization and the Fusion of Ghetto and Prison Culture," *Journal of Contemporary Ethnography* 46, no. 6 (2017): 673–98.

21. For an analysis of caring communities among heroin users, see Bourgois and Schonberg, *Righteous Dopefiend*.

Chapter Six

1. Leo R. Chavez, *The Latino Threat: Constructing Immigrants, Citizens, and the Nation* (Stanford, CA: Stanford University Press, 2008).

2. Chavez, *The Latino Threat*.

3. Chavez, *The Latino Threat*; Peter Brimelow, *Alien Nation: Common Sense about America's Immigration Disaster* (New York: Random House, 1995); Georgie Ann Geyer, *Americans No More* (New York: Atlantic Monthly Press, 1996); Arthur M. Schlesinger, *The Disuniting of America* (New York: W. W. Norton, 1992).

4. Chavez, *The Latino Threat*; Patrick J. Buchanan, *The Death of the West: How Dying Populations and Immigrant Invasions Imperil Our Country and Civilization* (New York: St. Martin's Press, 2002); Patrick J. Buchanan, *State of Emergency: The Third World Invasion and the Conquest of America* (New York: St. Martin's Press, 2006); Patrick J. Buchanan, *Suicide of a Superpower: Will America Survive to 2025?* (New York: St. Martin's Press, 2011); Victor D. Hanson, *Mexifornia: A State of Unbecoming* (San Francisco: Encounter Books, 2003).

5. Paulo Freire, *Pedagogy of the Oppressed* (New York: Continuum, [1970] 1993).

6. Michèle Lamont, *The Dignity of Working Men: Morality and the Boundaries of Race, Class, and Immigration* (Cambridge, MA: Harvard University Press, 2000); Michèle Lamont and Virág Molnár, "The Study of Boundaries in the Social Sciences," *Annual Review of Sociology* 28, no. 1 (2002): 167–95.

7. Gresham Sykes and David Matza, "Techniques of Neutralization: A Theory of Delinquency," *American Sociological Review* 22, no. 6 (1957): 664–70.

8. Irene I. Vega, "Conservative Rationales, Racial Boundaries: A Case Study of Restrictionist Mexican Americans," *American Behavioral Scientist* 58, no. 13 (2014): 1764–83.

9. Ulrike E. Stockhausen, *The Strangers in Our Midst: American Evangelicals and Immigration from the Cold War to the Twenty-First Century* (New York: Oxford University Press, 2021).

10. Stockhausen, *The Strangers in Our Midst*.

11. Stockhausen, *The Strangers in Our Midst*.

12. Jim Wallis, *Christ in Crisis: Why We Need to Reclaim Jesus* (New York: HarperCollins, 2019).

13. Stockhausen, *The Strangers in Our Midst*; Gastón Espinosa, *Latino Pentecostals in America: Faith and Politics in Action* (Cambridge, MA: Harvard University Press, 2014).

14. For a study that shows how US states with large immigrant populations have lower rates of driving while under the influence, see Alex Nowrasteh and Michael Howard, "Drunk Driving Deaths and Illegal Immigration," Immigration Research and Policy Brief No. 20, Cato Institute, July 6, 2021.

15. Robert Suro, "A Report on the Media and the Immigration Debate" (Brookings Institute, 2012); USA Green Card Center, "Bill O'Reilly and Geraldo Rivera Angry Fight Immigration," YouTube video, www.youtube.com/watch?v=Z3U9ENaTPLY.

16. Leo Löwenthal and Norbert Guterman, *Prophets of Deceit: A Study of the Techniques of the American Agitator* (New York: Harper, 1949).

17. Richard Wolin, "Our Prophet of Deceit: WWII-Era Social Scientists Explained Trump's Appeal," *Chronicle of Higher Education*, October 30, 2016, www.chronicle.com/article/our-prophet-of-deceit/.

18. Jean Guerrero, *Hatemonger: Stephen Miller, Donald Trump, and the White Nationalist Agenda* (New York: HarperCollins, 2020).

19. Guerrero, *Hatemonger*.

20. Russell Muirhead and Nancy L. Rosenblum, *A Lot of People Are Saying: The New Conspiracism and the Assault on Democracy* (Princeton, NJ: Princeton University Press, 2020).

21. Guerrero, *Hatemonger*.

22. Panayota Gounari, "Authoritarianism, Discourse, and Social Media: Trump as the American Agitator," in *Critical Theory and Authoritarian Populism*, ed. Jeremiah Morelock (London: University of Westminster Press, 2018), 207–27.

23. Gounari, "Authoritarianism, Discourse, and Social Media."

24. Arlie Hochschild, *Strangers in Their Own Land: Anger and Mourning on the American Right* (New York: New Press, 2016).

25. For an interesting analysis of how White Christian university students use techniques of neutralization to rationalize their support of Trump despite allegations of his sexual misconduct, see Madison Adams, "Supporting the President in a #NotMyPresident Context: Experiences of College-Aged Trump Supporters at a Southern University," *Qualitative Sociology Review* 17, no. 4 (2021): 82–102.

26. For how Trump makes this happen, see Guerrero, *Hatemonger*.

27. Amber Philips, "'They're Rapists.' President Trump's Campaign Launch Speech Two Years Later, Annotated," *Washington Post*, June 16, 2017.

28. Walter Ewing, Daniel Martinez, and Rubén Rumbaut, *The Criminalization of Immigration in the United States* (Washington, D.C.: American Immigration Council, 2015); Michael T. Light, Jingying He, and Jason P. Robey, "Comparing Crime Rates between Undocumented Immigrants, Legal Immigrants, and Native-born US Citizens in Texas," *Proceedings of the National Academy of Sciences of the United States of America* 117, no. 51 (2020): 32340–47.

29. Tim Wadsworth, "Is Immigration Responsible for the Crime Drop? An Assessment of the Influence of Immigration on Changes in Violent Crime between 1990 and 2000," *Social Science Quarterly* 91, no. 2 (2010): 531–53; Robert Adelman, Lesley W. Reid, Gail Markle, Saskia Weiss, and Charles Jaret, "Urban Crime Rates and the Changing Face of Immigration: Evidence across Four Decades," *Journal of Ethnicity in Criminal Justice* 15, no. 1 (2017): 52–77.

30. C-SPAN, "President Trump Walks across Lafayette Park to St. John's Church," YouTube video, www.youtube.com/watch?v=5ShnqmiKLE8.

31. *New York Times*, "Trump's Fraud Claims Died in Court, but the Myth of Stolen Elections Lives On," October 11, 2021.

32. Carleen Basler, "White Dreams and Red Votes: Mexican Americans and the Lure of Inclusion in the Republican Party," *Ethnic and Racial Studies* 31, no. 1 (2008): 123–66; Herbert J. Gans, "'Whitening' and the Changing American Racial Hierarchy," *Du Bois Review: Social Science Research on Race* 9, no. 2 (2012): 267–79; Jonathan Warren and France Winddance Twine, "White Americans, the New Minority? Non-Blacks and the Ever-expanding Boundaries of Whiteness," *Journal of Black Studies* 28, no. 2 (1997): 200–218.

33. Deyanira Rojas-Sosa, "The Denial of Racism in Latina/o Students' Narratives about Discrimination in the Classroom," *Discourse & Society* 27, no. 1 (2016): 69–94; Rudy Alamillo, "Hispanics Para Trump? Denial of Racism and Hispanic Support for Trump," *Du Bois Review* 16, no. 2 (2019): 457–87. On

color-blind ideology, see Eduardo Bonilla-Silva, *Racism without Racists: Color-Blind Racism and the Persistence of Racial Inequality in America* (New York: Rowman and Littlefield, 2009).

Chapter Seven

1. Tanya K. Hernández, *Racial Innocence: Unmaking Latino Anti-Black Bias and the Struggle for Equality* (Boston: Beacon Press, 2022).
2. Tatiana Flores, "Latinidad Is Cancelled: Confronting an Anti-Black Construct," *Latin American and Latinx Visual Culture* 3, no. 3 (2021): 58–79.
3. Christina A. Sue, *Land of the Cosmic Race: Race Mixture, Racism, and Blackness in Mexico* (New York: Oxford University Press, 2013).
4. Flores, "Latinidad Is Cancelled."
5. Sue, *Land of the Cosmic Race.*
6. David Torres-Rouff, *Before L.A.: Race, Space, and Municipal Power in Los Angeles, 1781–1894* (New Haven, CT: Yale University Press, 2013).
7. Hernández, *Racial Innocence*; Ian Haney López, "Protest, Repression, and Race: Legal Violence and the Chicano Movement," *University of Pennsylvania Law Review* 150 (2001): 205–44.
8. Haney López, "Protest, Repression, and Race."
9. Haney López, "Protest, Repression, and Race."
10. Philippe Bourgois and Jeff Schonberg, "Intimate Apartheid: Ethnic Dimensions of Habitus Among Homeless Heroin Injectors," *Ethnography* 8, no. 1 (2007): 7–31.
11. For an analysis of Black Mexican gang members, see Robert Weide, *Divide and Conquer: Race, Gangs, Identity, and Conflict* (Philadelphia: Temple University Press, 2022).
12. Janelle L. Wilson, "Here and Now, There and Then: Nostalgia as a Time and Space Phenomenon," *Symbolic Interaction* 38, no. 4 (2015): 478–92.
13. Fred Davis, *Yearning for Yesterday: A Sociology of Nostalgia* (New York: Free Press, 1979); Wilson, "Here and Now, There and Then."
14. Davis, *Yearning for Yesterday*; Wilson, "Here and Now, There and Then."
15. Svetlana Boym *The Future of Nostalgia* (New York: Basic Books, 2001).

Chapter Eight

1. Émile Durkheim, *Suicide: A Study in Sociology* (New York: Free Press, 1997).
2. Ashwin A. Kotwal et al., "Social Isolation and Loneliness among San Fran-

cisco Bay Area Older Adults during the COVID-19 Shelter-in-Place Orders," *Journal of American Geriatric Society* 69, no. 1 (2021): 20–29.

3. Durkheim, *Suicide*; Anne-Véronique Dürst et al., "Fighting Social Isolation in Times of Pandemic COVID-19: The Role of Video Calls for Older Hospitalized Patients," *Aging Clinical and Experimental Research* 34, no. 9 (2022): 2245–53.

Bibliography

Acuña, Rodolfo F. 1984. *A Community under Siege: A Chronicle of Chicanos East of the Los Angeles River,* 1945–1975. Chicano Studies Research Center, Monograph 11. Los Angeles: University of California.

Adams, Madison. 2021. "Supporting the President in a #NotMyPresident Context: Experiences of College-Aged Trump Supporters at a Southern University." *Qualitative Sociology Review* 17(4): 82–102.

Adelman, Robert, Lesley W. Reid, Gail Markle, Saskia Weiss, and Charles Jaret. 2017. "Urban Crime Rates and the Changing Face of Immigration: Evidence across Four Decades." *Journal of Ethnicity in Criminal Justice* 15(1): 52–77.

Alamillo, Rudy. 2019. "Hispanics Para Trump? Denial of Racism and Hispanic Support for Trump." *Du Bois Review* 16(2): 457–487.

Alaniz, Yolanda, and Megan Cornish. 2008. *Viva La Raza: A History of Chicano Identity and Resistance.* Seattle, WA: Red Letter Press.

Alonso, Alex. 2010. "Out of the Void: Street Gangs in Black Los Angeles." In *Black Los Angeles: American Dreams and Racial Realities,* edited by Darnell Hunt and Ana-Christina Ramón. New York: New York University Press.

Alvarez, Luis. 2008. *The Power of the Zoot Suit: Youth Culture and Resistance During World War II.* Berkeley: University of California Press.

Anderson, Elijah. 1999. *Code of the Street: Decency, Violence, and the Moral Life of the Inner City.* New York: W. W. Norton.

Arendt, Hannah. [1951] 1973. *The Origins of Totalitarianism.* New York: Harcourt.

Arnett, Jeffrey J. 2000. "Emerging Adulthood: A Theory of Development for the Late Teens through the Twenties." *American Psychologist* 55(5): 469–80.

Aron, Raymond. 1968. *Democracy and Totalitarianism*. New York: Praeger.

Bailey, Amanda, and Joseph M. Hayes. 2006. "California Counts: Population Trends and Profiles." *Public Policy Institute of California* 8(1): 1–27.

Baird, Adam. 2017. "Becoming the 'Baddest': Masculine Trajectories of Gang Violence in Medellín." *Journal of Latin American Studies* 50(1): 183–210.

Basler, Carleen. 2008. "White Dreams and Red Votes: Mexican Americans and the Lure of Inclusion in the Republican Party." *Ethnic and Racial Studies* 31(1): 123–66.

Bernal, Dolores D. 1997. "Chicana School Resistance and Grassroots Leadership: Providing an Alternative History of the 1968 East Los Angeles Blowouts." PhD diss., University of California, Los Angeles.

Billingham, Luke, and Keir Irwin-Rogers. 2021. "The Terrifying Abyss of Insignificance: Marginalisation, Mattering and Violence Between Young People." *Oñati Socio-Legal Series* 11(5): 1222–49.

———. 2022. *Against Youth Violence: A Social Harm Perspective*. Bristol, UK: Bristol University Press.

Blatchford, Chris. 2008. *The Black Hand: The Bloody Rise and Redemption of "Boxer" Enriquez, A Mexican Mob Killer*. New York: HarperCollins.

Bonilla-Silva, Eduardo. 2009. *Racism without Racists: Color-Blind Racism and the Persistence of Racial Inequality in America*. 3rd ed. New York: Rowman and Littlefield.

Bourdieu, Pierre. 1984. *Distinction: A Social Critique of the Judgment of Taste*. Cambridge, MA: Harvard University Press.

———. 1993. *The Field of Cultural Production*. New York: Columbia University Press.

Bourdieu, Pierre, and Jean Claude Passerson. 1990. *Reproduction in Education, Society, and Culture*. London: Sage.

Bourgois, Philippe. [1995] 2003. *In Search of Respect: Selling Crack in El Barrio*. 2nd ed. Cambridge: Cambridge University Press.

———. 1997. "Overachievement in the Underground Economy: The Life Story of a Puerto Rican Stick-up Artist in East Harlem." *Free Inquiry for Creative Sociology* 251: 23–32

Bourgois, Philippe, and Jeff Schonberg. 2007. "Intimate Apartheid: Ethnic Dimensions of Habitus among Homeless Heroin Injectors." *Ethnography* 8(1): 7–31.

———. 2009. *Righteous Dopefiend*. Berkeley: University of California Press.

Boym, Svetlana. 2001. *The Future of Nostalgia*. New York: Basic Books.

Brenneman, Robert. 2012. *Homies and Hermanos: God and Gangs in Central America*. New York: Oxford University Press.

Brimelow, Peter. 1995. *Alien Nation: Common Sense about America's Immigration Disaster*. New York: Random House.

Brotherton, David. 2015. *Youth Street Gangs*. New York: Routledge.

Buchanan, Patrick J. 2002. *The Death of the West: How Dying Populations and Immigrant Invasions Imperil Our Country and Civilization*. New York: St. Martin's Press.

———. 2006. *State of Emergency: The Third World Invasion and the Conquest of America*. New York: St. Martin's Press.

———. 2011. *Suicide of a Superpower: Will America Survive to 2025?* New York: St. Martin's Press.

Buscaglia-Salgado, José F. 2016. "Race and the Constitutive Inequality of the Modern/Colonial Condition." In *Critical Terms in Caribbean and Latin American Thought: Historical and Institutional Trajectories*, edited by Yolanda Martínez-San Miguel, Ben Sifuentes-Jáuregui, and Marisa Belausteguigoitia. New York: Palgrave Macmillan.

Camp, George M., and Camile G. Camp. 1985. *Prison Gangs: Their Extent, Nature, and Impact on Prisons*. Washington, DC: US Department of Justice, Federal Justice Research Program.

Chavez, Leo R. 2008. *The Latino Threat: Constructing Immigrants, Citizens, and the Nation*. Stanford, CA: Stanford University Press.

Collins, Patricia Hill. [1990] 2008. *Black Feminist Thought*. 2nd ed. New York: Routledge.

Collins, Randall. 2005. *Interaction Ritual Chains*. Princeton, NJ: Princeton University Press.

———. 2008. *Violence: A Micro-Sociological Theory*. Princeton, NJ: Princeton University Press.

Comfort, Megan. 2012. "It Was Basically College to US: Poverty, Prison, and Emerging Adulthood." *Journal of Poverty* 16(3): 308–22.

Connell, R. W. [1995] 2005. *Masculinities*. 2nd ed. Berkeley: University of California Press.

Connell, R. W., and James W. Messerschmidt. 2005. "Hegemonic Masculinity: Rethinking the Concept." *Gender & Society* 19(6): 829–59.

Contreras, Randol. 2013. *The Stickup Kids: Race, Drugs, Violence, and the American Dream*. Berkeley: University of California Press.

———. 2018. "From Nowhere: Space, Race, and Time in How Young Minority Men Understand Encounters with Gangs." *Qualitative Sociology* 41(2): 263–80.

———. 2019. "The Broken Ethnography: Lessons from an Almost Hero."
  Qualitative Sociology 42(2): 161-79.

———. 2019. "Transparency and Unmasking Issues in Ethnographic Research:
  Methodological Considerations." *Sociological Forum* 34(2): 293-312.

Courtwright, David T. 2001. *Dark Paradise: A History of Opiate Addiction in
  America.* Boston, MA: Harvard University Press.

C-SPAN. 2020. "President Trump Walks across Lafayette Park to St. John's
  Church." YouTube video, www.youtube.com/watch?v=5ShnqmiKLE8.

Davis, Fred. 1979. *Yearning for Yesterday: A Sociology of Nostalgia.* New York:
  Free Press.

Davis, Mike. 1990. *City of Quartz: Excavating the Future in Los Angeles.* New York:
  Verso.

Davis, Mike, and Jon Wiener. 2020. *Set the Night on Fire: L.A. in the Sixties.* New
  York: Verso.

Decker, Scott, and Barrik Van Winkle. 1996. *Life in the Gang.* New York:
  Cambridge University Press.

Desmond, Matthew. 2016. *Evicted.* New York: Crown.

———. 2018. "'Don't Mess with Me!' Enacting Masculinities under a Compulsory Prison Regime." In *New Perspectives on Prison Masculinities*, edited by
  Matthew Maycock and Kate Hunt, 91-121. New York: Palgrave.

Duneier, Mitchell. 1999. *Sidewalk.* New York: Farrar, Straus and Giroux.

Durkheim, Émile. [1912] 2001. *The Elementary Forms of Religious Life.* New York:
  Oxford University Press.

———. 1997. *Suicide: A Study in Sociology.* New York: Free Press.

Dürst, Anne-Véronique, Christophe E. Graf, Carmelinda Ruggiero, Dina Zekry,
  Virginia Boccardi, Lauretta Monney, Isaline Joss, Karine Vuilloud, Giulia
  Vespignani, Wanda Bosshard, Patrizia Mecocci, Christophe J. Bula, and
  Patrizia D'Amelio. 2022. "Fighting Social Isolation in Times of Pandemic
  COVID-19: The Role of Video Calls for Older Hospitalized Patients." *Aging
  Clinical and Experimental Research* 34(9): 2245-53.

Enriquez, Rene, and Ramon Mendoza. 2021. *The Mexican Mafia Encyclopedia.*
  2nd ed. Spartanburg, SC: Police and Fire Publishing.

Escobar, Edward J. 1993. "The Dialectics of Repression: The Los Angeles Police
  Department and the Chicano Movement, 1968-1971." *Journal of American
  History* 79(4): 1483-1514.

———. 1999. *Race, Police, and the Making of a Political Identity: Mexican Americans and the Los Angeles Police Department, 1900-1945.* Berkeley: University
  of California Press.

Escobedo, Elizabeth R. 2007. "The Pachuca Panic: Sexual and Cultural Battlegrounds in World War II Los Angeles." *Western Historical Quarterly* 38(2): 133–56.

Espinosa, Gastón. 2014. *Latino Pentecostals in America: Faith and Politics in Action.* Cambridge, MA: Harvard University Press.

Ewing, Walter, Daniel Martinez, and Rubén Rumbaut. 2015. *The Criminalization of Immigration in the United States.* Washington, D.C.: American Immigration Council.

Felker-Kantor, Max. 2018. *Policing Los Angeles: Race, Resistance, and the Rise of the LAPD.* Durham: University of North Carolina Press.

Flores, Edward. 2009. "I Am Somebody: Barrio Pentecostalism and Gendered Acculturation among Chicano Ex-Gang Members." *Ethnic and Racial Studies* 32(6): 996–1016.

———. 2014. *God's Gangs: Barrio Ministry, Masculinity, and Gang Recovery.* New York: New York University Press.

Flores, Tatiana. 2021. "Latinidad Is Cancelled: Confronting an Anti-Black Construct." *Latin America and Latinx Visual Culture* 3(3): 58–79.

Freire, Paulo. [1970] 1993. *Pedagogy of the Oppressed.* New York: Continuum.

Gans, Herbert J. 2012. "'Whitening' and the Changing American Racial Hierarchy." *Du Bois Review: Social Science Research on Race* 9(2): 267–79.

García, Jorge. 1986. "Forjando Ciudad: The Development of a Chicano Political Community in East Los Angeles." PhD diss., University of California Riverside.

Garcia, Mario T., and Sal Castro. 2014. *Blowout! Sal Castro and the Chicano Struggle for Educational Justice.* Chapel Hill University of North Carolina Press.

Garcia, MaryEllen. 2009. "Pachucos, Chicano Homeboys, and Gypsy Caló: Transmission of a Speech Style." *Ethnic Studies Review* 32(2): 24–51.

Garot, Robert. 2007. "Where You From!" *Journal of Contemporary Ethnography* 36(1): 50–84.

———. 2010. *Who You Claim: Performing Gang Identity in School and on the Streets.* New York: New York University Press.

———. 2012. "Gang Banging as Edgework." *Kriminologisches Journal* 44(3): 167–81.

Garrow, David J. 1986. *Bearing the Cross: Martin Luther King, Jr., and the Southern Christian Leadership Conference.* New York: HarperCollins.

Gear, Sasha. 2005. "Rules of Engagement: Structuring Sex and Damage in Men's Prisons and Beyond." *Culture, Health, and Sexuality* 7(3): 195–208.

———. 2007. "Behind the Bars of Masculinity: Male Rape and Homophobia in and about South African Men's Prisons." *Sexualities* 10(2): 209–27.

Geyer, Georgie Ann. 1996. *Americans No More*. New York: Atlantic Monthly Press.

———. 2014. "Race in California's Prison Fire Camps for Men: Prison Politics, Space, and the Racialization of Everyday Life." *American Journal of Sociology* 120(2): 352–94.

Gounari, Panayota. 2018. "Authoritarianism, Discourse, and Social Media: Trump as the American Agitator." In *Critical Theory and Authoritarian Populism*, edited by Jeremiah Morelock, 207–27. London: University of Westminster Press.

Gowan, Teresa. 2010. *Hobos, Hustlers, and Backsliders: Homeless in San Francisco*. Minneapolis: University of Minnesota Press.

Guerrero, Jean. 2020. *Hatemonger: Stephen Miller, Donald Trump, and the White Nationalist Agenda*. New York: HarperCollins.

Gutgsell, Jessie. 2015. "The Gift of Tears: Weeping in the Religious Imagination of Western Medieval Christianity." *Anglican Theological Review* 97(2): 239–53.

Hagedorn, John. 1998. *People and Folks: Gangs, Crime, and the Underclass in a Rustbelt City*. 2nd ed. Chicago: Lakeview Press.

Haney, Craig. 2011. "The Perversions of Prison: On the Origins of Hypermasculinity and Sexual Violence in Confinement." *American Criminal Law Review* 48: 121–41.

Haney López, Ian. 2001. "Protest, Repression, and Race: Legal Violence and the Chicano Movement." *University of Pennsylvania Law Review* 150: 205–44.

———. 2003. *Racism on Trial: The Chicano Fight for Justice*. Cambridge, MA: Harvard University Press.

Hanson, Rebecca, and Patricia Richards. 2019. *Harassed: Gender, Bodies, and Ethnographic Research*. Berkeley: University of California Press.

Hanson, Victor D. 2003. *Mexifornia: A State of Unbecoming*. San Francisco: Encounter Books.

Harding, David. 2010. *Living the Drama*. Chicago: University of Chicago Press, 2010.

Hernández, Tanya K. 2022. *Racial Innocence: Unmaking Latino Anti-Black Bias and the Struggle for Equality*. Boston: Beacon Press.

Hochschild, Arlie. 2016. *Strangers in Their Own Land: Anger and Mourning on the American Right*. New York: New Press.

Hunt, Geoffrey, Stephanie Riegel, Tomas Morales, and Dan Waldorf. 1993. "Changes in Prison Culture: Prison Gangs and the Case of the 'Pepsi Generation.'" *Social Problems* 40(3): 398–409.

Jewkes, Yvonne. 2005. "Men behind Bars: 'Doing' Masculinity as an Adaptation to Imprisonment." *Men and Masculinities* 8(1): 44–63.

Jones, Jonathan S. 2020. "Opium Slavery: Civil War Veterans and Opiate Addiction." *Journal of the Civil War Era* 10(2): 185–212.

Joseph, Peniel E. 2006. *The Black Power Movement: Rethinking the Civil Rights–Black Power Era*. New York: Routledge.

———. 2007. *Waiting 'til the Midnight Hour: A Narrative History of Black Power in America*. New York: Holt.

Katz, Jack. 1988. *The Seductions of Crime: Moral and Sensual Attractions of Doing Evil*. New York: Perseus.

Katz, Jesse, and Robert J. Lopez. 1993. "Mexican Mafia's Impact on Gangs Questioned." *Los Angeles Times*, September 28.

Kotwal, Ashwin A., Julianne Holt-Lunstad, Rebecca L. Newmark, Irena Cenzer, Alexander K. Smith, Kenneth E. Covinsky, Danielle P. Escueta, Jina M. Lee, and Carla M. Perissinotto. 2021. "Social Isolation and Loneliness among San Francisco Bay Area Older Adults during the COVID-19 Shelter-in-Place Orders." *Journal of American Geriatric Society* 69(1): 20–29.

Lamont, Michèle. 2000. *The Dignity of Working Men: Morality and the Boundaries of Race, Class, and Immigration*. Cambridge, MA: Harvard University Press.

Lamont, Michèle, and Virág Molnár. 2002. "The Study of Boundaries in the Social Sciences." *Annual Review of Sociology* 28(1): 167–95.

Lauger, Timothy. 2013. *Real Gangstas: Legitimacy, Reputation, and Violence in the Intergang Environment*. New Brunswick, NJ: Rutgers University Press.

Levant, Ronald F., and Shana Pryor. 2020. *The Tough Standard: The Hard Truths about Masculinity and Violence*. New York: Oxford University Press.

Levenson, Deborah. 2013. *Adios Niño: The Gangs of Guatemala City and the Politics of Death*. Durham, NC: Duke University Press.

Liebenson, Donald. 2018. "Robin Leach Defined the Wealth-Obsessed 80s, and We Never Got Over It." *Vanity Fair*, August 28.

Light, Michael T., Jingying He, and Jason P. Robey. 2020. "Comparing Crime Rates between Undocumented Immigrants, Legal Immigrants, and Native-born US Citizens in Texas." *Proceedings of the National Academy of Sciences of the United States of America* 117(51): 32340–47.

Lindegaard, Marie R., and Sasha Gear. 2014. "Violence Makes Safe in South African Prisons: Prison Gangs, Violent Acts, and Victimization among Inmates." *Focaal—Journal of Global and Historical Anthropology* 68: 35–54.

Lindhardt, Martin. 2011, "When God Interferes: Ritual, Empowerment, and Divine Presence in Chilean Pentecostalism." In *Practicing the Faith: The*

Ritual Life of Pentecostal-Charismatic Christians, edited by Martin Lindhardt. New York: Berghahn Books.

Lopez-Aguado, Patrick. 2018. *Stick Together and Come Back Home: Racial Sorting and the Spillover of Carceral Identity*. Berkeley: University of California Press.

Lopez-Aguado, Patrick, and Michael Walker. 2021. "'I Don't Bang: I'm Just a Blood': Situating Gang Identities in Their Proper Place." *Theoretical Criminology* 25(1): 107–26.

Löwenthal, Leo, and Norbert Guterman. 1949. *Prophets of Deceit: A Study of the Techniques of the American Agitator*. New York: Harper.

Macías, Reynaldo, Guillermo V. Flores, Donaldo Figueroa, and Luis Aragón. 1973. *A Study of Unincorporated East Los Angeles*. Los Angeles: Aztlán Publications.

Mars, Sarah G. Philippe Bourgois, George Karandinos, Fernando Montero, and Daniel Ciccarone. 2016. "The Textures of Heroin: User Perspectives on 'Black Tar' and Powder Heroin in Two U.S. Cities." *Journal of Psychoactive Drugs* 48(4): 270–78.

McCoy, Alfred. [1972] 2003. *The Politics of Heroin: CIA Complicity in the Drug Trade*. 2nd ed. New York: HarperCollins.

Mendoza, Ramon A. 2005. *Mexican Mafia: The Gang of Gangs—From Altar Boy to Hitman*. 2nd ed. Spartanburg, SC: Police and Fire Publishing.

Messerschmidt, James W. 1993. *Masculinities and Crime: Critique and Reconceptualization of Theory*. Lanham, MD: Rowman and Littlefield.

Mills, C. Wright. 1959. *The Sociological Imagination*. New York: Oxford University Press.

Moore, Joan. 1978. *Homeboys: Gangs, Drugs, and Prisons in the Barrios of Los Angeles*. Philadelphia: Temple University Press.

———. 1991. *Going Down to the Barrio: Homeboys and Homegirls in Change*. Philadelphia: Temple University Press.

Morín, Raul. 1963. *Among the Valiant: Mexican Americans in WW II and Korea*. Los Angeles: Borden.

Muirhead, Russell, and Nancy L. Rosenblum. 2020. *A Lot of People Are Saying: The New Conspiracism and the Assault on Democracy*. Princeton, NJ: Princeton University Press.

Musto, David F. 1991. "Opium, Cocaine, and Marijuana in American History." *Scientific American* 265(1): 40–47.

Myrdahl, Thomas, dir. 1971. *Chicano Moratorium: A Question of Freedom*. Produced by Nikolai Sherbin and Thomas Myrdahl.

Mysels, David J., and Maria A. Sullivan. 2010. "The Relationship between Opioid and Sugar Intake: Review of Evidence and Clinical Applications." *Journal of Opioid Management* 6(6): 445–52.

New York Times. 1991. "The 1990 Census: California." February 26. www .nytimes.com/1991/02/26/us/the-1990-census-california.html.

———. 2021. "Trump's Fraud Claims Died in Court, but the Myth of Stolen Elections Lives On." October 11.

Nowrasteh, Alex, and Michael Howard. 2021. "Drunk Driving Deaths and Illegal Immigration." Immigration Research and Policy Brief No. 20, Cato Institute, July 6.

O'Neill, Kevin L. 2011. "Delinquent Realities: Christianity, Formality, and Security in the Americas." *American Quarterly* 63(2): 337–65.

———. 2015. *Secure the Soul: Christian Piety and Gang Prevention in Guatemala.* Berkeley: University of California Press.

———. 2019. *Hunted: Predation and Pentecostalism in Guatemala.* Chicago: University of Chicago Press.

Padilla, Felix. 1992. *The Gang as American Enterprise.* New Brunswick, NJ: Rutgers University Press.

Pagan, Eduardo. 2009. *Murder at the Sleepy Lagoon: Zoot Suits, Race, and Riot in Wartime Los Angeles.* Chapel Hill: University of North California Press.

Peiss, Kathy. 2011. *Zoot Suit: The Enigmatic Career of an Extreme Style.* Philadelphia: University of Pennsylvania Press.

Philips, Amber. 2017. "'They're Rapists.' President Trump's Campaign Launch Speech Two Years Later, Annotated. *Washington Post*, June 16.

Powers, Charles T., and Jeff Perlman. 1970. "One Dead, 40 Hurt in East LA Riot." *Los Angeles Times*, August 30.

Quinones, Sam. 2015. *Dreamland: The True Tale of American's Opiate Epidemic.* New York: Bloomsbury Press.

Ramirez, Catherine S. 2009. *The Woman in the Zoot Suit: Gender, Nationalism, and the Cultural Politics of Memory.* Durham, NC: Duke University Press.

Ransby, Barbara. 2005. *Ella Baker and the Black Freedom Movement: A Democratic Vision.* Durham: University of North Carolina Press.

Ray, Ranita. 2018. *The Making of a Teenage Service Class: Poverty and Mobility in an American City.* Berkeley: University of California Press.

Reich, Adam. 2010. *Hidden Truth: Young Men Navigating Lives In and Out of Juvenile Prison.* New York: Oxford University Press.

Reynolds, Julia. 2014. *Blood in the Fields: Ten Years Inside California's Nuestra Familia Gang.* Chicago: Chicago Review Press.

Ricciardelli, Rosemary. 2020. "Unpacking Harm: Correctional Officer Framing of Sex Offenders and Protective Custody." *Howard Journal* 59(4): 465–83.

Ricciardelli, Rosemary, Katharina Maier, and Kelly Hannah-Moffat. 2015. "Strategic Masculinities: Vulnerabilities, Risk, and the Production of Prison Masculinities." *Theoretical Criminology* 19(4): 491–513.

Ricciardelli, Rosemary, and Mackenzie Moir. 2013. "Stigmatized among the Stigmatized: Sex Offenders in Canadian Penitentiaries." *Canadian Journal of Criminology and Criminal Justice* 5(3): 353–86.

Robbins, Joel. 2011. "The Obvious Aspects of Pentecostalism: Ritual and Pentecostal Globalization." In *Practicing the Faith: The Ritual Life of Pentecostal-Charismatic Christians*, edited by Martin Lindhardt. New York: Berghahn Books.

Robinson, Paul. 2010. "Race, Space and the Evolution of Black Los Angeles." In *Black Los Angeles: American Dreams and Racial Realities*, edited by Darnell Hunt and Ana-Christina Ramón. New York: New York University Press.

Rodgers, Dennis. 2006. "Living in the Shadow of Death." *Journal of Latin American Studies* 38(2): 267–92.

Rojas-Sosa, Deyanira. 2016. "The Denial of Racism in Latina/o Students' Narratives about Discrimination in the Classroom." *Discourse & Society* 27(1): 69–94.

Romo, Richard. 1983. *History of a Barrio: East Los Angeles.* Austin: University of Texas Press.

Rorabaugh, W. J. 2018. *Prohibition: A Concise History.* New York: Oxford University Press.

Sahagun, Louis. 2020. "A Day of Rage in East L.A." *Los Angeles Times*, August 23.

Sanchez, George. 1993. *Becoming Mexican American: Ethnicity, Culture, and Identity in Chicano Los Angeles, 1900–1945.* New York: Oxford University Press.

———. 2004. "What's Good for Boyle Heights Is Good for the Jews: Creating Multiculturalism on the Eastside during the 1950s." *American Quarterly* 56(3): 633–61.

Sánchez Jankowski, Martín. 1991. *Island in the Street: Gangs and American Urban Society.* Berkeley: University of California Press.

Sanders, William. 1994. *Gangbangs and Drive-bys.* New York: Aldine de Gruyter, 1994.

Sanyika Shakur. 1993. *Monster: The Autobiography of an L.A. Gang Member.* New York: Grove.

Scheper-Hughes, Nancy. 1992. *Death without Weeping: The Violence of Everyday Life in Brazil.* Berkeley: University of California Press.

Schlesinger, Arthur M. 1992. *The Disuniting of America.* New York: W. W. Norton.

Schneider, Eric C. 2008, *Smack: Heroin and the American City.* Philadelphia: University of Pennsylvania Press.

Sides, Josh. 2004. "Straight into Compton: American Dreams, Urban Nightmares, and the Metamorphosis of a Black Suburb." *American Quarterly* 56(3): 583–605.

Skarbek, David. 2014. *The Social Order of the Underworld: How Prison Gangs Govern the American Penal System.* New York: Oxford University Press.

Stockhausen, Ulrike E. 2021. *The Strangers in Our Midst: American Evangelicals and Immigration from the Cold War to the Twenty-First Century.* New York: Oxford University Press.

Stone, Mitchell R. 2007. *Historic Resources Technical Report for the Proposed Central Middle School No. 9 on the Site of Sunrise Elementary School, 2821 E. 7th Street Los Angeles, CA.* San Buenaventura Research Associates.

StreetTV. 2021. "Lowell Street Gets Put on the Greenlight." YouTube video, www.youtube.com/watch?v=U11iWleNbDE&list=PLQwhRJvmotyF1njucoIH1rmzAFgVXYMXM&index=4.

Stuart, Forest, and Reuben J. Miller. 2017. "The Prisonized Old Head: Intergenerational Socialization and the Fusion of Ghetto and Prison Culture." *Journal of Contemporary Ethnography* 46(6): 673–98.

Sue, Christina A. 2013. *Land of the Cosmic Race: Race Mixture, Racism, and Blackness in Mexico.* New York: Oxford University Press.

Suro, Robert. 2012. "A Report on the Media and the Immigration Debate." Brookings Institute.

Sykes, Gresham, and David Matza. 1957. "Techniques of Neutralization: A Theory of Delinquency." *American Sociological Review* 22(6): 664–70.

Toch, Hans. 1998. "Hypermasculinity and Prison Violence." In *Masculinities and Violence,* edited by Lee H. Bowker, 168–78. Thousand Oaks, CA: Sage.

Torres-Rouff, David. 2013. *Before L.A.: Race, Space, and Municipal Power in Los Angeles, 1781–1894.* New Haven, CT: Yale University Press.

Trammell, Rebecca. 2012. *Enforcing the Convict Code: Violence and Prison Culture.* Boulder, CO: Lynne Reiner.

United States Census Bureau. 2022. www.census.gov/quickfacts/eastlosangeles cdpcalifornia.

Urquhart, Michael A., and Marillyn A. Hewson. 1983. "Unemployment Continued to Rise in 1982 as Recession Deepened." *Monthly Labor Review* 106(2): 3–12.

USA Green Card Center. 2007. "Bill O'Reilly and Geraldo Rivera Angry Fight Immigration." YouTube video, www.youtube.com/watch?v=Z3U9ENaTPLY.

U.S. Bureau of Labor Statistics. https://data.bls.gov/pdq/SurveyOutputServlet. Accessed December 31, 2022.

Vega, Irene I. 2014. "Conservative Rationales, Racial Boundaries: A Case Study of Restrictionist Mexican Americans." *American Behavioral Scientist* 58(13): 1764–83.

Venkatesh, Sudhir, and Steven D. Levitt. 2000. "Are We a Family or a Business? History and Disjuncture in the Urban American Street Gang." *Theory and Society* 29(4): 427–62.

Vigil, James D. 1988. *Barrio Gangs: Street Life and Identity in Southern California.* Austin: University of Texas Press.

———. 2007. *The Projects: Gang and Non-Gang Families in East Los Angeles.* Austin: University of Texas Press.

Wadsworth, Tim. 2010. "Is Immigration Responsible for the Crime Drop? An Assessment of the Influence of Immigration on Changes in Violent Crime between 1990 and 2000." *Social Science Quarterly* 91(2): 531–53.

Walker, Michael. 2022. *Indefinite: Doing Time in Jail.* New York: Oxford University Press.

Wallis, Jim. 2019. *Christ in Crisis: Why We Need to Reclaim Jesus.* New York: HarperCollins.

Warren, Jonathan, and France Winddance Twine. 1997. "White Americans, the New Minority? Non-Blacks and the Ever-expanding Boundaries of Whiteness." *Journal of Black Studies* 28(2): 200–218.

Weide, Robert D. 2020. "The Invisible Hand of the State: A Critical Historical Analysis of Prison Gangs in California." *Prison Journal* 100 (3): 312–31.

———. 2022. *Divide and Conquer: Race, Gangs, Identity, and Conflict.* Philadelphia: Temple University Press.

———. 2022. "Structural Disorganization: Can Prison Gangs Mitigate Serious Violence in Carceral Institutions?" *Critical Criminology* 30(1): 1–20.

Wexler, Kathryn. 1995. "East L.A. Gangs' Uneasy Peace Hangs on a Wish and Prayer." *Washington Post*, March 29.

Wilson, Janelle L. 2015. "Here and Now, There and Then: Nostalgia as a Time and Space Phenomenon." *Symbolic Interaction* 38(4): 478–92.

Wright, Richard T., and Scott H. Decker. 1997. *Armed Robbers in Action: Stickups and Street Culture.* Boston, MA: Northeastern University Press.

Zohrabi, Azadeh. 2012. "Resistance and Repression: The Black Guerrilla Family in Context." *Hastings Race and Poverty Law Journal* 9(1): 167–90.

Index

Acuña, Rodolfo, 40–41, 292n36
addiction: community and, 190–91; to crack cocaine, 157–58; crime and, 66; to crystal meth, 252–53; to drugs, 68–70, 102, 106–11; in fatherhood, 159–60, 258–59, 260–61; to heroin, 130, 156, 208–9, 278–79; homelessness and, 138; Pentecostalism and, 153; poverty and, 64–65; in prison, 106; relapse, 198–99
Africa, 13
African Americans: Black people and, 25; in East LA, 238–39, 243, 247–49; Latino/as and, 13–14; in New York City, 21; in protests, 178, 292n44; racism against, 24–26, 158–59, 235–49; to white people, 178
Afro-Latino/as, 13, 25, 26, 235
aging: fatherhood and, 254–64; health issues and, 252, 272–73; as Maravillas, 265–72, 277–81; youth and, 251–52
alcohol, 162–64, 169, 259, 262
Alcoholics Anonymous, 109
American Me (film), 1, 288n16

anomie, 265–66, 272–73
anti-Blackness: from Chicanos, 236–38; Christianity and, 244, 247–49; by Maravillas, 158–59, 238–41, 246–47
anti-immigrant sentiment: against Chinese immigration, 30; by Maravillas, 202, 284; in East LA, 202–05, 207–13, 217–20, 228–31; Trump and, 215–17; in US, 201–7. *See also* immigration
Arizona, 31
Aryan Brotherhood, 78–79, 88
"Así Vas Pa Maravilla," 91
assimilation, 203–4, 219–20

bank foreclosure, 158
Bannon, Steve, 215
Bible: in Christianity, 107–8; conservatism and, 206–7; emotions from, 132; God in, 135; identity with, 119; Jesus in, 131; race in, 247–48
Biden, Hunter, 217, 225
bilingual education, 201
Black gangs, 4, 78–79, 88, 121
Black Guerrilla Family, 78–79, 88

Black people: African Americans and, 25; Afro-Latino/as and, 235; civil rights for, 77–78; in East LA, 237, 247–49; immigration and, 284; jazz and, 43; Latino/as and, 40–41, 120; as Maravillas, 238–39; in poverty, 23; in prison, 77, 79, 91–92; racism against, 24–25, 158–59, 235–36. *See also specific topics*

Black Power movement, 78

Blood In, Blood Out (film), 1

borderliners, 140–46

Bourdieu, Pierre, 185–86, 294n3

Bourgois, Philippe, 23, 60, 188, 237

boxing, 55–56

Boym, Svetlana, 250

bracing, 180

Brenneman, Robert, 122–23

Brooklyn Avenue, 149*fig.*

Brotherton, David, 4

Broucek, Francis, 288n10

Brown Berets, 38, 51–52

Cadena, Rodolfo, 77, 80

California. *See specific topics*

California Youth Authority, 197

Caló dialect, 32, 40, 193

Carranza, Venustiano, 290n3

cars, 7–11, 18, 147*fig.*

Castro, Sal, 37–38

Catherine of Siena (mystic), 131

Central America, 122–23

Chavez, Leo, 200–201

Chicago, 4

Chicanos: anti-Blackness from, 236–38; Blackness to, 242–43; Chicano empowerment, 13; in combat, 291n23; National Chicano Moratorium, 38, 46–47; nationalism to, 202–5; police and, 78; politics of, 37–38. *See also specific topics*

children: adults to, 47–50, 70–71; domestic violence to, 262–63; drugs to, 48–49, 159–60, 261; fatherhood and, 239–40, 277–78; heroin to, 48–49; juvenile hall, 53, 93; LA Child Guidance Clinic, 155; masculinity to, 50; protection of, 210–11; race to, 240–42; racism and, 25–26, 256; reconciliation with, 261–62; resentment from, 259–60; teaching, 257–58

Chinese immigration, 30

Christianity: anti-Blackness and, 247–49; Bible in, 107–8; borderliners and, 140–46; emotions in 121–27, 144; faith in, 97, 220, 272; gang life and, 115–21; God in, 105–6, 111–15; heroin and, 106–11; ideology of, 211–12; to Maravillas, 137–40; masculinity and, 127–36; Pentecostalism and, 105–6; to white people, 303n25

Christian Borderliners, 140–46

citizenship, 206–13, 218. *See also* immigration

City of Quartz (Davis, Mike), 178

civil rights, 77–78

Civil War, 42

class, 26, 42

Clinton, Bill, 214, 217

Clinton, Hillary, 213–14, 217, 225

clothing, 8–9

code. *See* street code

Cold War, 206

collective effervescence, 122

Collins, Randall, 72–73, 88, 122–23, 298n7

Colombia, 294n4

Coltrane, John, 43

Comfort, Megan, 295n11

competition, 100

conservatism, 206–7. *See also* politics

conservative media, 212–13

corrido music, 200, 230

COVID-19, 223–24, 247, 274–78

cowboy ethnographers, 20–21

crack cocaine, 4, 59, 154, 156–58

crime: addiction and, 62–64, 68–70; drugs and, 285–86; emotions of, 129–30; gangs and, 46–50; immigration and, 209–10, 218, 231; politics of, 41

crying: from anomie, 272–73; consequences and, 123; family and, 264; religion and, 108, 125–27, 131–36, 142

crystal methamphetamine, 186, 252–53

Cuba, 206

cultural capital, 185–86

Davis, Mike, 178

Davis, Miles, 43

Desmond, Matthew, 23

domestic violence, 262–63

domination, 294n3

drop-outs, 55–56

drugs: addiction to, 68–70, 102, 106–11; alcohol and, 163–64, 259, 262; to children, 48–49, 159–60; class and, 42; in community, 117, 198–99; crack cocaine, 4, 59, 154, 156–58; crime and, 138, 285–86; crystal meth, 252–53; drug dealers, 12, 47–50, 62–63, 78–79, 156–57, 183–84; drug rehabilitation, 98; drug-related health issues, 5–6, 154–55, 160–61, 267–68; drug taxes, 82–83; homelessness and, 18, 140–41; to Maravillas, 29, 43–44, 59–67, 116–17, 249; marijuana, 49–50, 60, 163; from Mexico,

106–7; to old-timers, 251–52; overdoses, 65; paint sniffing as, 54; PCP, 58, 60, 68, 92; in prison, 92–93; recovery from, 108–11, 140–46, 263–64; recreational, 42–43, 49; risk and, 73–74, 186–91; sex work and, 64. *See also specific drugs*

Duneier, Mitchell, 16

Durkheim, Émile, 121–23

East LA: African Americans in, 238; Black people in, 237–39, 247–49; education in, 53–54, 256–57; La Eme to, 82; history of, 29–30, 35–42, 291n33; Maravilla Historical Society in, 12; to Maravillas, 44–45, 178–79, 183–84, 202–5; March for Justice in, 39; murals in, 148*fig.*; New York City and, 270; police in, 69; politics of, 40–44, 200–202, 207–13, 222–27; protests in, 37–39; racism in, 30–35; reputation of, 83; resistance in, 37–40; schools in, 37–39, 256–57; Trump and, 213–22; unincorporated, 29; Whittier Boulevard in, 1–2, 7–11, 46–47, 148*fig.*, 152*fig.*

economics. *See specific topics*

education: bilingual, 201; drop-outs, 55–56; in East LA, 53–54, 256–57; to gangs, 53–54; in LA, 37–38; to Maravilla, 55; prison as, 72–73

Ellis, Anthony, 288n11

El Salvador, 228

La Eme: to East LA, 82; greenlight and, 3–4, 76–82; Maravillas and, 4, 82–88, 93–94, 98–99; to old-timers, 98–99; protection and, 81; victims of, 79–82; violence by, 88–89

emerging adulthood, 70–71, 295n11

emotions: in anomie, 265–68; from Bible, 132; from church, 124–29; death and, 281–82, 285–86; emotional energy, 93–94, 126, 129–30, 144–45; family and, 280; of fear, 182–83; God and, 128–29; in marginalization, 122–23; masculinity and, 71–74; from music, 130–31; of Pentecostalism, 121–22; of pride, 102; religion and, 97, 121–27; in social isolation, 278–79; violence and, 88, 96, 165–70

empowerment, 148*fig.*

English language, 204, 231

ethnicity, 24–26, 202–3, 207, 215–18, 228

ethnography: access in, 12–13; cowboy ethnographers, 20–21; history of, 29–30; race and, 23

Europe, 13, 42–43, 214

Evicted (Desmond), 23

Facebook, 253, 281–82

faith: in Christianity, 97, 220, 272; in God, 124–25; health issues and, 113; in Jesus, 111–15; in prayer, 118–19

family: crying and, 264; gangs to, 54; heroin and, 47–48, 66–67, 153–54, 159–60; morality and, 157; religion and, 107–108; single-parent families, 258

fascism, 214

fatherhood: addiction in, 159–60, 258–61; aging and, 254–64; children and, 239–40, 259, 272, 277–78; race and, 235–36; racism and, 240–41

fear: of prison, 71–73; in research, 19–22; of youth, 180–83

femininity, 32, 158–59

Flores, Edward, 128, 299n9

forgiveness, 128

Freire, Paulo, 201–2

gambling, 69–70

gangs. *See specific gangs*

gang studies, 287n2, 287n5

Garot, Robert, 179

gender, 64

geo-ethnic identity, 81

God: in Bible, 135; in Christianity, 105–6, 111–15; to Durkheim, 121–22; emotions and, 128–29; evidence of, 136; Jesus and, 123, 134; masculinity and, 143–44; nationalism and, 206–7; in Pentecostalism, 126–27; prison politics and, 119–21; salvation from, 136, 140, 142

Gold, 289n2

Gounari, Panayota, 215–16

Gowan, Teresa, 23

graffiti, 51

Great Depression, 30, 33

Great Shoe War, 79

greenlight: La Eme and, 3–4, 76–82; history of, 82–86, 98–101, 254; pride of, 101–2; protection during, 118–21; religion and, 118–21; research of, 19–20, 101–2, 197–98, 200; violence, 84–89, 98–102

Guatemala, 4, 145, 219, 228

guns, 56–57, 112, 114–15, 118, 194–95

Guterman, Norbert, 214–15

haircuts, 15, 151*fig.*

handball (*rebote*), 12, 14, 147*fig.*, 179–81

Hanson, Rebecca, 20

health issues: aging and, 252, 272–73; death from, 164; drug-related, 5–6, 160–61; in East LA, 162–63; faith and, 113; from heroin, 186–91; medicine for, 149*fig.*; Ménière's syndrome, 163–64; paralysis, 111–13;

from withdrawal, 109–10. *See also*
COVID-19
Hernandez, Tanya, 25
heroin: addiction to, 92, 130, 156,
198–99, 208–9, 278–79; to children,
48–49; Christianity and, 106–11;
family and, 47–48, 66–67, 153–54,
159–60; health issues from, 186–91;
methadone for, 164–65; in music,
91; in New York City, 271–72; in
prison, 78–79, 93; in US, 42–44;
users, 59–67; withdrawal, 60–63,
109–11
history: of East LA, 29–30, 35–42,
291n33, 292n34; gang studies and,
3–4; of greenlight, 82–86, 98–101; of
immigration, 289n2; of inflation,
40–41; of LA, 30–35, 178; of Mexico,
235–36; of pachucos, 31–35, 186; of
Pentecostalism, 298n7; society and,
3–4
Hitler, Adolf, 214
Hochschild, Arlie, 216
Holiday, Billie, 43
Holocaust, 214
homelessness: addiction and, 138;
community in, 161–62; drugs and,
18, 140–41; food in, 190; in LA,
141–42; Skid Row in, 131, 138, 278
Honduras, 219
Huerta, Victoriano, 290n3
Hunter College, 270–71

identity: of Afro-Latino/as, 13, 26;
with Bible, 119; of Blackness, 23–24;
with Christianity, 211; in community, 140–46; in East LA, 18;
geo-ethnic, 81; in Latin America,
235–36; with Maravillas, 101–2, 120;
with masculinity, 70–75, 195–96;
race and, 13; selling drugs and,

183–84; spatial, 178–85, 300n14;
with tattoos, 99; violence and, 7,
170–77
ideology: of Christianity, 211–12; of
masculinity, 155, 192–93; of street
code, 164–78; in US, 46
immigration: crime and, 207–13, 218,
231; criticism of, 203–5; from
Europe, 42–43; history of, 289n2; in
LA, 30; from Mexico, 30, 41–42,
226–27; in Pentecostalism, 206–13;
policy, 206–7, 210–11; research
on, 302n14; stereotypes of,
208–9, 219–20; in US, 200–202,
235–36. *See also* anti-immigrant
sentiment
inactive gang-members, 115–21,
140–46
incarceration. *See* prison
inflation, 40–41
inter-racial relationships, 239–42,
245–46
intimate apartheid, 237
Islam, 217, 221–22

jail. *See* prison
jazz music, 43
Jesus: in Bible, 131; faith in, 111–15;
God and, 123, 134; in Pentecostalism, 216; in prison politics, 115–21
juvenile hall, 53, 93, 237–38

Ku Klux Klan, 178, 222

LA. *See* Los Angeles
Lamont, Michèle, 202
language: Caló dialect, 32, 193;
community and, 204–5; English,
204, 228, 231; Spanish, 13–14, 24–25,
201, 228, 231; street talk, 186, 193; of
Trump, 217–18, 225

prison *(continued)*
  Mexican Mafia (La Eme), 76–101;
    music in, 90–91; Nuestra Family in,
    79–80; parole from, 156; politics, 19,
    83, 115–21; probation from, 114–15;
    race in, 77–82, 237–39; religion in,
    118–21; riots, 120–21, 237–38; shanks,
    91–92; tattoos, 94–95; violence in,
    77, 79, 81, 84–97; violent elites in,
    88–90; women in, 48
probation, 114–15
protests: African Americans in, 77,
    292n44; in documentaries, 292n45;
    in East LA, 37–39; against police,
    78; against racism, 236; riots and,
    37–39; against Trump, 220
public assistance, 153–54

race: in Bible, 247–48; to children,
    240–42; ethnicity and, 24–26;
    ethnography and, 13–15, 23–26;
    inter-racial marriages, 158–59,
    239–42; politics and, 235–37; in prison,
    77–80, 237–39; racist policy, 41; riots,
    33–35, 120–21, 237–39; in US, 30–35
racism: against Black people, 24–26,
    158–59, 235–49; by Chicano
    inmates, 77–80, 120–21; in East LA,
    30–35, 230, 242–45; against
    immigrants, 200–202; in prison,
    77–80, 237–39; protests, 37–40,
    77–78, 236; from white people,
    30–31, 33–35, 200–201, 206–7
Ray (film), 109–10
Ray, Ranita, 23
La Raza, 78, 80, 99, 188, 191, 195, 228,
    236–37, 239
Reagan, Ronald, 41
rebote (handball), 12, 14, 147*fig.*,
    180–81
reconciliation, 261–62

recovery, from drugs, 108–11, 140–46,
    263–64
religion: to borderliners, 140–46;
    crying and, 108, 125–28, 130–36, 142;
    emotions and, 97, 121–36; music
    and, 125–27, 130, 299n9; racism
    and, 247–48; Trump and, 220–21,
    303n25; xenophobia and, 206–07.
    See also specific religions
reputation: of Maravillas, 101–2;
    masculinity and, 72–75; pride in,
    170–74, 176–78; snitching and,
    170–74
resistance, 30–35, 37–40, 82–88,
    93–98, 148*fig.*
respect, 83, 164–78, 229–30
revenge, 86–87, 112–13, 169, 177–78,
    194–95
Richards, Patricia, 20
Righteous Dopefiend (Schonberg and
    Bourgois), 188
riots: prison, 120–21; protests and,
    37–39; race, 120–21, 237–39; Zoot
    Suit Riots, 33–35, 291n26
Robbins, Joel, 298n7
Rodgers, Dennis, 4
Romo, Richard, 30

Sánchez Jankowski, Martín, 46
SASSFA. *See* Southeast Area Social
    Services Funding Authority
Scheper-Hughes, Nancy, 23
Schneider, Eric, 43
Schonberg, Jeff, 60, 188, 237
schools, 37–38, 255–58
segregation, 31
selling drugs, 47–50, 62–63, 78–79,
    156–57, 183–84
sexist stereotypes, 63–64, 157–59
sex work, 64
shanks, 91–92

Skarbek, David, 78
Skid Row, 131, 138, 278
snitching, 74, 98, 116, 141, 170–75
social isolation, 274–80
social media, 213–14, 215–16, 281–82
South Asia, 206
Southeast Area Social Services
    Funding Authority (SASSFA), 156
Southern California. *See specific
    locations*
Southsiders (Sureños), 19, 80–87,
    97–102, 121
Soyer, Michaela, 268
space: race and, 11–17, 33–35; spatial
    identity, 13–14, 178–85, 300n14;
    spatial problems, 178–85
Spanish language, 13–14, 24–25, 201,
    203–4, 228–29, 231
Speed Racer (cartoon), 96
stereotypes: of Blackness, 235–36,
    243–44; of immigrants, 208–9,
    219–20; of Mexicans and Central
    Americans, 200–202; of Mexico,
    200–202; of minorities, 215–16;
    sexist, 63–64, 157–59
The Stickup Kids (film), 21
street code: for arguments, 164–77;
    Christianity and, 112–13, 115–21;
    from old heads, 193, 196–98;
    snitching in, 74, 98, 116, 141, 170–75
street fights, 57–59, 167–68, 170–78
street violence, 53–59, 164–78
style: Caló dialect and, 31–32, 40; of
    clothing, 7–11, 31–33, 249–51,
    291n26; of older Maravillas, 2,
    250–51; of younger Maravillas, 99;
    zoot suits, 31–33, 291n26
sub-oppressors, 201–2
Sureños (Southsiders), 19, 80–87,
    97–102, 120, 128, 133, 138
symbolic boundary work, 202

tando hats, 2, 10–11, 32, 250
tattoos, 55, 89, 96, 99, 101, 119, 132–33
tecatos (heroin users), 29, 59–65, 198
theft, 59, 61–63, 68, 176–77
Time (magazine), 201
Trammell, Rebecca, 78
Trump, Donald: anti-immigrant
    sentiment and, 214–17; conflicts
    over, 222–27; media and, 216,
    223–24; to minorities, 246; protests
    against, 220; religion and, 220–21,
    303n25
trust, 20–22

uncomfortable truths, 23–26
unemployment, 40–41, 159
U.S. News and World Report (maga-
    zine), 201

Vatos Locos, 53–59, 193–94. *See also*
    Maravillas
Venkatesh, Sudhir, 4
Vietnam War, 38–39
Vigil, James Diego, 46, 50
violence: assault, 84–94; children and,
    47–48; domestic, 259–60; drugs
    and, 15–16, 45; by La Eme, 77–80,
    81–82, 84–86; emotions and, 71–75,
    88–90, 96–97, 167–68; gambling
    and, 69–70; greenlight, 82–90,
    98–102; gun, 56–57, 112, 118,
    194–95; heroin and, 61–62; identity
    and, 7, 170–77; masculinity and,
    54–59, 71–75, 255–56; PCP and, 58;
    police and, 34–35, 37–39, 47–48; in
    protest, 37–39; in prison, 77, 79, 81,
    84–97; street, 57–59, 164–78;
    victims of, 111–13; violent elites,
    88–90, 92–97; in youth, 53–59; in
    Zoot Suit Riots, 33–35
violent elites, 88–90, 92–97

Walker, Michael, 180
Weide, Robert, 78–79
white people: African Americans to, 178; Christianity to, 303n25; Mexican-Americans and, 30, 33–35, 200–203, 206–7; racism from, 30, 33–35, 200–203; white women, 43, 63–64
Whittier Boulevard, 1–2, 7–11, 39, 46–47, 52, 141, 148*fig.*, 152*fig.*, 154, 183, 270
witchcraft, 100, 106–7, 196
withdrawal, 60–63, 109–11
women: drugs and, 47–49, 63–65; femininity, 32, 158–59; gangs to, 17; interviews with, 17–18; Latino/as, 191–92; low riders and, 7–11; objectifying, 63–64, 189; in prison, 48; doing research on, 20; sex and, 108–9; in street code, 143; white, 43, 63–64

Women in Chains (film), 238
World War I, 35–36
World War II, 33, 43, 214

xenophobia, 30, 200–205, 214–22, 228–31. *See also* anti-immigrant sentiment

youth: California Youth Authority, 197; drugs and, 132–33, 252–54; in East LA, 182–83; emerging adulthood in, 70–71, 295n11; in gangs, 76–77, 179–82; heroin in, 48–49; minorities and, 76–77; in 1930s and 1940s, 33–35; old-timers and, 7–11, 21–22, 183–85; politics of, 46–47; pride of, 181–82; pachuco and, 31–35

Zapata, Emiliano, 290n3
Zoot Suit Riots, 33–35, 291n26
zoot suits, 31–35, 291n26

Founded in 1893,
UNIVERSITY OF CALIFORNIA PRESS
publishes bold, progressive books and journals
on topics in the arts, humanities, social sciences,
and natural sciences—with a focus on social
justice issues—that inspire thought and action
among readers worldwide.

The UC PRESS FOUNDATION
raises funds to uphold the press's vital role
as an independent, nonprofit publisher, and
receives philanthropic support from a wide
range of individuals and institutions—and from
committed readers like you. To learn more, visit
ucpress.edu/supportus.